ANGIE ZELTER is a human rights, peace and environmental campaigner who sees herself as a 'global citizen'. She has been active in campaigning for many decades, having founded the Snowball Civil Disobedience Campaign in 1984, helped set up the Institute for Law and Peace in 1989, founded the North Norfolk Community Woodland Trust in 1991, founded Trident Ploughshares in 1997, initiated the International Women's Peace Service – Palestine in 2002 and Faslane 365 in 2005.

In 1996 Angie, as part of the Seeds of Hope – East Timor Ploughshares, took part in the disarming of a BAe Hawk meant to be used in genocidal bombings on East Timor. After spending six months in prison awaiting trial they won their case. In 1999 she and two other women disarmed a floating laboratory in Loch Goil, Scotland whose purpose was to mask the sounds of Trident submarines. After five months all three were acquitted in a landmark trial which concluded that the deployment of Trident nuclear missiles was illegal under international humanitarian law.

To date Angie has been arrested well over a hundred times, in 10 different countries, leading to over 30 convictions and deportations from Sarawak and Israel. But she has also won numerous acquittals and continues her non-violent resistance against inhumanity and corruption especially in the UK where she lives.

Angie received the International Peace Bureau Sean MacBride Peace Prize for 1997 (for the Seeds of Hope Ploughshares action) and in 2001 the Right Livelihood Award (on behalf of Trident Ploughshares).

All royalties from the sale of this book go to Trident Ploughshares.

Faslane 365

Edited by
ANGIE ZELTER

Luath Press Limited
EDINBURGH
www.luath.co.uk

First published 2008
Reprinted 2008

ISBN (10): 1-906307-61-x
ISBN (13): 978-1-906307-61-5

The paper used in this book is recyclable. It is made from low chlorine pulps
produced in a low energy, low emission manner from renewable forests.

Printed and bound by
Bell & Bain Ltd., Glasgow

Typeset in 10.5pt Sabon by
3btype.com

Acknowledgements

Thanks to David McKenzie for coming up with the name 'Faslane 365' and helping in those first crucial mobilising months when we met with groups around Scotland; to Adam Conway for his hard work, along with Petter Joelson, in putting up our website and keeping it going – it proved a crucial element in our campaigning; to Anna-Linnea Rundberg for taking a year away from her beloved Aaland Islands to look after our training needs; to Jane Tallents for keeping us focused on the people all around who are affected by our campaigning, and, along with Adam Conway, for keeping the legal and court support going; to Rebecca Johnson, who came into the steering group at a crucial time and brought her knowledge and under-standing of the bigger international picture into our discussions and plans, and for generously providing a safe haven in her flat on so many occasions; to David McLachlan, for his time with us on the steering group and for his thoughtful and steady encouragement when the going got tough and we wondered if we could manage to sustain the blockading. Thanks to the Faslane Peace Camp, where I was able to base myself for the year. I cannot mention all the wonderful people who have helped over the year, people like Olivia Agate, Janet Fenton, David Ferrard, Brian Larkin, Julia Mercer, Eric Wallace... you know who you are, the backbone of the peace movement. Love and thanks to all the thousands who shared their hopes and strengths by joining in the blockades. Finally, thanks to Gavin of Luath Press who supported our endeavours by agreeing to publish this book.

Contents

Contacts   277

Foreword

PROFESSOR PAUL ROGERS[1]

SOON AFTER THE Faslane Peace Camp started in October 1982, an 'embrace the base' demonstration took place down in Berkshire at another key nuclear weapons site, Greenham Common, where women's peace camps had done a huge amount to galvanise public opinion at a time of acute East–West tensions. The camps had been set up soon after Ronald Reagan had been elected as US President in 1980 largely on a platform of re-arming America. He went on to warn of the 'evil empire' of the Soviet bloc and both the Americans and the Soviets became immersed in a race to deploy highly accurate first strike nuclear missiles in Europe.

The focus of peace campaigning in Western Europe was the NATO decision to deploy ground-launched cruise missiles and Pershing two ballistic missiles, with campaigners in Britain bitterly opposing the two cruise missile bases at Greenham Common and Molesworth. There was also vigorous opposition to the Thatcher government's plan to replace the ageing Polaris missile force with Trident.

The autumn of 1983 was the peak of the campaigning, and many demonstrators were adamant that the nuclear arms race was extraordinarily dangerous and costly, as well as being irrelevant to the real issues of human security. They were widely decried as alarmists, but that very autumn saw events, far from the public eye at the time, which proved their point.

As part of its plan to test the deployment of the new mobile missiles, NATO began operation Able Archer, but this came at a time of near paranoia in the Soviet Union, where there was an ongoing leadership crisis. The moribund regime of Leonid Brezhnev had ended with his death the previous November, but his successor, Yuri Andropov, was already desperately ill and struggling to work from a hospital bed.

In September 1983, just a few weeks before the Able Archer exercise, a Soviet interceptor shot down a Korean Airlines Boeing 747 flying from the United States to Japan, killing all 269 passengers and crew, after it had twice entered Soviet airspace over the strategically crucial Sea of Okhotsk.

---

[1] Professor Paul Rogers is Professor of Peace Studies at Bradford University.

The Western reaction was one of outrage, and many analysts in Moscow believed that NATO and the Warsaw Pact were coming close to war. Under these circumstances, the Soviet intelligence agencies misread NATO's Able Archer exercise as preparation for a surprise attack and began to put a wide range of their own forces on alert. Fortunately for us all, some NATO analysts realised what was happening, and the NATO exercise was scaled down.

None of this came into the public domain for nearly a decade, but it turned out to be one of the worst crises of the whole cold war, certainly on a par with Cuba in 1962. It was powerful evidence in support of the anti-nuclear protestors and their warnings of potential disaster, and now forms part of our post-cold war knowledge of how dangerous that 45-year period was for everyone. We now know much more about the many accidents with nuclear weapons, the nuclear bombs lost at sea and never recovered, and the crises that were played out behind closed doors.

Any kind of sensible conclusion would be that we were extraordinarily lucky to come through the cold war without an out-and-out nuclear catastrophe. Even the notion that nuclear weapons kept the peace is nonsensical – they merely exported war to the rest of the world. For nearly half a century, proxy wars were fought in Korea, Vietnam, Afghanistan, the Horn of Africa and many other places, killing at least ten million people, maiming tens of millions and crippling the development prospects of even more.

Perhaps the most extraordinary aspect of that era was the willingness of the nuclear powers to plan for the first-use of nuclear weapons, a strategy that persists right through to the present day both for NATO and Russia. NATO's 'flexible response' policy, which included nuclear first-use, was pro-gressively developed and adopted 40 years ago, and was codified in a doc-ument MC13/3, with the anodyne title *Overall Strategic Concept for the Defence of the NATO Area*. Supported by 7,000 tactical nuclear weapons deployed in Europe for much of the cold war era, NATO was prepared to fire first in the belief that a nuclear war, once started, could be controlled before utter disaster ensued.

Forty years later we remain in the remarkable position that all three nuclear-armed members of NATO – the United States, Britain and France – still have first-use options in their nuclear planning. Most of the tactical nuclear weapons may have been withdrawn in the early 1990s, but enough remain to keep the posture intact. Britain got rid of its last tactical nuclear bombs a decade ago, but in a neat sleight of hand, modified some of the Trident warheads to turn them into small tactical nuclear weapons that could be used in 'small wars in far-off places'. These warheads are still really powerful – equivalent to several thousand tons of conventional high explosive – but they are seen as useable in regional conflicts.

Successive governments have been deeply reluctant to raise the issues of nuclear war-fighting and first-use, and in recent years the term 'tactical' has been quietly abandoned. The preferred term until recently was 'sub-strategic', but even this has now been banned, encouraging people to believe that Trident and its replacement are no more than rather expensive insurance policies. This is also claimed to be true for the Trident replacement. The lengthy White Paper published last year devotes just two short phrases to the issues of first-use and small warheads. There is just enough to confirm that current policies will be maintained but everything is done to minimise the public awareness of this.

Britain's Trident replacement forms part of a wider trend by the nuclear weapons states to modernise and maintain their nuclear forces for decades to come. Quite apart from the criminality of being willing to kill millions of innocent people, the nuclear postures are simply irrelevant to the real needs of international security. Even so, that doesn't make it easier to campaign and argue against them. During the cold war there was an almost universal awareness of the dangers of nuclear war, and most people thought there was a small risk of an utter catastrophe. Even if they thought that the risk was low, they were still worried. It was as though we were on the edge of an abyss, yet we might not fall in.

Twenty years later it is more of a slippery slope – the risk that nuclear proliferation, first-use postures and modernisation will ultimately lead to the use of nuclear weapons in war for the first time since Nagasaki, tipping us over, bit by bit, into an acceptance that they are useable weapons. That is one of the greatest dangers but it is much more complicated than the relative simplicities of the cold war era. Furthermore, new generations of younger people have grown up with no personal knowledge of that era and little understanding of the present-day nuclear dynamics.

What we have to recognise are the real threats to world-wide human security – the deepening socio-economic divisions, the marginalisation of most of the world's people, and the hugely dangerous effects of environmental constraints, especially the impact of climate change. We need people-centred ideas of sustainable security, moving away from what is best described as the control paradigm or 'liddism' – keeping the lid on problems in an effort to maintain the status quo rather than addressing the underlying global issues.

A few months ago, a group of retired defence chiefs from France, Germany, the Netherlands, Britain and the United States published a report calling for a renewed grand alliance of Western Europe and North America from Finland to Alaska.[2] This would revitalise NATO, connect the US and Canada more closely to the European Union and lead to a 'New Atlantic Century' in which global security would be ensured by the power and influence of this cluster of elite states. One of the recommendations was the maintenance of effective nuclear forces with a commitment to nuclear first-use. It was a classic example of 'old thinking' but was persuasive for those seeking a response, built on strength, to an uncertain and volatile world.

Faslane 365 and what it stands for is the antithesis of that attitude, challenging not just the nuclear status quo but also the whole idea that a few states can maintain power in their own interests in an interconnected world. It has also come at a time of renewed debate over Britain's nuclear weapons. Partly this has come from the antagonism to Trident in Scotland – much stronger than that in the rest of the UK – partly through wide opposition to the government's plans to replace Trident, and partly from the impact of Faslane 365 itself.

Moreover, the Faslane action is much more than an anti-nuclear witness since it has also been an empowering process for the many people involved in it. As well as introducing new generations to nonviolent action it has reawakened a wider interest in the nature of security, in opposition to the deep-rooted belief that a few 'civilised' elite states have some kind of right to determine the future of all our security. If the abject failure of the last few years of Mr Bush's 'war on terror' does not amply demonstrate that, it is difficult to know what will.

In the following pages we have a remarkable and powerful group of contributions, ranging from numerous first-hand accounts of the year of action through to analyses of nuclear policy, Scottish opposition and the wider international potential for disarmament. What comes through is a message of hope that ordinary people can achieve real change. Faslane 365 is doing much to revitalise a critically important debate, with a determination to ensure a nuclear free Britain, which could be a huge step on the way to understanding how a more peaceful world might be achieved.

---

[2] *Towards a Grand Strategy for an Uncertain World: Renewing Transatlantic Partnership*, Noaber Foundation, Lunteren, 2007.

You Should Visit Faslane

ADRIAN MITCHELL[3]

You should visit Faslane. You'll be in great company. You'll meet veterans of Greenham Common and the early Aldermaston marches, all of them keeping on keeping on – still laughing and singing and organising against the mass murder of the innocents. You'll meet the new generation of protesters – compassionate and determined. Young or old, they are practical visionaries and great company.

You should visit Faslane. It's quite a sight to see, especially in sunlight. Stand on the road and face the perimeter of the base that nurses our killer submarines. Sparkling, spiralling, vicious razor wire, hedge after hedge of malicious steel. Beyond the steel, a maze of buildings. Beyond the buildings an enormous shoebox, huge, a larger than life, bleak block, which they call the shiplifting shed. A gormenghastly surgery where they operate on nuclear subs.

So far, so nightmarish. But raise your gaze above the base and you will see the gently sloping green, brown and blue hills, gracefully descending to the waters of the loch. And, above them, a vast, light-blue Scottish sky. Beyond the monster factory, the angelic beauty of Scotland.

This is a double vision – Blake saw such things. In one poem he saw London as a dirty murder shop. But in another he saw the streets of Marylebone and Kentish Town 'builded over with pillars of gold/And there Jerusalem's pillars stood'. Blake was talking about the New Jerusalem, that great city of mutual friendship and love. He didn't see it as a Utopia for the far-off future. He spent his life building the New Jerusalem, with his wife and his friends, with his drawings and paintings and poems and songs and illuminated books.

You should visit Faslane. The demonstrators who are there all the year round are today's builders of the New Jerusalem. Join them for as long as you can. Help them if you can. You may well feel, as I did, that you want to join them in their blockade of the nuclear base by sitting down with other demonstrators to block the base. I hope you do.

Look, I'm 74, and not very brave. But I did the nonviolence workshop

---

3 Shadow poet laureate Adrian Mitchell was one of nine peaceful protesters arrested at the Faslane blockade on 6 December 2006. This was an open address to *Red Pepper* readers advocating a visit to Faslane and speaking of his hopes to return.

the night before, and when it came to lying down on the road I was happily going limp, smiling widely and singing 'We Shall Overcome'. I was arrested and charged along with nine others for breach of the peace. I spent 23 hours in the Dumbarton local nick – a room to myself with toilet, paper and pencil, and room service (tea, meals, water and blankets). Next morning I was sent back to England with a printed warning that I shouldn't do it again. I hope I will.

The police who carried us away and the ones in the Dumbarton nick were courteous and gentle throughout. One of them even advised me to turn vegetarian to avoid the worst meals, and, when I finished the book I'd brought, handed me another – a hefty autobiography by somebody called Greg Dyke. So do take enough of a paperback book to last 24 hours. But since you're interested in changing the world, you should certainly visit Faslane.

Introduction

ANGIE ZELTER

DURING THE EARLY PART of 2005 I became increasingly concerned that the UK peace movement was not showing its strength nor exerting enough influence – it was not translating its concerns into action that would create the changes our society needed to make. I was horrified that nuclear weapons were proliferating once more, a new nuclear arms race was beginning, and that we had squandered the peace-dividend opportunities of the end of the cold war. The powerful nations of the world were still locked into war-fighting over exploitative, resource conflicts. What could we as a peace movement do about it? I came up with what my friends and colleagues called a 'mad plan' for sustained, civil resistance against the UK's nuclear weapons. The plan, later to be called 'Faslane 365', was conceived from within a personal perspective that is probably shared by many of us within our movement for just and equitable social change.

This perspective includes a belief that we human beings have caused massive global damage over the last few centuries – forest destruction, desertification, species extinction, the genocide of whole peoples, long-lasting and serious pollution, wars, refugees, torture and gross human rights abuses. The wake-up call of climate change may have finally brought us a unique opportunity to make the links, understand and put right our destructive behaviours. It is now obvious that it is only by acting together in full mindfulness that we can save our planet Earth and our own humanity.

Everything is linked and if we work deeply to cure one ill we will come into contact with the need to cure another. The key is for us to know ourselves as global citizens. We all belong to one fragile Earth and we must carry this knowledge into every area of our lives and politics.

At the root of it, is the necessity to have compassion for all people and all living things – to love. We must act as if we could be anyone, anywhere on this planet. We must have the imagination to feel and know what it is like to be an Iraqi or a Palestinian under military occupation, or an asylum seeker awaiting her fate in a detention centre, or an impoverished, hungry, dispossessed labourer working to produce cash crops for a transnational corporation, or the last stand of ancient old-growth trees looking out over a devastated clear-cut, or a turkey in an intensive factory farm. Our policies and actions must be viewed from the perspective of all, and any, living beings. To put ourselves in the place of another is a necessity, not a luxury.

It is our ability to close off, to deny the implications of our actions on others, to rationalise rather than to be wise, that has led us to this critical turning point for life on Earth. And nothing epitomises more this denial and lack of imagination in the UK today than our threat to use weapons of mass destruction. As McSorley once said, nuclear weapons are the tap-root of violence in our society. The fact that we can allow Trident nuclear weapons to exist and allow our neighbours and friends to work on maintaining and preparing for their use symbolises a corrupt and spiritually bankrupt society that has lost its way.

To plan for the replacement of Trident, in breach of Article VI of the Non-Proliferation Treaty, while condemning other, less powerful nations for trying to get their own nuclear weapons, is a hypocrisy that undermines international law, encourages the continuation of state terrorism, and is indicative of our cultural collapse.

Nuclear weapons do not exist in a vacuum, they exist in a web of lies, evasions, and power abuses, they exist to prop up an exploitative, narrow, selfish and ultimately *destructive* culture.

When looking at the foreign policy of the UK over the last 500 years, we can view it from the eyes of millions of victims all around the world as a sordid history of stealing scarce resources of gold, minerals, timber, oil and food. First by war and conquest, then by slavery and colonialism, and now by unfair and unethical 'trading' rules that ensure multinational corporate power, long-lasting debt bondage and control over vast stretches of other people's lands and seas. These power abuses have caused millions of deaths, horrendous poverty, and vast ecological destruction. Africa, one of the richest continents on earth, is just one example of where Britain has abused economic and military power to exploit natural resources and leave a wave of destruction behind.

Military power is *not* often about self-defence – the lie that lies behind our society's acceptance of it. It is about forcing other people to do what we – in our infinite ignorance – think we want. Thus, our foreign policy has consistently led us not only to war and occupation but also to backing repressive regimes, selling arms and torture equipment to human rights abusers and turning a blind eye to the subjugation of vast numbers of people all over the world.

Behaviour like this not only affects others in distant far-off places but destroys and distorts our own culture. It is one of the reasons for the cultural disintegration that you can see in the despairing, confused and angry eyes of people around.

Any campaigning against nuclear weapons must thus also work for the open transformation of British foreign policy, from control of other people's resources to regional self-sufficiency, global cooperation and fair trade. People have a right to grow their own food and save their own seeds, to use their own water resources before being forced to trade in luxury items like tea, coffee and out-of-season fruit and vegetables, and to have clean, safe rivers and lands rather than the contamination caused by gold, oil and other mineral extraction. This is not just an issue of foreign policy, it is also one of economic policy. We need to put human rights and environmental safeguards ahead of profit and change the global trade agreements to make sure they do not undermine our efforts to cooperate for the sake of the planet rather than profit.

All of these issues at their heart are about real security. Everyone on Earth has a right to a clean, safe and secure environment, to live and to love. Real security cannot be found at the end of a gun – the wars in Afghanistan and Iraq have shown very clearly that you cannot bomb a country into democracy or liberty or safety. Violence just creates more violence. We have to deal with the root causes of violence – and to do this we must be honest and compassionate. We must not take more than our fair share of the resources of the world and our policies must be respectful of the rights of every other life form to have its space on this planet. We have to put our own society right before blaming others.

To put into practice the changes our society will have to make we need to transform the most destructive forces. We need to dismantle Trident, re-commit ourselves to international humanitarian law and get out of all the current wars and occupations that we are involved in. We must stop supporting repressive regimes and stop our arms trade. We must recognise that all these aspects of the industrial war machine not only use up vast amounts of scarce human and mineral resources but also account for massive energy and carbon wastage causing huge environmental and societal destruction and poverty. These are all issues that we need to address co-operatively in order to survive the challenge of climate change. We have to divert resources to life-enhancing work. And in the process we will revitalise and renew our own culture and put the heart and soul back into ourselves.

In our society it is the politicians who will have to join with us against the state abuse of power and ensure that international law is upheld and Trident dismantled. And they need people power to push, encourage and support them to act in the best interests of the global community.

To enact social change on such a scale we need to have all the elements of a movement for social change active – ranging from analysis, debate, education, letter writing and lobbying, to demonstrations and nonviolent civil resistance. In a society such as ours where we have no constitution, no real separation of powers, where democracy is crumbling as people feel more and more disempowered, where responsible appeals to the 'authorities' to deal with the criminal activities of the state are not heeded, we need a nonviolent street presence to show more directly our concerns and requests for change. Sometimes we even have to disrupt what is going on – we have to engage in nonviolent civil resistance campaigns like Faslane 365.

This was my personal perspective, from which arose the idea of the 'mad plan'. Called mad not because people thought it was a bad or crazy idea but because it seemed much too ambitious. How could we expect to be able to mobilise groups of 100-plus people to come and blockade the base every single day for a whole year? The peace movement was at another low ebb and there were so many more direct problems that needed to be addressed. On the other hand, Trident Ploughshares had built up a great deal of experience in training and empowering people to engage in civil resistance and had kept up the political pressure for nuclear disarmament in Scotland by organising disarmament camps at Faslane and Coulport over the last six or seven years. The annual Big Blockades had attracted much publicity and some of the high-profile court cases had brought the issue of international law being broken by deploying nuclear weapons right into mainstream discussion.[1] However, by 2005 the energy was beginning to slacken and the camps and the Big Blockades were not bringing in many new people. There was a waning of people pressure just at the time when it seemed to me the opposition to nuclear weapons should be increasing. However, many people were struggling with trying to make a living alongside a massive feeling of political disempowerment after the anti-war protests of millions of people had failed to prevent the war in Iraq.

---

[1] The story of Trident Ploughshares and people's disarmament efforts has been told in Angie Zelter, *Trident on Trial: The Case for People's Disarmament*, Luath, 2001.

The 'mad plan' would have remained just that, except that a group of friends with whom I had worked in Trident Ploughshares – Adam Conway, Anna-Linnea Rundberg and David Mackenzie (all of whom have contributing chapters in this book) – decided to try and make it happen. With four of us working together we began to meet. David Mackenzie came up with the name – Faslane 365 – and we began the hard work translating mad ideas into reality. And of course the idea developed and changed over the year, as all implemented visions do. But that vision of 100 blockaders at the gates of Faslane every day for a year gave us the energy at the start to facilitate the reality that emerged as Faslane 365. This book is about the extraordinary events of this year-long blockade of Faslane.

Faslane is the naval base where the UK's weapons of mass destruction are based and is thus a prime military target. Faslane is about 30 miles north west of Glasgow. Glasgow is Scotland's commercial capital and largest city, with a population of around 600,000. Faslane is the home port of four nuclear-powered Vanguard submarines, equipped with US Trident missiles and up to 200 nuclear warheads, each of which can deliver around eight times the destructive power of the bombs that flattened the cities of Hiroshima and Nagasaki in Japan in 1948. The spare warheads are stored at Coulport, which is very close to Faslane.

During 2006–7 the whole non-proliferation regime was threatened by the renewal and modernisation of nuclear weapons systems by the UK, US and France. The nuclear weapon ambitions of Iran and Korea were also in the limelight. It was a year of political upheaval and controversy, with Westminster voting for the replacement of Trident and Scotland voting against it. Chapter 2 – 'Focusing on Scotland to Break the Nuclear Chain' – written jointly by David Mackenzie and Rebecca Johnson, explores this political context, and Chapter 4 – 'International Security, Law and Abolition of Nuclear Weapons' – written by Rebecca Johnson, analyses the international ramifications of the UK's stance over the years.

Faslane 365 came at this most crucial time and managed to keep the spotlight in Scotland on nuclear weapons at Faslane. The campaign encouraged a renewed nonviolent confrontation with the state to pressurise it to implement its promises of disarmament. I summarise this story in Chapter 1 – 'People Power'. There is a long history of demonstrations and nonviolent civil resistance opposing nuclear weapons in Scotland, and this is remembered and honoured in Chapter 3 – 'A History of Scottish Anti-Nuclear Protest' – written by Helen Steven.

Vital questions of what real security should look like and how the nuclear threat distorts not only the UK's foreign and defence policies but also environment, development and economic policies, were raised by the inclusion of a wide variety of civil society groups taking part in Faslane 365. The linked issues of poverty, arms sales, war and occupation, refugees and asylum seekers, carbon footprints, morality, international law and spirituality are all explored through the stories, songs and witnesses of various blockading groups. These personal stories and thoughts from the blockades themselves are interspersed throughout the book to bring the campaign to life.

Since it is often not realised how much hard work and organisation these seemingly 'spontaneous' civil resistance campaigns need, I have included a few chapters to give an insight into the organisation and behind-the-scenes work of Faslane 365. They are also included in order to share experience and power. The whole campaign was designed to be as autonomous as possible and this was facilitated by the liberal sharing of information and training materials. Thus you will find Chapter 5 – 'What the Hell Do You Need Training For?' – written by Anna-Linnea Rundberg, exploring the nonviolent workshops that all groups were encouraged to participate in. And linked in with the trainings were legal briefings and encouragement to groups to organise their own legal support. Adam Conway deals with this in Chapter 6 – 'We Fought the Law... and the Law Ran and Hid' – where he gives an account of the process, and some of the experiences, of both providing legal support and of going through the courts.

Jane Tallents, in Chapter 8 – 'Local Impact around the Rosneath Peninsular' – looks at the impact on the local community of the disruptions caused by a year-long blockade and how this affected the campaign as a whole.

Another very necessary part of any nonviolent civil resistance campaign is the stance one takes with the police. I explore this in some detail in Chapter 9 – 'Policing the Blockades' – in order to give people a glimpse into this little-known process.

And finally, to provide a deeper probe into the thought and philosophy that went into so many of the blockades I have included an example from the academics' blocks – Chapter 7 – 'Critique in Action: Academic Conference Blockades' – written jointly by Justin Kenrick and Stellan Vinthagen.

As I write this the sun is shining through the sycamore leaves onto the ferns and the little stream that I can see out of my caravan window here at Faslane Peace Camp. A nuthatch perches upside-down on the goat willow. The traffic going into the Faslane naval base thunders past on my other side.

Eleven thousand people going in and out, working to service and deploy weapons of mass destruction that are a constant threat to all life on earth. I am pondering the different viewpoints and philosophies, hopes and fears that are symbolised by these two realities. The view into the trees and water, the quiet life that slowly passes through its seasons, has been my constant companion over this extraordinary year of blockades. It is what sustains me. The mountains and lochs dominate the view around the base and remind me of a geological timescale of millions of years, putting into a different perspective our human toils to prevent the loss of our natural world. The constant stream of dedicated, wonderfully compassionate people who have joined in this year of blockades has provided the hope, companionship and cooperation that have been essential to living and working to rid the world of nuclear weapons. I hope that this book will not only record part of the history of the peace movement in the UK but will also inspire readers to have faith in their power to act and change the world they live in. I dedicate this book to all the thousands who have made the pilgrimage to Faslane and who believe that they can make a difference.

Nun Blood and Nuclear Insanity

A.L. KENNEDY

I was speaking at Faslane in December, saying 'Hi' to the blockaders – who have considerably more spine than me; I've still not been arrested after years of visiting – and to the police.

That's the thing about addressing gatherings of activists. I know that everyone in the audience knows more than me about the issues we're discussing, does more to resist the things we should all be resisting, and is generally an all-round better person. So I tend to aim myself towards the police. A bit of humour to help us bear thinking about the horror, to give us all a bit of ginger – and a bit of a chat for the police.

This may be especially important at Faslane because the blockade has been consistently well-disciplined and focused and, partly as a consequence, many of the police are sympathetic to the blockaders. And you wonder, how much more would it take for the coppers to come over, risk their jobs, risk their families' economic security and just come over, to really uphold the law, look to the light?

So, as the sleet sleeted, I talked about why we were there, outside the gates, outside the fence. Inside the fence, of course, there are an undisclosed number of nuclear warheads kind of rented at obscene expense from the US and not really under our control, but nevertheless constituting The United Kingdom's Nuclear Deterrent. Which worries me. For lots of reasons.

Never mind that there isn't really a credible threat that it actually defends us against, or that it's got a cheap, unstable propellant. (That's three words you don't want in the same sentence as 'nuclear missile' – 'cheap, unstable propellant', anyone else feel queasy?) And by cheap, I mean it would only cost a few hospitals and maybe some really well-equipped schools.

Forget about that, and the fact that Trident is locked into a 'missile defence' system that only works if it's used pre-emptively – and how does Tony Blair square his Christian values with first-use of nukes, for Christ's sake? Let's not get into any of that, let's just discuss basic safety.

Because I know people – maybe you know some, too – who break into nuclear facilities, into Faslane. They break into places surrounded by fences and razor wire and motion sensors and CCTV and guards and dogs and... who are these people?

I happen to know.

For a start, they're nuns. Not ninja nuns, not SAS-trained nuns – just nuns. They break into all sorts of nuclear bases, they pour blood onto missile silos, which upsets military people no end – nun blood, it freaks them out. Nuns can get into these places? I mean, that whole vow of silence and black-clad thing would work, but the wimple, you could see a wimple from miles off. And then there are those French nuns with that kind of hang glider effect on their heads – Little Sisters of the Perpetual Take-off. They'd be obvious, surely? Any security officer worth their salt would notice something. Wouldn't they?

Who else breaks in? Little old ladies. This is to do with nature, of course. As ladies get older, their sexual drives become enhanced, their orgasms become longer, deeper, higher, just more. And as gentlemen get older – well, things don't go quite so smoothly. So lots of spare energy amongst the ladies and some of them become activists.

Little old ladies. They sabotage submarines, for crying out loud. Little old ladies.

Who else? With the greatest possible respect, people who are hippies and crusties. So that's nuns, little old ladies, hippies and crusties.

Not your first pick for a stealthy, lightning commando raid on anything beyond the sweetie bins at Woolworths. Yet they get in – time and time again.

Does anyone else worry about the security in these places? We all know the war on terror is commercially-satisfying hogwash, but given that our 'intelligence' is now based almost entirely on sadistic millennialist fantasy and the gibberish produced by torture victims, do we actually have any guarantee that our nuclear threat won't be used against us, right here at home?

I know, I know – we're supposed to trust our leaders and have confidence in science (and its ability to kill lots of people we don't know) and the Pentagon. But then you discover that, just for an example, the US military is developing plans to weaponise sharks. Maybe they've turned to sharks because that whole weaponising dolphins thing didn't work out well in PR terms. You can't have Flipper being blown to chunks without a really good excuse. So nobody likes sharks: weaponise them. Great idea. If you're in a cartoon. And I would just point out that our Coalition is fighting a war in Iraq, a desert country, and Afghanistan, a desert country with big fucking mountains; and is thinking about a war in Iran, a desert country... I mean, if Wicked Islamist Fanatics take over Seaworld, we're sorted, but otherwise, less so.

Then there was the plan to attach cameras to flies and turn them into Spy Flies. Again, a good idea – in Cartoonworld. It could work – little tiny cameras fixed to little tiny, innocent-looking flies that could wander in through a window and carry out surveillance. I just have a nagging feeling that none of these people have ever tried to get a fly to go where they want. Fly herding isn't easy. So you have to get the covert operatives to creep up on the terror suspects, or the rogue librarians, or the school kids who've voiced non-conformist opinions, and smear them with jam – that way the flies might get to them. Along with lots of other amateur flies and maybe some armed wasps.

Sanity isn't really our watchword here, is it? But then, if you look into the history of somewhere like the Pentagon – which I do, from time to time – you don't find a hell of a lot of sanity there either.

For instance, did you know that a major architect of cold war policy, and that means the West's nuclear policy, was one James Forrestal? He was appointed the United States' first secretary of defence and, guess what – he was paranoid. I don't mean, he used to think people were bad-mouthing him around the water-cooler; I mean he suffered from paranoid delusions. He was mentally ill. And mentally ill people deserve our compassion and adequate health care and support, but they shouldn't really be put in charge of formulating foreign policy, amassing vast nuclear arsenals and bringing the world to the brink of particularly appalling destruction. James Forrestal, remember the name. Married to an alcoholic. They had nothing in common beyond a vast hatred and fear of communists. Great fun at Washington parties.

Eventually he killed himself. And didn't anybody ever think – maybe this is a clue, maybe this way of thinking ends in self-destruction of some kind? Apparently not. Or maybe we just didn't hear about it. There are lots of nuclear truths we don't get to hear about – like that whole pre-emptive use thing. Or the fact that the guy who won the Pulitzer Prize for describing the wonders of the bomb and the Nagasaki raid, *New York Times* reporter William Laurence, was working for the Pentagon. Did you know that, at the same time that he was ignoring a load of facts about suffering and radiation and risk, he got a photographer to pose in the bomb crater at the New Mexico test site and the photographer died of cancer?

Did you know that the 'missile gap' that was used to terrify successive US presidents was always in the US's favour? That it was Eisenhower who coined the phrase 'military-industrial complex'? That influential US military men ignored peace moves from Japan to make sure they'd get to use the bomb and see if it worked? That scientists who worked on the bomb and then tried to resist its use were muzzled? Did you know that several influential government and military thinkers in the US (including Henry Stimson, who was in charge of the war department throughout the Second World War) thought the best post-war plan was to share nuclear technology with Russia in order to prevent an expensive and potentially disastrous arms race? Did you know that everything we've been led to believe about the bomb is based on lies? Lies and death.

And, of course, nuclear weapons break all manner of international laws, while our commitment to participation in new nuclear development breaks some more treaties and controls too. Which is why it's strange when the blockaders are on one side and the police are on the other. Some laws you should obey and some you can ignore – is that it? You can't smoke in a Scottish pub, but you can threaten everyone on earth with death?

Because that's what's beyond the fence at Faslane – death. And it's something that the police know about. They have to look at the dead, find them, tell husbands that wives are gone, mothers that children are gone – they do things I couldn't do. It's their job – upholding the law, dealing with the victims. But at Faslane they stand outside the fence and the gate and they defend it. They defend death. The special death they keep here.

If I stood on the platform with a gun and I had a child with me and I threatened that child with a gun, you can bet the police would stop me. And if I had 10 children with me and my gun – oh, you can bet I'd be stopped. They'd move heaven and earth to stop me.

Behind the fence is a gun at the head of every child on earth. It's more than a threat to kill. It's a threat to vaporise victims, so their relatives can't even mourn over a body, have nothing to bury. Or maybe your son or your sister was a little further from the blast and gets turned into carbon, an unrecognisable mineral fragment. Or maybe your daughter gets torn by shrapnel and burned and dies slowly with no water to drink and no one to tend her wounds – maybe it takes her hours to die.

Or maybe she's burned inside, maybe the radiation poisoning takes days to kill her, weeks, breaking down every organ in her body, rotting her alive. Or maybe your child survives and then cancer doesn't get him for years, or he makes it, only has the nightmares and the guilt, but all of his children are poisoned in the womb.

Death beyond imagining, death for generations, a hell so terrible we let it rest beside our cities, we let it be – because we cannot think how terrible it is, our minds cannot hold it. Death behind the wire at Faslane, promised and nourished by Blair; death's more efficient replacement on the way. Death defended against breaches of the peace. Stupid death, expensive death, appalling death, unnecessary death. And why, in God's name, do we need more death?

An Angel, a Squirrel and a Big Red Bus: Manchester at Faslane

SARAH IRVING and RED SQUIRREL

A collection of affinity groups and individuals from Greater Manchester came to Faslane not once but four times during the year-long 365 campaign. Travelling by car, minibus, train and on one memorable occasion a big red Routemaster bus, over 100 people – veterans and newcomers, arrestables and supporters – made the trip to defy the British state's intention of wasting billions of public pounds on Trident renewal.

Some figures loom large in many people's memories of their involvement in Faslane 365.

Most frequently mentioned is Betty Tebbs, an 89-year-old veteran of nearly 60 years of anti-nuclear campaigning. Betty was arrested in June for thumb-locking herself to Alan and Neville, both in their 70s, and blocking the road to the South Gate for over an hour.

As Alan Johnson put it, 'the most memorable occasion was our June 2007 visit. I say this because, not only was it the most effective blockade I have taken part in, but it was the one that gave me the most pleasure and also provided the most media coverage. After 40 years of activity in the CND, Betty Tebbs, 89 years old and registered blind, took part for the first time in a blockade at Faslane and along with Neville, two Matts and Ben, we held up the traffic at the South Gate for an hour. This was reported in the *Manchester Evening News*, the *Big Issue*, *Red Pepper*, 17 local newspapers and on Sky TV. If the amount of publicity is an indicator of success then this was a successful operation.'

Olive, one of the support team that day, notes that both her best and worst memory of several trips was, 'watching Betty, 89, lying down in the human chain across the back exit road with the midges biting and being so practical about it.'

A close second to Betty in many people's minds was Secret Squirrel, a 7ft-high squirrel outfit occupied by Pete. After a number of visits in support roles, a change of job meant that Pete could at last notch up an arrest at Faslane, and he did it in style! Pat, a veteran Faslane campaigner, remembers this as one of the funniest occasions of her many actions, 'the sheer exasperation on the face of the policeman who bent down to separate the Squirrel, Ali and me when he saw we were thumb-cuffed together, and we realised we would keep the gate blocked for longer while they called up the cutting team.' Secret Squirrel's adventures didn't end with being arrested, as the costume's head was taken into trophy custody by a cutting team of MOD police and had to be rescued from the base itself by detectives from Strathclyde police.

A close second to Secret Squirrel in the costume stakes was November's Angel, a feathery white outfit which was built to disguise a heavy metal four-arm lock-on. As Helen, one of the team that was meant to form a star-shaped block in the road, said of her experience, 'one of my worst memories was realising the planned decoy wasn't going to happen and we were now in fact the decoy, and feeling myself get dragged off as soon as I hit the floor.'

Pete, watching this event, remembers 'hearing Helen's plaintive cry of "I'm locked on" as she was dragged away from the Angel lock-on'. But not all was lost, as Helen recalls 'turning round after sadly being dragged off to see that Chris was locked on and not going anywhere for two hours.' And the same team successfully blocked the road on another occasion, recalled by some for Debs's cry, in answer to passing heckles of 'get a job!', of 'I'm a grocer...!'

Reasons Why

These examples show the creativity and diversity of Manchester's contribution to Faslane 365. Some of the Manchester bloc, like Roy, who went on the Aldermaston marches at the age of 16, have been involved in the anti-nuclear struggle for decades. Others, like Secret Squirrel's arrest companion Ali and members of the samba band who livened up the November 2006 visit, had never been before. As Mai put it, 'the demos provided a reaffirmation about the issues and the decency and humanity of the protesters.'

Inspirations for joining in were diverse. Olive and Pat expressed their fury, saying respectively that they were 'appalled at our government's renewed investment in nuclear weaponry' and that 'It always makes me cry – from fear, shame, despair, rage... the obscenity, the immorality, the hypocrisy, the misuse of power, the oppression that the abuse of the public purse means to vulnerable people at home and abroad...'

Pete's reasoned response was that, 'I believe that a decision not to replace Trident could be a "turning point" in the way that Britain develops both its foreign and domestic policies and implements solutions to the real challenges that face people in the UK and internationally. Threatening to use, or using Trident missiles would not only be illegal but is also a massive waste of resources that could be better used to bring real security. My government doesn't seem to be listening – and so I felt it was time to go and protest and to say "not in my name".'

Personal Inspirations

Debbie pointed out that as well as pursuing her political goals, getting involved in Faslane 365 'was a wonderful opportunity to work with a group of people who I've known for a long time (as well as an opportunity to make new friends). It has had a lasting effect on my life, nudging me towards spending more of my free time on activism. I had lost touch with this important aspect of myself.'

Other people echoed the personal importance of getting involved – or re-involved – in the campaign against Trident through the year of 365 campaigning. The impetus of a national campaign brought together new groups of people to inspire one another and pass on experience, new skills and energy. Roy, a veteran of decades of anti-nuclear campaigning, observed that 'the strength and ingenuity of people never fails to uplift me' and Pat, also with many years of involvement behind her, emphasised 'the strength and joy from working with others'.

Practical Lessons

Even some of these extraordinarily experienced campaigners flagged up the practical skills they picked up or were reminded of through the year of Faslane 365. Pat emphasised, 'The importance of good press work before, during and after actions; that we don't have to be daunted at apparent failure, there are enough of us, with enough energy and new ideas, to keep trying other methods, the importance of practicing lock-ons lots beforehand!'

Pat's memories also remind us that such practice and attention to detail are a vital part of the whole narrative of coming to Faslane, and what seemed like hard work at the time takes its place amongst the tales to tell afterwards: 'we had a laugh in the bushes behind the service station when Jacqui, Hilary and I were practicing walking up carrying the banner with lock-ons disguised – poorly – as banner poles and trying to synchronise our dropping down to the floor and locking on. Each time one of us would roll over on her back like some ungainly turtle and bring the others, locked on to her, down too. We realised of course that eventually we would all want to lie down, it was just that the litter-strewn earth behind the service station wasn't the most pleasant place to practice in.'

Pete also mentioned 'the need to be closer than the YHA in Glasgow, getting people to practice in affinity groups beforehand, that politically the London (national) media is not really interested in Faslane (too far away from London desks) and, as well as continuing to protest at Faslane, the need to bring the demonstrations closer to the "centre".'

Olive, too, raised 'the importance of meticulous forward planning when people intend to get arrested.' And Helen recalls how, when things came together on a highly successful day of action with groups from all over Europe, 'it was a really organised, sorted process, and it worked and we managed to get locked on this time.'

The last word goes to Rae Street, another Faslane long-timer, who draws together the personal and political importance of the 365 campaign in its ability to reinvigorate debates and tactics, to draw in new people and to inspire ongoing resistance to the replacement of Trident: 'Faslane 365 gave us a chance locally to reinvigorate the contribution of direct action to campaigning. I enjoyed (yes, enjoyed) the planning meetings which old and new friends organised. You might have said we just went for the fun and camaraderie. But of course we had a more important mission. Bumping along in the minibus to Scotland (blessing our generous drivers), chuntering at the latest appalling government decisions, I reflected how just for these days the sense of frustration at being beaten back by inane government arguments on why we needed a "nuclear deterrent" was being dispelled. When I was arrested I felt free.'

On Vacation

EMMA BATEMAN

I do non violent direct action, which mostly consists of sitting around drinking tea, eating biscuits and discussing peace, so perhaps it should be more correctly called non violent direct inaction, although we do sometimes chain ourselves together and lie down in an appropriate place. While I am in full agreement with the anti-nuclear, pro-choice, anti-war, pro-peace-and-love ethics of the hippy generation, I am really in it for the free holidays.

The campaign of the moment is Faslane 365. People are flurrying up to Scotland to abolish the nuclear base at Faslane. Faslane is a serene green grey landscape on the edge of a deep blue loch with a smattering of seagulls ducks and swans. Of course if you look over here, there is a hulking black metal beast of a naval base where unsightly submarines with weapons of mass destruction break the surface, but as long as you keep looking the other way, everything is perfect.

In our busy today lives, holidays are hard work. The tourist is under extreme pressure to have a fun filled holiday because when all your friends demand 'what did you do!' you are obliged to have had the most thrilling time ever. If you say you took a city mini break and slept all weekend you are deemed to have failed at your holiday.

So we are offering an alternative. Subsidised travel in a jolly community bus, and when you arrive at Faslane, you are not expected to do anything other than lie down in the road and relax. There is no compunction to sightsee or exert yourself at all. In the peace movement, the longer you can lie still in the road, the more heroic you become. And if you are a shy and stilted lonely single looking for love or friendship or just someone to talk to who doesn't make desperate signs of 'got to go' as soon as you arrive, we can lock you on to another blockader of your choosing and you will have a captive audience until the police come and cut you apart.

The police are very friendly. They will take a nice holiday snap of you and chat about what you have been up to before escorting you to your free accommodation in the exclusive Dumbarton police station cells. The cell cuisine is incredible. For some fussy folk 'incredible' may veer towards 'incredibly inedible', however I like the food, but I do have the advantage of being a terrible cook which means that meals concocted by anyone else are far superior to my own home cooking and so are a real treat. For those who are disdainful of the fare viewing the experience as a chance for a diet detox retreat can be very positive.

Personally, I have found Strathclyde police to be endearingly courteous, and for those from the lower orders like myself, cell accommodation provides a rare opportunity to indulge in the bourgeois luxury of being waited upon by uniformed staff which is normally the preserve of those who sojourn at the Dorchester or Ritz. If you require cell service refreshment just ring the bell and an officer will oblige.

On one trip north I encouraged my mother to tag along. My mother tends to regard this peace campaigning caper as a tad peculiar. It's not that she wants a nuclear holocaust to engulf us, she just thinks that people who try to stop it are oddly extreme. So I asked her to come along on a kind of open day to see what we do. And it was great because it was near Christmas and we had the opportunity to see each other when we weren't drunk or falling asleep in front of the TV, which is how most families get through the trauma of spending quality time together.

Seeing busloads of jubilant blockaders got me musing on how we could use trips to Faslane to raise the self esteem of the underclass and socially overlooked; the broken, helpless and bleak. I thought about gathering reams of street people and old people from dead rest homes and taking them on a delightful Scottish excursion.

Elderly blockaders are tactical troops in the peace war. Scotland can be chilly and the advantage old people have is that once you get them down on the ground, their arthritis and rheumatism set fast and they are very tricky to move until they thaw. I am sure that such a well intentioned community project that strengthens hearts and changes minds should attract copious political praise.

Getting out of an armchair and into the road makes you powerful. Many people don't like the look of the world turning around them and for a short space they feel they can alter its revolution.

On the road between tea and biscuits they become polite potent rebels.

CHAPTER I

People Power

ANGIE ZELTER

THE IDEA BEHIND FASLANE 365 was to encourage and support people to sustain civil resistance against nuclear weapons, to make our opposition to Trident replacement visible and to provide the political pressure for change in a year when the Scots would hold an election that might bring an anti-Trident party into power.[1]

There are hundreds of thousands of people in the UK who are against nuclear weapons but their views are not often publicised or taken into account in decision-making, nor are they often visible. Many people in other countries might believe that the vast majority of UK citizens support their government's warmongering and the possession of nuclear weapons. However, as this book testifies, there are thousands who have felt strongly enough about the necessity for nuclear disarmament to come and join the blockades at Faslane in an inspiring year of people power.

I had been coming up to the Faslane Nuclear Naval Base for many years and felt very strongly that this was the nuclear base where sustained civil resistance had the most chance of success. The base is near to a small town called Helensburgh where there is a good-sized active CND group, and quite a few locals also support the Faslane Peace Camp,[2] which is right next to the approach road to the South Gate of the Faslane Base. The majority of Scots are against nuclear weapons and this made it a much easier country

---

[1] Our civil resistance and work helped enable that to actually happen and as I write in October of 2007 the anti-nuclear Scottish National Party are, with the Green Party, in a minority government. This minority government is exploring ways to rid Scotland of nuclear weapons and as part of this process Faslane 365, along with other active parts of civil society, were invited to join a Trident summit to discuss ways forward.

[2] Faslane Peace Camp is the longest-running peace camp in the UK and celebrated its 25th birthday in June 2007.

to campaign in than England.[3] But perhaps the most important feature was the base itself. Placed right next to the Gare Loch it is a long, thin base with only three entrances. There is one main entrance – the North Gate – that can be blocked easily by 15 people, a South Gate which is reached by a long approach road that can be blocked by as few as four people and an Oil Depot Gate that can be blocked by three people. I thought that if groups of 100 people could be encouraged to take on a day of blockading then they could probably block the base for a whole day each, perhaps by coming in three or four separate waves, especially if they were willing to use lock-ons.[4]

If groups could be mobilised to be part of a rota of blockades that would cover a whole year then perhaps the civil resistance pressure would give strength to the anti-nuclear movement and enable nuclear disarmament to become a reality. To encourage groups to seriously commit themselves to disruption of the base I decided that it would be best to have them come for two days each and to overlap with the groups before and after, having the first day as their 'main' day, when the blockading would take place, and the second day to collect people from police stations and support the following group. Otherwise I feared that groups would just turn up for a few hours in the middle of the day and then go home again and thus the base would merely have to change its shift times to carry on its business as usual.

My first task was to see if I could persuade anyone else that this was practical and possible. I took the idea first to my friends and colleagues in Trident Ploughshares (TP)[5] and suggested that we attempt to find at least

---

[3] Aldermaston in England was the other candidate for such a sustained civil resistance campaign but it is a huge complex with many different entrances, very difficult to shut down completely, and although near to London there was no strong or visible local opposition. Nevertheless, another campaign called Block the Builders has organised regular blockades at Aldermaston to try to stop the building of the testing facilities for the new nuclear warheads being designed and manufactured there.

[4] Lock-ons are made from sections of plastic or metal pipe inside which two people clip together with karabiners fastened to their wrists. Sometimes tubes are reinforced with concrete or layers of various materials. Sometimes people lock on in a group. Other equipment like D-locks, bike locks or chain and padlocks are used to lock people together and more recently people have used superglue to fix themselves to each other or to heavy immovable objects.

[5] Trident Ploughshares is a campaign to disarm the UK Trident nuclear weapons system in a nonviolent, open, peaceful and fully accountable manner. www.trident ploughshares.org

100 groups to cover the first 100 days and not to go ahead unless we managed to get these first 100 groups. There was doubt that we could manage to get that number of people involved in civil resistance but there was enough enthusiasm to at least go ahead and test the waters. Four people from TP agreed to work to take the idea further.[6] It was also decided that it would be best to set up an entirely separate campaign organised on autonomous principles, that was not 'owned' by any particular NGO, like TP, even though it would obviously build on their and other direct action organisations' work. Our resource pack thus stated, 'All who participate will contribute, but no one organisation will "own" the continuous blockade.'

David Mackenzie and I decided to visit other groups to see what their response would be. We visited a few in Glasgow and Edinburgh and found enough interest to continue. More importantly, we found that David McLachlan, a minister of the Church of Scotland and a member of Clergy Against Nuclear Arms, was willing to join our steering group.[7] Our steering group started meeting regularly and began the design of leaflets, resource packs and other necessary mobilising materials. And at the beginning of January 2006 I spent almost a month travelling around Scotland visiting and talking with peace and justice groups. I then returned to concentrate on England and Wales, leaving David to continue in Scotland.

These first few months of mobilising were perhaps the most exciting and the most difficult. The rota was completely empty! How could we persuade people it would be worth their time and effort to mobilise for something that might not even take place?

We just told them how important it was at this particular time when the UK was at war trying to stop other countries getting nuclear weapons, when the UK was talking about replacing its own nuclear weapons, when resource

---

[6] Adam Conway, Anna-Linnea Rundberg, David Mackenzie and myself, Angie Zelter.

[7] By the end of October 2005 the steering group consisted of Adam Conway, Anna-Linnea Rundberg, David Mackenzie, David McLachlan and Angie Zelter. Mel Harrison from Theatre of War joined the group for a couple of months at the end of 2005, before she became too busy with work against the US base at Lakenheath and had to leave. Rebecca Johnson joined in February 2006, Jane Tallents in March 2006, and Brian Larkin in January 2007. Both Davids had to leave in 2007 due to other commitments. At the end of the campaign in October 2007 there were six people in the steering group – Adam Conway, Rebecca Johnson, Brian Larkin, Anna-Linnea Rundberg, Jane Tallents and Angie Zelter.

conflicts were increasing and a new nuclear arms race was beginning. We explained how nonviolent civil resistance had worked in other places at other times, how we would support them by sharing our skills and knowledge and how good they would feel to be part of such an ambitious campaign. We often showed an inspirational video called *The Big Blockade*.[8] We suggested that if they had the vision and conviction to book a date in the rota then it would encourage others to do so. Enough agreed. And when we got to March 2006 and only had 14 bookings, with only another possible 31 other groups still deciding on dates, it was clear that there was already such momentum from these participating groups that they wanted to go ahead even if we did not reach the 100 goal we had aimed for.[9] Some blockading was better than none. And as with all ideas, as more and more people joined in and owned it for themselves, it changed and took on a life of its own.

Surprisingly, it was often our closest allies that felt unable to commit to the blockades at the beginning. They felt very disempowered. For instance, early on, the Scottish CND executive told us the idea of Faslane 365 was 'dangerously flawed' and that 'the government won't let you do it'. We had to work hard to get them to join in and when we did it was mainly due to the number of other groups that were supporting the blockades – it would have looked strange if the group best known for nuclear disarmament had not supported them. There was reluctance, and hesitation too, from many other local CND and peace groups,[10] who had grown weary of the continual protest work they had had to sustain for so many decades. It was certainly time to bring in new energy and new hope. And this is what Faslane 365 did. We put out the call to blockade to a variety of peace and justice groups, solidarity and human rights groups, environmental and international groups, religious and pagan groups – anyone who we thought might desire nuclear disarmament.

---

[8] *The Big Blockade* video followed people from Stirling CND who had taken part in a previous Trident Ploughshares Big Blockade. The film explored the fears and hopes of a local teacher, GP, school janitor, museum curator and school children and followed them throughout the Big Blockade.

[9] By the time the blockades started on 1 October 2006 only 50 groups covering 56 days were in the rota but by the end of the Faslane 365 year we had 131 blockading groups, which covered 188 days. The year finished with a Big Blockade on 1 October 2007, which brought the grand total up to 132 groups covering 189 days.

[10] With the notable exceptions of Yorkshire, Manchester, East Anglia and Welsh CND.

Many of the precursors to Faslane 365 had been too centralised, causing a core group of people to wear themselves to shreds to keep the civil resistance going. They were providing most of the infrastructural support for the direct action and this was not healthy for themselves or the movement.[11] This time we wanted to empower people and groups to organise themselves as independently as possible. This was essential if we wanted to keep going for a year. So, right from the start, we decided to encourage autonomy and to make available all of the materials we had developed over our years of campaigning. We would make the tools of resistance easily accessible in printed and electronic versions and we would try and set up training workshops to transfer skills.

Thus we designed an initial leaflet but encouraged people to adapt it or create their own for their specific group. We printed a resource pack to distribute at our mobilising meetings but made sure it was up on the website too so people could print out individual pages and adapt it as they saw fit. The website[12] was designed to be as informative as possible, including photos and maps of the base and the gates to be blockaded, a guide to organising one's own legal support along with maps of police stations, how to write a press release, how to arrange transport and accommodation and how to arrange workshops to learn a whole variety of things. Information was never allowed to be bottle-necked by the steering group but was shared as quickly and efficiently as possible amongst participating blockading groups. We even organised a survey of vehicles in and out of the various gates at the base over random days and times so that groups would be well enough informed to make their own decisions about when it would be most effective to place their blockades. And each blockading group was given its own unique section on the website to put up its leaflets, press releases, pictures and reports. We encouraged groups to read each other's pages and to contact each other, especially the groups before and after them in the rota.

We envisaged that our steering group would just facilitate the rota of blockades, find trainers for the nonviolence workshops, encourage a collective experience by maintaining a website and write a monthly newsletter, to monitor, record and feedback information about the blockades to all the participating blockading groups. We also committed to provide some overall legal

---

[11] See p.101, 'Globalised Resistance' by Petter Joelson and Anna Sanne Göransson, for some insight into this dilemma.

[12] www.faslane365.org.

support until the finish of all prosecutions, and to communicate, over the year, with the police to encourage nonviolence from everyone involved. Of course, inevitably, the reality was not quite as autonomous as we had hoped and the steering group was hard pressed at times to provide the support required,[13] especially during the first three months, but it was much better than if we had not made this attempt. By the second half of the year, when some of the blockading groups were returning for a second turn in the rota, we discovered that groups were much more confident and self-sufficient. They booked their own accommodation, knew where the police stations were, took their own pictures and uploaded them onto the website, and provided their own trainings. The culminating Big Blockade showed an even greater degree of self-sufficiency, especially apparent in the blockading groups who had decided to lock on at various times in the day providing waves of blockaders, and in groups taking the initiative to block Coulport as well as Faslane, and in some groups even deciding to block in the three days following the Big Blockade.[14] If only we could have started the year with this level of preparation!

I think we underestimated how 'domesticated' people were, how unsure of their own abilities, how fearful of being arrested, how difficult it was for the few strong local facilitators of the blockading groups to bring in new local people and to delegate the organising work. We had also underestimated how factionalised our society is. Some of the initial mobilising meetings that were organised in geographical areas attracted audiences of up to 70 or 80 people from a variety of different social justice groups but even though volunteers came forward to take the process on, they found it hard to work together and many supporters were lost in the process of follow-up meetings. The average number of people actually making their way to

---

[13] The support included providing a welcome at the gates, extra banners, fold-up chairs, tea urns, water and mugs, portable loos, access to the internet and troubleshooting, to mention just a few things.

[14] Bradford decided to block the North Gate of Faslane on the following day, 2 October 2007, with a banner that said 'Faslane 366 to be continued...'. Then on 3 October the Finnish group blockaded the South Gate along with a few Peace Campers, and on the night of 3 and early morning of 4 October the Swedish group sent three people walking into Coulport and another group swimming in from the south and north sides of the base. All got in. None are being taken through the courts.

Faslane in a blockading group often fell to below 30 – a more comfortable size to organise around. The target of 100 people was daunting for many local organisers. Perhaps we could have done more to encourage groups to use the fish-bowl type facilitation[15] for later meetings or other techniques for equal participation. Nevertheless people and groups did what they could and were empowered in the process. It was a learning process for everyone who took part.

Faslane 365 Nonviolence Guidelines

We are committed to always acting in a way that causes no harm to ourselves or others. We ask that everyone taking part in Faslane 365 respect and follow these guidelines:

- Our attitude will be one of sincerity and respect towards the people we encounter.
- We will not engage in physical violence or verbal abuse toward any individual.
- We will carry no weapons.
- We will not bring or use alcohol or drugs other than for medical purposes.
- We will clear the blockade to allow emergency vehicles in or out of the base and then resume the blockade afterwards.

We wanted to make sure that the year of blockades would stay nonviolent and that our actions would be in accordance with our aims for a peaceful world, so we made two simple commitments an essential requirement for all those taking part:

All groups need to agree to a basic set of non-negotiable guidelines that stress nonviolence and respect for all. All groups must also commit to

---

[15] A method of consensus decision making which involves representatives from each small (affinity) group sitting in a circle, with each group behind its representative. The discussion is only carried out by the representative but everyone can hear it. When necessary each small (affinity) group can call back its representative to discuss further or make a decision, and this is then taken back to the circle of representatives for further discussion. The circle works by consensus, as does each small group. There can be several embedded fish bowls if the numbers of people are very large.

the main demand: Trident must be taken out of deployment and the government should make a timetable for dismantling the weapons together with a commitment not to develop any new nuclear weapons.

We had aimed to enable different groups working on varied important current issues to come up to Faslane and make the links and this was explicitly stated in our resource pack under a section called 'Making the Links'. We knew that there was a whole range of related issues but also knew how hard it is to mobilise people around a common platform and how debilitating it can be for everyone to have to agree on everything before action can be taken. We thus felt it would be good to encourage groups working on a single issue to gather their supporters together and take on their own individual block in the rota. This would enable undiluted single-issue messages to be made with an underlying common message of No Nuclear Weapons. We hoped that this would strengthen the anti-nuclear movement, as well as give a forum for issues that some people might not even have realised were related.

To give just a few examples: the Palestinian Solidarity group on 8 November 2006 made links between Western support for Israeli nuclear weapons, illegal Israeli occupation of the West Bank and Gaza, human rights abuses and the UK–Israeli arms trade; the Irish group on 9 December 2006 highlighted the possibility of a peace process in conflict zones when nonviolent people pressure is applied; the Health Professionals group on 25 January 2007 emphasised the waste of resources and the health impacts of the whole nuclear chain; the Environmentalists on 26 and 27 April 2007 made the link between military and civil nuclear power and the radioactive pollution of environments across the world; and the Unity group that came up to support the blockades on 18 May 2007 made the links between wars and refugees.[16]

Of the roughly 130 groups that took part around half were from geographical areas – 48 from the UK (30 from England, 14 from Scotland, three from Wales and one from Northern Ireland) and 13 international groups, mostly from other European countries but some from as far away as Japan. The other half were special interest groups. For instance, 15 religious groups took part, 13 peace groups, six political parties or groups of political representatives like the Scottish Councillors, six music and arts groups including choirs and dancers, six professional groups like teachers, lawyers and

---

[16] To gain an overall picture of the kinds of groups that participated there is a full list of participating groups in Appendix 1.

Faslane 365 – Making the Links

Governments that are so busy spending our money and wasting the world's resources on building up military capabilities are failing to address the most serious challenges facing the world. Of what conceivable use are nuclear weapons against the real mass destruction that threatens our security and the lives of millions: the oil-and-industry-driven heating of the planet; destruction of our habitat and environment; and the institutionalised poverty that destroys the hopes and lives of thousands each day?

Representing a quick and violent 'fix' to complex threats and challenges, nuclear weapons epitomise the abuses of power and skewed values that fuel terrorism and the growing levels of violence in our homes and on our streets. Trident is thus inextricably related to a wide range of economic, humanitarian, peace and justice issues.

The yearlong blockade of the Faslane nuclear base that will start on 1 October will provide an opportunity for a wide range of people to oppose the deployment and replacement of Trident, while simultaneously highlighting the important issues they are working on, such as poverty, peace, environment, globalisation, economic equity and social justice. Bringing together the people and organisations working for a better world will help to expose the myriad crimes and distortions wrought by the nuclear mentality and globalised dominance of military-industrial corporations.

If we succeed in cutting the cord that binds our country to nuclear weapons, we will find that we have gone a long way towards cutting or at least loosening the hold of the military mindset and the dominant corporations, giving us a better chance to turn things around on a host of connected issues.

Faslane 365 is asking for 48 hours of your time to make the connections: to publicise and work on your issues while helping us physically to close the Trident nuclear base.

academics, 10 environmental and solidarity groups like Unity, Greenpeace, and Palestinian Solidarity, and six women's groups including Women in Black and Grannies. There was also a great input from eight youth blocks, with the UK student community joining together to cover six days in a block in the summer.

Work was put into getting organisations and individuals to sign the statement of support whether or not they could actually join in and this helped to raise the awareness of the blockades. Perhaps this had most impact in the run up to the Scottish elections when we approached various Scottish political parties to take on a block for their party. The Greens were the first political party to take on a block on 15 October 2006 and Green MSPs and MEPs supported the parliamentary block on 8 January 2007 as well as supporting many of their local geographical groups. The Scottish National Party took on a block on 21 October 2006 and many of their MSPs signed the statement of support, including Alex Salmond, who later became First Minister of Scotland. SNP councillors from Glasgow decided to hold their own councillors' block on 8 August 2007. Solidarity and the Scottish Socialist Youth also participated in the blockading rota with their own blocks. The Welsh Party, Plaid Cymru, must not be forgotten. Having been anti-nuclear for many years they supported their Scottish colleagues by coming along to several blocks. Plaid Cymru councillors, AMS and MEPs supported not only the two overlapping Welsh blocks from 13 to 15 November 2006, which came with choirs and red dragons, but also the elected representatives' block and the Big Blockade at the end. Our arguments on the illegality and criminality of the Trident system helped legitimise our disruption of the Faslane nuclear base, thus making it possible for law-makers to feel comfortable about upholding the law by trying to stop preparations for war crimes.

The issue of international law has been an important underlying foundation for the whole year and was explicitly addressed in the small but important lawyers' blocks on 9 January and 13 September 2007. With Westminster 'reserving' issues of defence under the devolution settlement and trying to prohibit the Scottish Executive having any say over military issues it was important to point out time and time again that Westminster cannot reserve illegalities, cannot force Scotland to break international law, that defence must be real defence and not preparation for war crimes. The starting date for the year of blockades, 1 October, was specifically chosen to make these links, it being the anniversary of the judgement of the major war criminals at the Nuremberg tribunal at the end of the Second World War. The Big Blockade which celebrated the end of Faslane 365 was similarly on 1 October.

There has been a fascinating mix of people coming to Faslane. I cannot hope to tell you about all the different groups, each of which was special and valuable, but scattered in between the chapters of this book are some of the blockading groups' reports on their actions in their own words.

Women did the first blockade of the year, making a link with the Greenham Common Women's Peace Camp of 25 years before, which succeeded in getting rid of cruise missiles and eventually closing the Greenham Common airbase – a reminder that the peace movement has been, and can again be, very successful if it sustains nonviolent civil resistance. Women held another block at the end of the year, bringing to the fore the long-lasting impact of war on women and children. This tied in with the Grannies for Peace block, on 23 August 2007, when photos of grandchildren were tied to the fence and the impact of nuclear weapons on the coming generations was highlighted.

The family block brought together children, babies and parents, who played amongst the rocks, in and under the rainbow umbrellas, blew bubbles, dressed up in fancy costumes and made a blockade of Action Man toys dressed up as peace protesters – a safe way of joining the blockade without getting arrested!

Probably the youngest to actually blockade and get arrested was 13-year-old Catherine Holmes, who locked on with her teddy bear with the Edinburgh group on 13 October 2006.[17] And the oldest may have been Betty Tebbs, who at 89 years of age thumb-locked herself to others from Manchester and lay down in the rain, with the midges biting, blocking the south entrance to the base on 12 June.[18]

We held two Power of the Word and Song blocks (6 December 2006 and 5 June 2007), to which famous writers, poets, actors and musicians came to celebrate the creativity of our world and to speak out against the injustice and cruelty that holds humanity back from its full potential. Billy Bragg, David Ferrard, A.L. Kennedy, Gerry Loose, Adrian Mitchell, Roger Lloyd Pack, Rebecca Thorn and Theo Simon were just a few of those who joined in speaking and singing out. Various choirs, socialist and radical in their outlook, decided to hold their own special block, singing protest songs on 3 and 4 June 2007. They put the words and music on their web page beforehand and on the days at the base they taught each other their favourite songs as well as performing to each other at either side of the North Gate. They then massed themselves in front of the gates and sang powerfully and movingly until the police warned them off the road. They

---

[17] See 'Teddy Bear Lock-on', p.20.

[18] See 'An Angel, a Squirrel and a Big Red Bus: Manchester at Faslane', p.xxvii.

continued to sing and support those who remained seated in front of the gates and were then taken off by the police.

The two academic blocks (7 January and 27 June 2007) were another occasion when distinguished and famous people joined the blockades. The professors, researchers, lecturers and students engaged in deep discussions in small seminar groups in front of the gates of Faslane. They were glad to meet colleagues from different disciplines, to know they were not alone in their concerns, and were intellectually challenged by the varied papers presented. Professor Sir Richard Jolly and his academic wife and children were amongst those both contributing to the discussions and being arrested for blockading. The debates continued into the police vans and cells and onto plans for publishing the papers in book form.

One of the academics, Professor John Hull, a theologian of international repute, who also happens to be totally blind, found the occasion so stimulating that he decided to organise a block of theological students. These came up on 10 June 2007 and the students organised their service with a specially prepared hymn book and then went into the road to block it. When writing up their experiences, John described the 'Faslane pilgrimage' as 'an official part of the ministerial formation offered' by the Queen's Foundation for Ecumenical Theological Education in Birmingham. He described it as a useful start in 'preparing students to lead a counter-cultural church'.

Faith groups had quite an impact, with various religious leaders making their way to Faslane, including the Bishop of Reading, who managed to get the gates to Faslane closed and then processed in front of them and blessed the congregation as peacemakers. Clergy Against Nuclear Arms organised several of these services and vigils over the year. On 27 October 2006 around 90 Quakers from the south of England met for worship at the gates and then 25 blocked the road and were arrested. This was followed by Northern Friends on 12 November, when a further 16 Quakers sat down and were arrested. 4 March 2007 saw Quakers from the north of England witness, with ten more arrests for disrupting preparations for war crimes at Faslane. Then on 25 May another group of Quakers came to worship and witness. Some individual Quakers also came up from Bath and from Mosedale to do their bit, and then a final group was up in early September, when four were arrested. None of the yearly total of 41 arrested Quakers were proceeded against in the courts.

Cyclists did two blocks, the first on 12 October 2006 emphasising a more sustainable and healthy lifestyle by cycling as opposed to nuclear propulsion and missiles, and the second on 5 September 2007 seeing four of them strip off all their clothing and display a banner saying 'Renewing Trident is Naked Aggression'.

Another amusing block was carried out by 16 banana activists, all 'arrested' for blockading the North Gate. The bananas, using miniature arm locks and D-locks made of foil, managed to disrupt the base for some minutes and were assisted by three human supporters wearing Banana Support jackets. Their banners read 'Trident is Bananas' and 'Bananas say No Trident'. The police were amused, as was passing traffic, as the supporters – a large French contingent who had just been let out of the police cells after their action the previous day – cheered and shouted 'Libere la Banane'. Behind the banter and good humour the serious issue of economic exploitation of poorer nations and the link with military power were being highlighted. A few days later more humour was celebrated on April Fool's Day with the Rebel Clown Army engaging in wondrous stilt-walking, juggling and teasing foolishness, which brought everyone down to size.

The geographical groups that formed the bulk of the blockades often found specific links to their own areas. Thus York came dressed as Vikings and said 'The Vikings slaughtered tens of thousands of people but they did so over half a millennium. Trident could do the same in a minute.' Nottingham came dressed as Robin Hood and his Merry Band, including Maid Marion and Little John, and numbered around 50. They succeeded in blocking the North Gate for over four hours with their plaster of Paris and cement lock-ons. Their banner read 'Stop robbing the poor NHS to fund WMD'. The East Anglian block emphasised the links between the US and the UK and talked of the US nuclear bombs stored at Lakenheath in Suffolk.

The internationals must not be forgotten. They formed an important part of the year, making links between UK nuclear weapons and policies in their own countries and emphasising the essential point that UK nuclear weapons affect everyone in the world, they are not merely a concern of the UK. They also saw NATO as an illegal nuclear alliance that has continued to lock the military in an outdated 'if you are not with us then you are against us' war-fighting mentality.

The Finns and Swedes came along first on 16 and 17 October 2006 and did one of the most effective blockades of the year with Finns putting up a tripod and lock-ons just before the entrance into the South Gate that blocked traffic going to the North Gate too. That took over two hours to remove. The Swedes meanwhile had locked on at the North Gate with steel tubes that also took quite a time to get through. It all took place during the rush hour at 7am. Forty-three Scandinavians were arrested in total that morning! They then joined us once more for the Big Blockade on 1 October 2007.

The Spaniards were a joyful exuberant bunch, belonging to the Conscientious Objection Movement, who poured red paint all over themselves on 17 March 2007. The police did not want to get their uniforms dirty and so kept out of the way until they had been given white paper suits and could hardly be distinguished from the protesters. Meanwhile the Spaniards sang and danced at the gates, looking quite festive in their red spattered garb and keeping the atmosphere nonviolent and light. Serious passion against nuclear weapons and the knowledge of what is happening in our world wisely mixed with an ability to enjoy life and protest at the same time.

The French joined in with their blockade on 26 and 27 March 2007 and on the following two days were joined by a German group who organised their 24 blockaders into four lines, one behind the other, walking up the main road towards the South Gate approach road in their lock-ons. When police refused to let them walk up to and into the approach road leading to the South Gate, and thus to get out of the main road, they lay down where they were and it took three hours to get them cut out, creating huge tail-backs. The Belgian Friends of the Earth group came on 2 and 3 January and the Belgian Bomspotting group on 17 and 18 September.

These blocks were not only good in themselves but also cemented the ties between the peace movements in these countries. Useful contacts were made and discussions held about future nonviolent pressure to be applied in the coming years at NATO HQ in Brussels.

The Japanese block was a very special one as they were taken to various peace gardens where Japanese cherry trees had been planted by previous visiting Hibakusha.[19] They brought exhibition materials of the nuclear devastation they had witnessed so people could more clearly visualise the horror of nuclear weapons. They decorated the fences with thousands of paper cranes and then took part in a bamboo blockade.

Most groups managed to get extensive local or special interest press coverage of their actions. The health professionals had articles in medical magazines and also produced a video that they distributed on DVDs. Seize

---

[19] 'Hibakusha' is the Japanese word for survivors from Hiroshima and Nagasaki, the two Japanese cities that were destroyed by US nuclear bombings at the end of the Second World War.

the Day, a well-known folk group, mobilised their fans to blockade, videoed their action and songs, put it up on YouTube, and got local Somerset coverage as well as Scottish coverage. Manchester drove its blockading group and supporters all the way to Faslane in a big red double-decker bus with the side billboard stating 'Manchester Says No Trident'. It was a Number 365 bus, of course! The Leicester group got ITV central news coverage when one of their supporters, a pensioner of 94, was interviewed outside the gates of Faslane. The Welsh, Japanese and Scandinavian groups also got extensive coverage in their own language press as well as in Scotland.

Greenpeace got brilliant coverage for their wonderful blockade. They had sent the *Arctic Sunrise* along the Gare Loch with lots of fast rigid inflatable boats that managed to get tens of people into the high-security waters around the submarine berths, resulting in a full blockade of the base for a whole morning as the bandit alarms sounded. And then the captain brought the ship right up to the boom, where it dropped its anchor, blocking access to the submarine area. The navy had to laser the anchor chains free, making a hole in the side of the Greenpeace ship, which had to be towed right into the base for repairs before being released some days later.[20] Captain Waldemar used to be in the Argentinian navy and I think he was amused to be able to take on the British navy in this nonviolent manner! The traffic queuing up to get into the South Gate[21] was treated to a full view of the police boats chasing the Greenpeace boats. I chatted to some of the workers waiting to get into Faslane and some actually said the blockades were making them re-evaluate their work in Faslane, with one man saying he was going to leave.

Over the year, the continual coverage in the press helped keep the pressure for nuclear disarmament in the public mind and on the political agenda.

The groups not only took part in wonderful creative nonviolent blockading but also produced some stunning banners. Being based at the Peace Camp, near the South Gate of Faslane, I was able to easily observe the vast majority of the blocks and take pictures of the blockades and their banners. I enjoyed designing a series of 16 cards and a commemorative poster that recorded the diversity of messages and actions, providing a great

---

[20] Forty-seven Greenpeace activists were arrested but only six are being taken through the courts, including the captain.

[21] When any protester gets into the base, the bandit alarm goes off and all gates are closed until they have been apprehended.

visual record of the year. Some of these photos appear on this book's cover. Most of the groups took photos of their own and they were posted on the website. The latest posted photo appeared on the home page, which changed almost every day. Groups were also able to post their blockade reports to encourage the groups yet to come.

The year of blockading ended with a Big Blockade because many of the participating groups wanted to meet other blockading groups and get a feel of their joint strength. They wanted to celebrate the successful conclusion of a year of resistance. It was a great day, with around 700 people coming along in their great diversity and with 189 people being arrested throughout the day.

The year of blockades is over now and the inevitable question is, what did it achieve? Are we any nearer nuclear disarmament? It is always difficult to evaluate such a diverse campaign and even more difficult to know the ultimate consequences of our actions. However, some indications are already apparent.

On the political side it does seem as if Faslane 365 helped to keep nuclear disarmament on the Scottish agenda and helped get a pro-nuclear disarmament executive elected. The new Scottish government is committed to nuclear disarmament and many of the NGOs who have been working for nuclear disarmament over the last few years were invited to a summit of key stakeholders held in Glasgow on 22 October 2007. As Bruce Crawford, Minister for Parliamentary Business, stated in his invitation to Faslane 365, the summit is to 'reflect the views of the majority of Scots and carefully consider which aspects of the UK government's plans to replace Trident impact on our responsibilities in Scotland under devolution. I made it clear that we will do all that we can, in the light of those responsibilities, to persuade the UK government to change its stance both on the replacement programme and on the general principle of maintaining and deploying nuclear weapons in Scotland.' Several of the groups involved in organising Faslane 365 blockading groups were also invited, including Trident Ploughshares. The summit provided a forum for us to engage with others on how Scotland can use the tool of international law to extricate itself from complicity in preparations for war crimes. The potency of this tool has not yet been fully recognised by politicians, who feel bound by the devolution reservations to Westminster. The Scottish government pledged to set up a working group to take the ideas that came out of the summit forward.

Another result and follow-up to the year of blockades and our insistence that international law is being broken at Faslane and Coulport was the organising of a high-level delegation to the Lord Advocate with a summary of the legal case against Trident. I organised this, along with the Edinburgh Peace and Justice Centre, and many of the delegates were people whom we had met through their involvement with Faslane 365 blockades, including professors, lawyers and religious leaders. The energy raised by the year is being slowly translated into other actions and pressures for nuclear disarmament.

As part of an evaluation of the campaign itself it is useful to look back at a session we had way back in October 2005, when we put up on a board the possible pluses and minuses of the proposal for Faslane 365.[22] Of the 27 potential minuses – which included things like burn-out amongst activists, taking energy away from other nuclear sites like Aldermaston or Devonport, repressive reaction from the police and military, difficulty of finding arrestables and the failure of the rota leading to depression and lack of hope, the possibility of failing to maintain nonviolence – only one actually took place – there was an impact on locals because of the blocking of the roads. This was difficult to deal with but we managed it reasonably well and it is examined in Chapter 8. Of the 27 potential pluses, nearly all have taken place – new people joining in and a revitalisation of the peace movement, empowerment for individuals and a rise in energy and actions, new and extended contacts and networks, a voice and space for political empowerment, breaking down the reluctance to engage in civil resistance, a transformation of the political scene. Of course the pluses are not all down to us but at least we did not stop them from taking place!

However, it might be useful to examine why we could not get more groups to join in and why so few people (relatively) actually felt able to blockade.

To begin with let us acknowledge the contribution made by those who came and did not blockade. They still felt brave enough to come, moved enough to make their personal arrangements and give up their free time, empowered enough to do their own thing, to add their voices and strength to the year of blockades. And this was vital, we are all interconnected and of course this ultimately is what people power is all about. It is not about the convictions of one or two people but about the different convictions of many people expressed in myriad ways. These people felt that their particular

---

[22] See Appendix II for a complete list of these pluses and minuses.

activities were just as important as blockading and wanted to do their protest in their own way, wanted to support the year of blockades but did not actually want to blockade. And thank goodness they came. Their contribution was essential. Without them we would have been a much weaker presence. One policeman said to me that he was more impressed by the group that came up from London and sang for two days solid in the rain at the gates of Faslane than by the group that came up, blockaded for an hour and then disappeared after the arrests had taken place. Everyone who came up did their bit in their own way to add to the pressure for change, the call for nuclear disarmament.

At the same time, I found myself continuously wondering why people felt unable to blockade.

Only an average of six people per day actually blockaded until they were arrested. Some blockaded only until asked to move by the police, finding it difficult to disobey a policeman! Some groups of 20 or 30 protesters had no blockaders with them at all. Some individuals of course were doing essential support roles like legal observing, driving, press work, but there were many more who only felt comfortable demonstrating and felt unable to blockade – to 'break the law'. This despite the fact that there is a strong body of law that supports us trying to prevent preparations for mass murder and the vast majority of us plead not guilty. Maybe the non-arrestables are more persuaded by the local Helensburgh magistrates who find us guilty nevertheless or maybe they are not so interested in the law anyway and are against nuclear weapons for purely moral reasons.

Some groups came all the way up to Faslane, with all the effort that it took to arrange for time off work, to raise funds for travel and accommodation, to prepare themselves, and then they only demonstrated or did a vigil or took part in a religious service or meditated or danced. It still fascinates me why blockading until arrested is such a difficult step to take. Perhaps because it was never a difficult step for me, I find it hard to understand. Perhaps because I believe passionately that the state could not continue to get away with such wrongdoing if we did not let it, that if we 'disrupted' more and were less 'obedient' we could change our society, that we could actually have brought the base to a standstill. Perhaps we are afraid of our own strength – scared of the unknown, of the impact of our own power.

As I raised this issue with people, I heard very consistent answers. People feel afraid of being arrested, of having a criminal record, of what impact it might have on their job prospects or careers if their bosses find out, fears about whether they will be allowed to travel to other countries if they have a criminal record, not wanting to take any of these possible risks for something that they feel will probably not stop nuclear weapons from being deployed anyway, not wanting to spend a night in a police cell, having to get home for work or family commitments. Each person has a myriad of fears and practical problems to overcome before they manage to take their first arrestable action.

Nevertheless, one of our successes over the year was helping to support people in this step. The vast majority of people who were arrested were first-time arrestees and all of them felt proud of their actions and much stronger for having overcome their fears. The nonviolence workshops were undoubtedly of prime importance in allowing people a safe environment to explore their fears and hopes and prepare for arrest.[23]

A classic tactic of the police was to make use of these fears: by telling those that were present on a Friday that they would be held over the whole weekend and not released until Monday if they blockaded; or by allowing them some time to blockade and then going up to them and saying – look, you have blockaded for a while but now we are going to arrest you if you continue, so the blockade will end anyway now whatever you do, why not get up and leave now because you will not achieve any more than you have already. You will be getting arrested for nothing! Very persuasive! It is easy to forget at this point how much more trouble and pressure is caused by having to remove people, process them and take them to police stations, how many more points of interaction there are between protester and 'authorities', how much more costly it is to society and thus how much more pressure is brought to bear to 'solve' the problem.

Then there is the 'lawful protest' via the 'unlawful blockading' issue. It is interesting to see how many people (especially police, judges and politicians) smugly point to the ability of UK citizens to demonstrate lawfully as a sign of our wonderful democratic rights, even though this 'right' is under great threat from the current erosion of civil liberties. Many do so in the belief that demonstrations are a good in themselves, as if the matter ends there. You often hear people say, 'Well, you have had your protest, why don't you go away now?' But isn't protest a tool to awaken the public conscience, to make discontent and concerns highly visible to society at large, so that

---

[23] The workshops and trainings are dealt with in more depth in Chapter 5.

something is done about an issue? In a functioning democracy, the issues raised by the protests should then be examined, and protesters legitimately expect their concerns to be addressed. We do not protest for the sake of protest but to effect social change, to have wrongs put right. Until those wrongs are righted the protests continue. When the issues raised by demonstrations and protest are not addressed then we have to move to nonviolent civil resistance, whereby we nonviolently resist the status quo and try to disrupt the functioning of that part of society that we feel is immoral, unlawful or inhumane.

For me this is what this year was about – creating change. People power showed its strength, from protest and presence, vigils and prayer, to civil disruption. We have finished the year with more people engaged in working for nuclear disarmament and a stronger social change movement just at the time when we need it, to tackle the serious security issues that confront this planet. So perhaps one of the most important off-shoots from Faslane 365 was one hoped for at the very beginning – the transference of information, skills and confidence, leading to the empowerment of local affinity groups around the country who can work together over the long term. I have heard back from many of the blockading groups that they have gained a great deal from their participation, that they feel they are part of a real and lasting 'affinity' group, that they feel able to tackle together various local issues now. Many are committed to taking nonviolent civil resistance actions at nuclear bases or facilities nearer to them and to keeping up responsible and non-violent people power over the coming years.

Teddy Bear Lock-on

CATHERINE HOLMES[24]

Nuclear weapons are immoral. They are indiscriminate and cost billions of pounds. The government say that they are for security yet it's a strange kind of security which puts our people more at risk from terrorists and any other enemies. What right do the governments of America and Great Britain have

---

[24] At 13, Catherine Holmes was the youngest person to be arrested for peaceful direct action at Faslane during the year of blockades. Catherine was one of the Edinburgh group blockading on Friday, 13 and Saturday, 14 October 2006.

that they should own these bombs? Owning them is illegal and they are not above the law. They may be more powerful and rich than other countries but why should this be a reason to bully smaller countries? The recent nuclear test in North Korea was deemed 'a risk to national security and peace' by George Bush; however he seems to forget that his country owns billions of pounds worth of these weapons. By replacing – or even retaining – these weapons of mass destruction, our governments are failing to abide by the Non-Proliferation Treaty.

Earlier this year, in September, along with many other people from different places across Britain and the world, I walked from Faslane to the Scottish parliament in Edinburgh in an effort to bring about awareness amongst the local people and MSPs of Scotland. Amongst the walkers there was a real sense of community and it was a pleasure getting to talk to people who you don't normally get the chance to. Long-term peace protesters such as Bruce Kent were joined by church and trade union leaders as well as young people like myself. On the walk we went through many areas where it was clear to see funding was needed and it was apparent to everyone on the walk that if we weren't spending so much money on Trident then all these areas could be improved, along with the lives of the people who live there. The support of local people we passed on the walk was incredibly encouraging, with people tooting horns and shouting support. It was obvious that the majority of locals were against Trident. It's just a shame no one else listens to them.

Following on from the walk there were many meetings with people from the walk as well as people who weren't able to join us. At a meeting with ex-senator Douglas Roche and peace writer and Jesuit Gerry Hughes it was pointed out with reference to the Nuremberg trials after the Second World War, that there is no difference between putting innocent people in ovens and throwing ovens at innocent people.

All through my life I have known about what's going on in other countries and I've been educated by more than the media and school. I've had the chance to go to a talk with a man called Moazzam Begg who had been taken to Guantanamo Bay and kept as a prisoner there for years without getting to speak to his family and without being found guilty or even tried for anything. Listening to him speak in such a gentle and forgiving way was so inspiring and seeing someone who has been through so much come out the other end peaceful and not at all full of hate or anger was incredible.

Ever since I was young I have been signing petitions, going on marches and demonstrations, hearing people talk about their experiences in Africa, Palestine and other places, and learning about things which are hidden from us by the government, like the munitions depot at Beith. I think that this is a really important part of demonstrating against things which we believe to be wrong in the world. However I began to feel that I wasn't being listened to, and so I decided that I wanted to be part of a direct action. This is why I decided to go to Faslane and make my views heard.

To prepare for this I worked with an affinity group so that we knew and trusted each other to take care and act safely. We took nonviolence training to help with being peaceful whatever happens and showing respect to the police and people working at the base. We practised our action, locking our arms inside a giant teddy, over and over, going through all the different things that might happen, so on the day, it all went according to plan – one policeman even said he had to hand it to us that he hadn't seen it coming.

While I was lying in the road being cut out of the lock-on one of the police officers made a comment about my age. Surely they know that there are innocent children much younger than myself being killed in Iraq because of depleted uranium. We asked one of them if they actually knew what was behind that big tall fence with the guards and the dogs yet she just shrugged. It made me wonder why they hadn't asked themselves what we were actually protesting against. I guess they were just doing their jobs.

One of the major problems in our society today is the fact that there is little education about what our government is actually doing in Iraq or in Palestine or even just up the road at Faslane. If people knew what was really going on there would be many more questions asked and much more pressure on the government to get rid of Trident. If Britain were to get rid of our nuclear weapons I am sure many other countries would follow. No wonder they feel the need to own weapons of mass destruction when the Western world has enough to do the damage of Hiroshima hundreds of times over.

Trident, War, Refugees, Asylum Seekers and Unity[25]

PHILL JONES[26]

Glasgow, the nearest city to Faslane, where all of Britain's nuclear weapons are based, has more than 5,000 asylum seekers[27] living in it, more than any other city in Britain.[28] Due to the city council's policy of housing only families,[29] there are 1,400 families, two thirds of which are single-parent families, from about 50 different countries, living in Glasgow. Many of these families have been in Glasgow for four, five or even six years, waiting for a decision from the Home Office about their asylum application and battling heroically against the institutional racism of the UK's immigration system.

Some might suggest it's because Glasgow is the furthest major city from London and the south east of England, and it's probably only a coincidence that the nearest city to Britain's Trident nuclear submarine base also plays host to so many people trying to get official recognition as refugees. It probably is only a coincidence, but on reflection it's not difficult to make connections between these two facts and discover why it was appropriate for Unity – the union of asylum seekers in Scotland – to come to Faslane as part of the Faslane 365 campaign.

For a start, more than anything else, it's wars that cause refugees.

If you're like me, in the past you've maybe associated the word 'refugee' with an image of someone living in a camp, probably somewhere in Africa, having fled famine or some other natural disaster. This is the image used

---

[25] In memory of Solyman Rashed, a 28-year-old asylum seeker, who after being held in a detention centre for 15 months gave up his claim for asylum in the UK, voluntarily returned to his home town, Kirkuk, in Iraq, and was killed by a car bomb two weeks later.

[26] Phill coordinates the Unity Centre in Glasgow.

[27] An asylum seeker is someone applying for official recognition as a refugee in the UK.

[28] This is more than double the number living in any other city outside of London.

[29] Under the dispersal programme Glasgow is the only council in Scotland to accept large numbers of asylum seekers. The council's contract with the National Asylum Support Service (NASS) is to house families only. Single asylum seekers are housed by a private company, Angel, and the YMCA.

'Blockaders', Jill Gibbon

repeatedly by the UN, by aid agencies, refugee support groups, charities and so on. It's an image we're all familiar with, staring out of charity shop windows on every high street or from leaflets coming through our letterboxes. It's an image designed to trigger sympathy and compassion. An image used to provoke donations. But it is a gross misrepresentation.

During the First World War, civilians made up fewer than five per cent of all casualties. Today, 75 per cent or more of those killed or wounded in wars are non-combatants. Civilians caught up in fighting abandon their homes and flee war in their thousands. Looking at the global statistics on refugees is like looking at a roll call of the world's bloodiest conflicts.

According to the United Nations High Commissioner for Refugees (UNHCR), the number of refugees worldwide went up in 2006 for the first time in five years due to at least one million Iraqi civilians fleeing from their war-torn homeland. Globally in 2006 there were about 9.9 million refugees.

This figure however does not include 4.3 million Palestinians being looked after by the UN Relief and Works Agency. Palestinians make up the largest group of refugees globally. Afghans make up the next largest group as 2.1million people have fled Afghanistan over the last decade. Iraqis are the third largest group.

It's important to remember that the figure of 1 million Iraqi refugees does not include the number of Iraqis internally displaced, those people who have been forced from their homes but remain within the country. This rose by 660,000 in 2006, to a total of 1.8 million. Worldwide, the number of internally displaced people receiving UNHCR assistance in 2006 was about 13 million.

Refugees from Sudan, where there is ongoing strife between the Arab-led government and the black African population of the country's Darfur region, make up the fourth-largest group with 686,000.

Somalia, with about 460,000 of its population having fled during two decades of fighting between different warlords, has the next largest number of refugees, while about 400,000 people have fled from civil wars in both the Democratic Republic of the Congo and Burundi.

From these figures it is clear that war and conflict is the largest cause of refugees by far. The seven largest groups of refugees in the world all come from war-zones, not from areas affected by natural disasters. It is 'man-made' disasters that most people flee from.

The three largest groups of refugees, which when combined make up over half of the world's 14.2 million refugees, come from wars or conflicts

Global refugee populations

1	Palestinians	4.3 million
2	Afghanistan	2.1 million
3	Iraq	1 million
4	Sudan	686,000
5	Somalia	460,000
6	DRC	400,000
7	Burundi	400,000

that the West, and in particular the policies of the US and the UK governments, are directly responsible for. What's clear is that these refugees have not been created by obscure conflicts with long-forgotten and intractable origins. Instead over half of the world's refugees have been created directly by the policies pursued by the US and UK governments.

And that's without looking at the role of the UK and the US in, for example, the global arms trade that fuels the conflicts, or in supporting multinational corporations that destabilise governments. Or for that the matter, the role of Western countries in drawing up arbitrary national borders in the colonial and post-colonial period.

So, as Trident is one of the more potent symbols of UK military and foreign policies and an important symbol of British military power, it is more than appropriate for people who have fled war to be at Faslane.

But there are other connections as well which we all would do well to consider. Essentially, both Trident and the issue of immigration are to do with national identity and national responsibilities. And racism.

In a nutshell, lots of British people remain dedicated to the idea of Trident because it gives them a strong feeling of security against the dangerous, 'alien' rest of the world. At the height of the cold war this went as far as people saying it was better to be 'dead than Red'. It's claimed that Trident is to defend 'our way of life'. To do this somehow gives us the right to prepare to incinerate thousands, if not millions, of innocent people, all to defend something supposedly unique to us in the UK, or shared with the US or shared with all the other countries of NATO (depending on how parochial or not the politicians feel they need to be).

The intention to destroy so many people, rehearsed rigorously and repeatedly (and expensively) under the surface of the North Atlantic, implies belief in some kind of superiority of 'our' way of life over 'other' people's ways of life. How else could you actually justify it?

And this idea that we in the West believe we are superior becomes completely exposed when looking at the issue of nuclear weapons proliferation. Look at the knots people get into through trying to explain exactly why Iran or North Korea or India or Pakistan shouldn't have nuclear weapons when at the same time we intend to upgrade ours.

Basically, it boils down to the fact that we think we're superior. And that is how Trident is sold to us – as part of global 'realpolitik'.

But of course that is not the real world. We don't have Trident to defend 'our way of life', just as we didn't go to war with Iraq because there was a possibility that British troops sunbathing in Cyprus might be attacked by chemical weapons in 45 minutes. We have Trident to project power in the world in order to protect the economic interests of the UK.

In exactly the same way we are also told to be worried about immigration because of the threat it poses to our way of life. We are told to be scared of the 'alien' ways of life that migrants bring with them. Horrific predictions of trouble and bloodshed (whole rivers of it, apparently) have been repeatedly made to highlight the danger of immigration.

Yet isn't it strange that all those campaigning against being 'swamped' by immigrants wouldn't dream of campaigning against the civil liberties of people leaving the UK, who are 'deserting' our way of life in Britain and presumably 'swamping' the way of life in Spain, France or Australia? As emigration from the UK historically has been just as high, if not higher than immigration, where is the campaign for stronger 'emigration controls'?

The reality of course is that migration is such a part of human history that no government can stop it. For all the claptrap about 'our' 'unique', 'threatened' way of life, the reality is that the history of Glasgow, of Scotland, of Britain, of Europe, of the World, is a history of mass-movement and migration (and inter-marriage!)

And, in reality, immigration controls are more to do with controlling the labour market (and using cheap migrant labour as a way of undercutting labour demands for better pay and conditions) than anything to do with 'protecting' our way of life.

Within the constant movement of people around the world, asylum seekers and refugees have a special position. They are people who have not left their homes through choice but have been driven, primarily by force and violence. In other words, they are especially vulnerable and need special protection and assistance. And how we go about providing that perhaps has a lot to say about us.

In comparison to the 14.2 million refugees worldwide last year, only 23,610 people applied for refugee status in the UK, about 0.1 per cent of the global total (and equivalent to a minuscule 0.04 per cent of the UK's population.)

At the same time, the UK also operates the Gateway Protection Programme, where people already registered as refugees with the UN are allowed indefinite leave to remain in the UK. The system works by allowing people who are registered with the UNHCR and living in refugee camps to apply to enter the UK to live in safety. In this way the UK claims to be doing its share in supporting 'genuine' refugees and, at the same time, justifies placing excessive restrictions on people who have made their own way to the UK to claim asylum.

The only problem with this is that the Gateway Protection Programme only has places for 500 refugees a year. That's right. 500. You have not misread that number. It is not a typing error. Currently the UK's policy is to accept only 500 refugees annually out of a worldwide population of 14.2 million refugees.

Five hundred out of 14 million. It's a pitifully tiny, tiny number.

Equally pitiful is the reality that of the 24,000 or so people making their own way to the UK in 2006 to claim asylum, only two in 10 were given permission to stay in the UK by the Borders and Immigration Agency of the Home Office. On appeal another two out of 10 also won refugee status – which meant, if nothing else, that in the opinion of the judges of asylum tribunals, the Home Office wrongfully refused refugee status to at least as many people as it initially granted status to.

In total about only 8,000 out of 24,000 people claiming asylum last year got permission to stay in safety in the UK.

Just as the huge potential destructive power of Trident and what it could do to millions and millions of civilians and non-combatants reveals an insanity and immorality at the heart of the state's military and foreign policy, so the way in which people who have been refused asylum are treated reveals how brutal the state can be towards those it regards as having no rights.

For those refused refugee status the Home Office claims to have a robust policy of enforcing their removal. In Glasgow, almost two thirds of the families have had their cases refused. In September 2006, the Home Office doubled the number of immigration enforcement officials based at the Glasgow asylum reporting office, and the number of Strathclyde police seconded to assist the enforcement teams was similarly increased.

Early in the mornings Home Office officials carried out regular 'dawn raids' on the homes of asylum seeker families to detain and forcibly remove them from the UK. Wearing stab-proof vests and dark blue overalls, the Home Office enforcement teams broke into people's homes using the same methods employed for drug dealers and violent criminals. Often the children of the families wet their beds in fear as the police bashed their doors open with battering rams.

Surrounded by 10 or 12 officials crowding into their home, parents were separated from their terrified children and put into handcuffs. Given only 15 or 20 minutes to grab what possessions they could carry, the families were taken from what had been their home for as many as six years and put into cages in the back of vans with blacked out windows. Often children were taken in separate vans from their parents.

Once detained, families were taken to special immigration prisons or 'removal centres'. For those families taken to removal centres near Heathrow or Gatwick, the journey from Glasgow took over 14 hours and the only stops were for toilet breaks in police stations or army bases en route.

Each morning, in households throughout Glasgow, mothers would wake early, rise, get dressed, pack, and watch out of their windows for the arrival of the immigration police, terrified at what might happen to them.

In 2005 there were growing protests against the forced removals of families of asylum seekers in Glasgow. A weekly vigil began outside the Home Office reporting centre at Festival Court on Brand Street, near the Ibrox football stadium, every Saturday.

At the end of 2005 a series of early-morning blockades was held at the reporting centre to stop the immigration enforcement teams from carrying out the dawn raids, and the gates of the reporting centre were locked shut with chains and padlocks so that the enforcement vans could not leave.

At the same time as friendships grew between the people on the vigils and those required to report every week at the Home Office, a series of meetings were arranged in people's living rooms in the different parts of Glasgow where large numbers of asylum seekers had been housed.

From these living room meetings grew the idea of organising a union to stand up and campaign for greater rights for asylum seekers. Large public meetings were held, attended by 100 or 200 asylum seekers at a time. At these gatherings local committees were formed to represent asylum seekers and to campaign against dawn raids, for the right to work and for an end to the detention of children.

In March 2006, Unity – 'the union of asylum seekers in Scotland' – held its first demonstration. One hundred asylum seekers stood outside the reporting centre holding signs demanding an end to dawn raids and for the right to work.

On the same day, local Scottish supporters opened the 'Unity Centre' less than 100m from the reporting centre. Since then the Unity Centre, run entirely by volunteers and financially supported entirely by donations, has been open five or six days a week from 10am to 6pm to support families required to report every week or every month.

When the Home Office attempted to increase the number of forced removals it was carrying out in Glasgow, Unity and other support networks organised early-morning protests and vigils. In one part of Glasgow, local residents and asylum seekers gathered in their hundreds in early-morning vigils to watch out and protest against the brutal and terrorising dawn raids.

Then, following one particularly tense protest during a dawn raid that left one asylum seeker knocked unconscious by the action of the police, the public and political outcry shamed the Home Office into stopping the policy of dawn raids. From September 2006, the Home Office was carrying out two dawn raids a morning. Since January 2007 there have been no more than half a dozen dawn raids in Glasgow thanks to the major protests and direct action triggered by the formation of the union of asylum seekers and the Unity Centre.

And here is another connection between Trident and Faslane and the asylum seekers living in Glasgow. In Scotland, the combination of direct action, solidarity, collective action, protests and political pressure exerted through the devolved Scottish parliament stopped the Home Office in its tracks and made it reverse its policy of brutal dawn raids against families.

And as I write, in October 2007, the Home Office is in the middle of a process in which many of those 5,000 or so asylum seekers living in Glasgow are being granted permission to stay in the UK indefinitely as the Home Office realises that it will never be able to overcome the opposition and resistance to its attempts to forcibly remove them.

It doesn't take a genius to realise that a similar combination of people power and political action may well be successful in stopping the MOD's plans to replace Trident at Faslane.

For all of those reasons it was more than appropriate for Unity, the union of asylum seekers in Scotland, to be at Faslane as part of the Faslane 365 campaign.

CHAPTER 2

Focusing on Scotland to Break the Nuclear Chain

REBECCA JOHNSON and DAVID MACKENZIE

ON 22 OCTOBER 2007, three weeks after Faslane 365's closing Big Blockade, the Scottish government held the first ever Summit for a Nuclear Free Scotland. The meeting in Glasgow involved Scottish members of parliament from both Westminster and Holyrood, Church and Faith leaders, councillors, trades unionists, prominent lawyers, journalists and peace activists, including several members of the Faslane 365 steering group. Opening the summit, Deputy First Minister of the Scottish government, Nicola Sturgeon MSP, paid tribute to Faslane 365 for mobilising public opinion and providing impetus and arguments for Scotland to reject Trident. The government has subsequently established a working group on 'A Scotland without Nuclear Weapons', which will have direct input from organisers and participants in the Faslane 365 blockades.

Even without the explicit acknowledgement of the impact of the year's blockading, the Scottish summit was vindication of Faslane 365's strategy. At a time when there were many other calls on activists' time and resources, Faslane 365 chose this strategy because 'Scotland is the key to world nuclear disarmament'. This observation from Bill Bicksell, a veteran of the US anti-Trident campaign, explains why we put so much energy into inspiring people to demonstrate at Faslane rather than spreading our resources between the UK parliament and various other nuclear facilities and military bases: Scotland is the weakest link in the worldwide nuclear chain.

Britain's Trident delivery platforms are home-ported in Scotland, the warheads are stored in Scotland, the majority of the population in Scotland opposes UK nuclear weapons, and since the partial devolution of 1998, Scotland is seeking to forge a different identity in the world.

Faslane is not more accessible or dangerous than the Atomic Weapons Establishments (AWE) at Aldermaston and Burghfield, where the nuclear warheads are designed and made. Nor is Britain more important than the other nuclear weapon states, although it is a core maxim of direct action that responsibility for change starts at home. We focused on Faslane because we believed that concerted action here could tip the debate sufficiently to make it impractical for the UK to deploy its nuclear weapons in Scotland. A central part of Faslane 365's strategy has been to take the default option – Trident Lite – out of the running. A combination of circumstances – environmental, political, military, geographical and psychological – come together to make the continued deployment of UK nuclear-armed submarines dependent on a country where the majority of people do not want them.

If Trident becomes undeployable in Scotland, there are no alternatives in England or Wales that could feasibly be adapted. The problem is not just finding somewhere to home-port the nuclear submarines but finding somewhere *sufficiently safe and secure* to store and handle the vulnerable nuclear warheads. Devonport and Milford Haven are arguably the only viable ports for submarines, but they are not ideal. Experience suggests that any proposal to build a warhead handling facility like Coulport within reach of either harbour would attract massive Nimby ('not in my back yard') opposition that would greatly invigorate anti-nuclear opposition in England and Wales. So instead of falling back on the incumbent nuclear weapon system and continuing business as usual, the British government would have to seriously consider different types of nuclear weapon system that would not need nuclear submarines.

Sir Michael Quinlan, head of the Ministry of Defence (MOD) during Mrs Thatcher's first government (1979–83), when Trident was procured first time round, lobbied hard for Trident to be renewed, even as he acknowledged in 2006 that if Britain didn't have nuclear weapons already there would be no good reason to acquire them. The weighing of new options – as opposed to continuing business as usual – would inevitably raise deeper questions about the role and utility of tactical/non-strategic nuclear weapons in the 21st century and cause debate about nuclear doctrine and use that governments would prefer not to address. The process of such a debate would heighten awareness and public engagement on the issues. As opposition grew and the public and decision-makers looked more closely at the financial and opportunity costs, as well as the local and environmental factors associated with each option, opposition to retaining and renewing nuclear weapons would undoubtedly increase. Taking all things into consideration, it is likely that within a few years of trying to justify building and deploying a different type of nuclear weapon system using other bases in England or Wales, a prudent British government would make a virtue of necessity and become the first of the NPT nuclear weapon states to eliminate its arsenal in full compliance with its Article VI obligations. Like a reformed smoker, Britain would then become one of the strongest, most effective voices on behalf of nuclear abolition for all, showing how nuclear disarmament could be technically and verifiably achieved. And we would be pushing at a door that has already been opened by civil society and the majority of states parties to the Nuclear Non-Proliferation Treaty (NPT).

Faslane 365 was timed to mobilise opposition and increase the Scottish and grass roots impact on the UK debate over renewing Trident. In view of Tony Blair's determination and the prevailing political conditions in the Westminster parliament, it was predictable that the first vote would support Trident replacement. Our strategy took a longer view. By disrupting the submarine base directly over an extended period of time, the blockades increased awareness of the financial and environmental costs of deployment, including policing and security, and made the illegality and immorality of the renewal of Trident into an election issue before the Scottish parliament elections on 3 May 2007. In addition, in view of the dangerous weakening of the NPT, illustrated by the failure of the 2005 Review Conference, Faslane 365 was part of a wider movement to hold the nuclear weapon states accountable and show that future security depends on the full implementation of the NPT's disarmament obligations by all.

Because of the creation of a semi-autonomous Scottish parliament in 1998 with devolution of responsibilities (albeit not defence or foreign policy), a campaign based on Faslane gave the best opportunity to have direct political impact and to challenge the politicians, courts and police to address the illegality of nuclear weapons deployment and use. As we wrote in one of our first mobilising articles, published in *Peace News* in August 2006:

> To break a chain, it is necessary to apply maximum pressure at the weakest link. Britain's decision on whether to get another nuclear weapon system to give us nuclear 'status' beyond 2025 is the weakest link in the worldwide nuclear chain. If we can get one nuclear weapon state to start the process towards real disarmament, it will have far-reaching impact. Scotland's role as the site for berthing the submarines weakens the chain even further. Time and again, Scottish and Welsh people and politicians have proved much less supportive of Britain's nuclear weapons and imperial aspirations than the English. As things

currently stand, the Scottish parliament will not be consulted about whether a new generation of nuclear weapons will be deployed on the Gare Loch, but they will be expected to find the money to support the Faslane base in all sorts of ways.

The Debate over Next-Generation Trident

Just before the 2005 UK general election, Tony Blair mentioned that the next parliament would need to decide on a follow-on to Trident. Though the current Trident system would not be decommissioned until the 2020s, Blair seemed determined to ensure that his legacy – like Margaret Thatcher's – should include a future generation of nuclear weapons. Though the Labour government would go through the motions of a public debate and demo-cratic decision-making process over the next couple of years, Blair's government had already committed funding to build the next generation of nuclear weapons for Britain. According to evidence provided by the Aldermaston Women's Peace Camp(aign) to the House of Commons Defence Committee, decisions were taken as far back as 2002 to fund 'new build' capabilities at Aldermaston, including a supercomputer and Orion laser.

In 2000, the government had awarded a 10-year contract worth £2.3 billion to AWE Management Limited (a private company comprising US arms manufacturer Lockheed Martin, British Nuclear Fuels and SERCO) to run AWE Aldermaston and Burghfield. Following publication of a site development plan in July 2002, the government extended AWEML's contract to 25 years in January 2003, increasing its value to £5.3 billion.[1] In July 2005, another £350million was granted for each of the next three years, amounting to a further billion pounds.[2] These increased levels of investment pre-empted the debate about future nuclear policy and showed that the government was already banking on AWE continuing to research, design and make new nuclear weapons well into the future.

Even so, the House of Commons Defence Committee instituted a three-stage inquiry on 'The Future of the UK's Strategic Nuclear Deterrent' in late 2005. After receiving strong criticism from the Defence Committee for not cooperating in the first phase of its Inquiry, the government finally issued a

---

[1] See memorandum from Aldermaston Women's Peace Campaign, House of Commons Defence Committee, col. 986, Ev 121–125.

[2] House of Commons, Hansard, 3 November 2005, col. 1,259w.

White Paper on 'The Future of the United Kingdom's Nuclear Deterrent'. Introduced personally to the House of Commons by Blair on 4 December 2006, the White Paper's 36 glossy pages put forward his best arguments for an early decision to procure new nuclear submarines to carry UK nuclear weapons and keep Britain in the nuclear weapon business well beyond 2050. Yet the government's arguments for renewing Trident as an 'insurance policy' to 'deter' future threats had already been discredited and rebutted in reports and analyses from civil society. Though most British newspapers, television and radio had failed to cover Trident renewal until they saw the White Paper, the Faslane 365 blockades had ensured that the issue got into the main Scottish media. After December, articles about the role and utility of nuclear weapons and deterrence began belatedly to appear in the mainstream press south of the border.

Tony Blair, however, was determined not to allow the public debate much time to get going for fear that common sense would prevail and that Labour Party politicians would heed their constituents' views and ask awkward questions about Trident replacement. He cut short debate in his own cabinet, giving them sight of the White Paper only a few hours before he presented it on their collective behalf to the House of Commons. Shortly after, there was a month-long break while parliament recessed for Christmas and New Year, and in February it was announced that the vote would take place on 14 March 2007. This was just one week after publication of the Defence Committee's report on the government's White Paper, which posed questions about the renewal plan that it said should be answered before any decision was taken. The government did not bother to respond.

Government White Paper Advocates Trident Lite

The White Paper considered four options: air-launched cruise missiles; Trident missiles on surface ships; a land-based Trident system; and another submarine-based Trident system. Despite the fact that Trident had been designed with the cold war and Soviet Union in mind, the government plumped for renewing it with a 'lite' version of the current system, with perhaps three submarines rather than four. Under pressure from the Foreign Office and international and domestic critics of the decision, the government pledged 'a 20 per cent reduction' in 'our stockpile of operationally available warheads', noting also that 'our current holding [of Trident D5 missiles] has reduced to 50,' from 58, 'as a result of a number of test firings'.

Contrary to how positive it might sound, the carefully worded 'reduction' does not commit Britain to change the number of nuclear warheads and missiles that are currently deployed, armed and ready to launch on the order of the Prime Minister. The MOD has made clear that the UK posture of deterrence will still require continuous at-sea patrols, which new nuclear reactors on the submarines will make possible even if there are three rather than four boats. Normally the patrol would be carried out by one submarine, equipped with 16 missiles and 48 warheads. On 15 November 2007, the Defence Secretary, Des Browne, announced 'that we have now reduced the number of operationally available warheads from fewer than 200 to fewer than 160'[3] thereby confirming the view of Nukewatchers that 160 was close to the actual number of warheads in the stockpile in 2006 and that there would not therefore be a genuine 20 per cent reduction in Britain's arsenal. The lower numbers are welcome, but attrition due to testing, wear and tear, as well as the desire to keep manufacturing and storage costs down, does not amount to sacrifice or disarmament and should not be rewarded as if it did. With 160 warheads in the arsenal, Britain has more than enough to continue deploying three submarines at current levels with 48 warheads each. That would amount to more than 800 times the explosive power of the Hiroshima bomb. However, to deploy this Trident Lite system into the 2050s, Britain will have to convince Lockheed Martin and the US government to keep producing D5 missiles for a decade longer than the Pentagon currently envisages for the US Trident system.

In its security and defence justifications for renewing Trident, the White Paper gives the impression of being stuck in a time warp, clinging to notions of nuclear deterrence that former US Secretaries of State George Shultz and Henry Kissinger publicly recognised in a *Wall Street Journal* op-ed won't work in the changed security environment.[4] The UK government has tried to avoid such questions by labelling British nuclear weapons 'the nuclear deterrent' or, simply, 'our deterrent'. The subliminal effect is meant to reassure us that this isn't a weapon that might be used, but a 'deterrent' to prevent use. When Blair introduced the White Paper to the House of Commons, he used

---

3 Des Browne, response to question from Mr Hancock on Trident missiles, House of Commons, Hansard, 15 November 2007, col. 366w.

4 George P. Shultz, William J. Perry, Henry A. Kissinger and Sam Nunn, 'A World Free of Nuclear Weapons', *Wall Street Journal*, New York, 4 January 2007.

'deterrent' or 'deterrence' to describe British or American nuclear weapons and policies 23 times.[5] By contrast, the term 'nuclear weapon' appeared only six times, in relation to North Korea, Iran, Russia and China, as well as in the term 'nuclear weapon states'. In other words, *they* have nasty dangerous nuclear weapons (or ambitions to acquire them), while *we* (and our allies) have a nice safe deterrent.

Through banners, interviews and press releases, and by using humour and satire, the participants in Faslane 365 exposed and ridiculed the government's use of linguistic and political spin to try and lock the concepts of nuclear weapons and deterrence together in people's minds. Meant to make people trust in deterrence, the White Paper was designed to shut off questions about whether nuclear weapons do deter. It sounds absurd, for example, to ask 'does the deterrent deter?' Faslane 365 reminded the world that such political spin and chicanery says nothing about the real world, where life, death and our very survival may depend on whether nuclear weapons contribute to deterrence and security or not. Naming a cat 'dog' does not give it the ability to bark.

The White Paper's case for gaining public acceptance (and MPs' votes) for renewing Trident rested on its unproven (and unprovable) assumptions and statements about deterrence. They know that the public is more likely to consent to nuclear weapons that are there in order not to be used, especially if they magically prevent anyone else from using nuclear weapons against us. The idea of renewing Trident becomes far less attractive when put in terms of nuclear weapons that a political leader in the future might decide to launch against another country, where they could kill hundreds of thousands of people. Especially when, having ratcheted up the terrorist threat after 11 September 2001, Tony Blair admitted to the House of Commons, 'I do not think that anyone pretends that the independent nuclear deterrent is a defence against terrorism'.[6]

Though the 2006 White Paper went further than its predecessors to try and explain the usefulness of Trident's particular capabilities in terms of range, readiness and the diversity of targets it can hit simultaneously, it does not go into detail on targeting doctrine and strategy. Information on this is

---

[5] Tony Blair, House of Commons, Statement on Trident to the UK parliament, 4 December 2006.

[6] House of Commons, Hansard, 19 October 2005, col. 841.

classified in Britain, but available in an unclassified version from the United States, with which UK doctrine and targeting are harmonised. UK officials insist there are some critical differences between British and American doctrines and targeting policies, but have failed to provide information on what these differences are and why.[7] So what is Trident designed to hit?

In accordance with declarations to NPT parties since 2000, UK nuclear weapons are not currently targeted at anyone in particular. However, hundreds of military and civilian targets anywhere in the world are on the 'potential target' list and can be programmed in as quickly as it takes to key the coordinates into a computer.

Though the UK increased the 'notice to fire' from hours to days in 1998, this is only an operational and communication extension. The UK's current policy requires that whenever the submarines go on patrol they are equipped with armed warheads attached to primed missiles able to be launched at a moment's notice once they receive the order, which, according to the White Paper, can only come from the Prime Minister. If the cabinet has been incapacitated, what then? There is a letter in the submarine's safe telling the captain the Prime Minister's wishes, which may include: 'Put yourself under the command of the United States, if it is still there'; 'go to Australia'; 'retaliate'; or 'use your own judgment'.[8] While accepting that the Prime Minister's authorisation is the political requirement, recent reports that the Royal Navy has resisted attempts to install 'permissive action links' (PALS) to prevent unauthorised arming and use of the UK's nuclear weapons indicate that the commanders on board the submarines possess the physical capability to launch Trident without receiving additional codes or authority from the Prime Minister if they believe war has commenced and the government is dead or incommunicado.[9]

---

7   See Appendix 1 on Nuclear Doctrine in: Rebecca Johnson, Nicola Butler and Stephen Pullinger, *Worse than Irrelevant? British Nuclear Weapons in the 21st Century*, Acronym Institute, London, October 2006.

8   Richard Norton Taylor, 'Go to Australia or Use Your Own Judgment', the *Guardian*, 28 June 2007.

9   Meirion Jones, 'British Nukes Were Protected by Bike Locks', *Newsnight*, BBC News, 15 November 2007. For confirmation that Trident does not have permissive action links, see House of Commons, Hansard, 28 November 2007, col. 454W.

When unpacked and analysed, as the White Paper avoids doing, nuclear deterrence turns out to be a very dangerous and immoral concept to keep around in the 21st century. It relies on the threat to unleash millions of tonnes of nuclear explosive power and long-lived radiation on people in far off places in order to induce leaders or terrorists not to threaten us. If it works for us, then it ought to work for other states, like Iran, Libya or North Korea. As such, it becomes a recipe and fuel for nuclear proliferation. If it doesn't work, then it is a very expensive distraction – a false promise that gets in the way of putting our resources and abilities to work on much surer approaches to reduce conflicts and threats and build genuine, collective security based on international justice and respect.

Deterrence, if and when it works, is the product of the interplay of multiple instruments. As well as hard and soft power, psychological, cultural and communications factors play important but not necessarily predictable roles in deterrence. It is inappropriate – and counterproductive – to rest the weight of security and deterrence on a single weapon system as 'the deterrent'; if that were justifiable, all governments would feel duty-bound to provide such protection to their populace. At issue is not whether deterrence is a useful concept for defence, but whether nuclear weapons are a sensible, essential – or even useful – component of deterrence in the 21st century. They are not. Adherence to a policy of nuclear deterrence in a proliferating world increases the risks of its failure, and may then cause nuclear weapons to be used, which would be catastrophic.

Relying on the threat to use nuclear weapons risks and diminishes our humanity, making it harder to stop other kinds of violence or weapons being used for political ends – including terrorist bombs, incendiary bombing from the air, rape, torture, death camps and rampaging gangs armed with guns or machetes. If nuclear war is upheld as a last resort by nations that pride themselves on being 'civilised', others may try to justify the most abhorrent uses of violence for their purposes too, since the mass destructive effects of nuclear weapons are manifestly worse.

In addition to fundamental contradictions in how the White Paper characterised the security and deterrence arguments for Trident, the government deliberately understated the costs, putting a price tag of only £20 billion on Trident renewal. Economists researching the costs on behalf of the Liberal Democrat Party found that this figure would barely cover the cost of building three new nuclear submarines. If the Trident Lite option advocated in the White Paper were built and deployed for 30 years beyond 2024, the true costs would need to take into account the research and testing facilities at Aldermaston and 30 years of deployment at sea, refitting expenses, nuclear warhead transports and maintenance costs for Faslane, Coulport and Burghfield. The Liberal Democrats therefore calculated the cost of Trident replacement to be at least £76 billion at today's prices. Even this figure did not adequately count decommissioning costs for the nuclear submarines or facilities and adjunct military and policing expenses associated with deploying nuclear weapons, which would be likely to take the cost past £100 billion.

House of Commons Defence Committee Report

Chaired by James Arbuthnot MP (Conservative), the all party House of Commons Defence Committee's third report, titled 'The Future of the UK's Strategic Nuclear Deterrent: the White Paper', argued that 'Decisions on the future of the UK's nuclear deterrent should be taken on the strategic needs of the country, not on industrial factors'.[10]

Calling on the government to 'do more to explain what the concept of deterrence means in today's strategic environment', the committee raised questions about the circumstances in which the government envisages using nuclear weapons. Noting that terms like 'self-defence', in 'extreme circumstances', and in defence of the UK's 'vital interests' should be clearly explained, it raised concerns that 'ambiguity does not lead to a lowering of the nuclear threshold' and was 'unclear whether this has significance as a non-proliferation measure [and] unclear that this reduction has any operational significance'. The committee also called on the government to be much clearer about how it intended to fulfil its stated commitment to 'achieve nuclear non-proliferation'.

First Parliamentary Debate on Trident, 14 March 2007

The government ignored the Defence Committee's concerns and forced the vote through the House of Commons on a 'three-line whip'. This is the strongest

---

[10] House of Commons Defence Committee, 'The Future of the UK's Strategic Nuclear Deterrent: the White Paper', Ninth Report of Sessions 2006–07, HC 225–1 (London, The Stationery Office, 7 March 2007), available at www.publications.parliament .uk/ pa/cm200607/cmselect/cmdfence/225/225i.pdf. The quotes are from the report's executive summary.

possible voting instruction, and generally carries penalties for party members who go against it. The government's motion was: 'this House supports the government's decision as set out in the White Paper "The Future of the United Kingdom's Nuclear Deterrent" (CM6994) to take the steps necessary to maintain the UK minimum strategic nuclear deterrent beyond the life of the existing system and to take further steps towards meeting the UK's disarmament responsibilities under Article VI of the Non- proliferation treaty.'

After several hours of debate, the motion was carried by 409 votes to 161.[11] This appears pretty conclusive, but the voting analysis and tenor of the debate indicate a more substantial opposition to Trident renewal than the numbers superficially convey. MPs from most of the other parties, notably the Liberal Democrats, Scottish National Party (SNP) and Plaid Cymru, voted against. A majority of MPs – from whatever party – representing Scottish constituencies voted against. Several Scottish junior ministers and ministerial aides and one Welsh aide chose to resign their government jobs in order to vote against the government whip. Altogether 88 Labour MPs opposed outright, while a number of others failed to vote at all, suggesting they also opposed but were less courageous. Moreover, 95 Labour MPs had voted for an amendment from Jon Trickett MP, supported by senior Labour and Liberal Democrat MPs, which called for a delay on the grounds that the government had failed to make an adequate case for replacing Trident.

The Conservative leader, David Cameron, had boasted that he would win the vote for the Prime Minister, and he did! Since some senior Tory MPs spoke against Trident renewal and called for greater resources to be devoted to more effective non-nuclear means of defence and deterrence, Cameron clearly felt he should make sure of his party's votes by copying Blair and imposing a three-line whip of his own. The whipped Labour and Conservative MPs delivered 409 votes for the government. The linkage made in the resolution between Trident renewal and taking further nuclear disarmament steps enabled some MPs to salve their consciences, while others pointed to promises of a further vote given by the Foreign Secretary, Margaret Beckett, on behalf of the government. Indeed, some claimed during the debate that they were only voting in favour of the resolution on the

---

[11] For a summary, with excerpts from the debate, see Rebecca Johnson, 'Blair Wins Trident Vote after Telling UK Parliament that the NPT Gives Britain the Right to Have Nuclear Weapons', *Disarmament Diplomacy*, 84 (Spring 2007), pp 60–70. The full debate is available from Hansard, for the date 14 March 2007.

understanding that further decisions – including about the warheads – would be put to parliament before any irrevocable decision was finalised.[12]

Scotland Votes to Be Nuclear Free

British nuclear weapons have never been very popular in Scotland, as opinion polls have shown over the decades. In 2001, Professor William Walker (University of St Andrews) and Professor Malcolm Chalmers (University of Bradford) published a detailed analysis of the potential implications of Scottish devolution on UK nuclear policy.[13] Noting that there were few if any feasible alternative sites for deploying nuclear submarines in England or Wales, they identified five serious challenges to Westminster's assumptions that they would continue to be able to site nuclear weapons at Faslane and Coulport:

1   Considerable scepticism about nuclear deterrence and status among Scottish political elites, as well as the wider population.

2   London's apparent failure to recognise that there are 'special and distinct' problems for Scotland arising from the fact that UK nuclear weapons are based at Faslane and Coulport.

---

[12] In full, the exchange was as follows:

Nick Palmer (Lab): Does the Secretary of State accept that all these issues must be subject to review over the years, and that many of us who will support her today reserve the right to review our positions when the warheads are considered in the next parliament?

Margaret Beckett: As my hon. Friend is aware, we are not making any decision about the warheads in this parliament, so the matter will inevitably come before a subsequent parliament...

Frank Field (Lab): Is the Foreign Secretary saying that we are making a decision today to keep all our options open, or are we making a decision that would commit a future parliament to large expenditures when we go through the big gateway decision in due course?

Margaret Beckett: My right hon. Friend will know that that question was raised with the Prime Minister a few moments ago and he answered it clearly. It is the decision of principle that we are required to make today. It is inevitable that there will be future discussions, and there will be decisions down the road as the programme proceeds. Hansard, 14 March 2007.

[13] Malcolm Chalmers and William Walker, *Uncharted Waters: The UK, Nuclear Weapons and the Scottish Question*, Tuckwell Press, East Linton, 2001.

3   Under the devolution legislation of 1998, Scotland's institutions have no say over matters relating to defence and security – including nuclear weapons deployment – although their cooperation is necessary.

4   'Fuzzy' boundaries of responsibility between London and Edinburgh.

5   The possibility that one day Scotland could become fully independent.[14]

Trident renewal has served to highlight the tensions over the devolutionary arrangements agreed in 1998, which reserved decision-making powers on national security, defence and foreign policy to London. The special protocols on defence issues also give the final say to Whitehall on matters that affect Trident, but which would otherwise be under the control of the Holyrood parliament, such as economic planning, roads and the environment. Even Scots who do not favour constitutional independence are alienated by decisions pushed through the Westminster parliament that ignore public opinion in Scotland and sideline the votes of Scottish MPs. This factor is more persuasive in Trident's case since nuclear weapons raise critical questions of international law.

A positive feedback loop therefore exists between Trident and the extension of devolution. A stronger devolutionary position will strengthen the anti-Trident cause while a more powerful public rejection of Trident will be a prime motivator for increased devolution. This explains why, within three months of the 14 March vote on Trident in the UK's Westminster parliament, the Scottish elections on 3 May gave the Scottish National Party (SNP) – a party that has long been committed to making Scotland nuclear free – a one-seat majority over the Scottish Labour Party. Opinion poll data showed that for traditional Labour voters who switched to the SNP in 2007, opposition to Trident was a major factor. Six weeks later, Patrick Harvie, Green Party MSP for Glasgow, tested the water with a resolution opposing Trident replacement. It was resoundingly carried by 71 (a mixture of SNP, Green, Liberal Democrat and Labour MSPs) to 16 (all Conservative). The Scottish Labour MSPs divided, with some voting in favour and 39 choosing to abstain. So, of 126 members of the Scottish parliament who voted, only 16 (12.7 per cent) actually voted in favour of renewing Trident.

After this confirmation of support, work has begun on laying the paving stones to make Scotland nuclear free. On 15 October the First Minister, Alex

---

[14] Ibid., pp.48–49.

Salmond, sent a letter to NPT states parties with embassies in Edinburgh or London, informing them of the new Scottish government's policies, and asking for support as Scotland explores 'the possibility of taking up observer status at future NPT meetings, so that we can more directly and effectively represent the aspirations and interests of Scotland's people'. A week later, as noted above, the government convened a high-level Summit for a Nuclear Free Scotland, which generated a number of proposals and ideas for political, legislative and educational initiatives. Though national security, defence and foreign policy are reserved to Westminster, plans are afoot to challenge the transporting of nuclear warheads on the roads using Scottish and European Union environmental and safety regulations. The Scotland Act also specifies that 'observing and implementing international obligations, obligations under the Human Rights Convention and obligations under Community law' are not reserved matters. Other initiatives would address the illegality of nuclear weapons head-on by challenging Trident deployment and renewal on grounds that Westminster cannot reserve and impose on Scotland something that is contrary to international law and Britain's international and treaty obligations.

A Cautionary Look Forward

Faslane 365 made a difference in 2006–07 because we mobilised sustained direct action based around diverse groups that each took responsibility for demonstrating or blockading for one or more days. The fact that Trident's opponents are in government now in Scotland does not, however, mean that we have won. We cannot complacently assume that the present relatively high levels of awareness and opposition will grow or even be maintained without continued action and input. Over the years the polls on Trident have varied, and on occasions the size of the opposing majority has been slight, even in Scotland. The heightened levels of awareness this time round were largely due to the blockades and arguments about the potential of Trident, the immorality of its use and illegality of its deployment. For some the deciding factor was that Trident was imposed on Scotland by London; for others that it increased dependence on the United States and may thus have contributed to Tony Blair's decision to back George W. Bush's war on Iraq.

Peace campaigners and activists have been working in Scotland against the deployment of nuclear weapons for decades, both at Faslane and further west at Holy Loch, where the US kept a base for its nuclear armed submarines and ships during the cold war (Holy Loch was closed in the early 1990s).

Illustrating this history of resistance to nuclear weapons, June 2007 saw the Faslane Peace Camp commemorating 25 years of its caravan-based living opposition behind a picket fence and rows of banners close to the South Gate of the Faslane nuclear base. In 1998, a new grass roots group, Trident Ploughshares, started building up a broader community of 'Pledgers' who committed themselves to take nonviolent actions to disarm Trident, including the holding of periodic Big Blockades that attracted hundreds. Over time, however, such campaigns – though still important – had become almost routine, both for activists and for the base. A scheduled Big Blockade would successfully close the Faslane or Coulport bases for a day or two, but if they were held only a few times during the year, it became apparent that they were treated practically as training exercises for the police, while the base prepared in advance to ensure that key workers were on site in time and the rest were encouraged to work from outside or enjoy a day off. Such plans made it possible for the military to minimise the disruption arising from an occasional blockade, but this would be impossible if the blockades were of longer duration.

It has required continuous grass roots action to grow the awareness and enable people to believe that their actions can bring about the political change they desire. Faslane 365 helped to get more coverage than usual into the Scottish media, but the most important factor has been local coverage of the concerns and experiences of the steady stream of activists that have put their bodies, their careers and their freedom on the line to get rid of Trident. Even so, public awareness and opposition in Scotland will need to grow stronger and be more solidly grounded to provide the significant public backing a Scottish government will need to take forward its challenge to Westminster over Trident. This is no time for complacency, as there is nothing intrinsic or irreducible in Scottish opposition to Trident – it has to be continually worked for. This is also true of what is perhaps the strongest institutional site of opposition to nuclear weapons – the churches. The anti-Trident stance of the Church of Scotland required a vigorous and sustained struggle in the 1970s and 80s and can still not be taken for granted.

It is also significant (and some might say ironic) that one Scottish institutional nexus – the police, the criminal justice system and the judiciary – which had an identity separate from the rest of the UK long before the establishment of the new Scottish parliament, has been more resistant than most to recognising the changing security environment and its responsibilities to uphold international law and human rights. As most blockaders would agree, the policing at Faslane has generally been carried out with restraint and good humour; but institutionally the police and judicial authorities have shown no appetite for recognising their responsibilities where there is prima facie evidence of breaches of international law by the state. The refusal of Strathclyde Police to investigate well-founded allegations of UK collusion in arms trafficking by the United States through Prestwick Airport during the Lebanon war of 2006 is a prime example. Similarly, the Crown has consistently refused to act on strong prima facie cases where state activity is involved, and it was hardly the finest hour for the Scottish judiciary when the Lord Advocates' Reference on the legal points arising from the 1999 Loch Goil/Maytime case determined that the UK's deployment of Trident warheads under the policy of deterrence was not unlawful and that the actions of the 'Trident Three' were not justified under the doctrine of necessity or under international law,[15] giving instead a muddled judgement that amounts to judicial approval for these weapons of mass destruction.

In conclusion, Faslane 365 may not have succeeded in blocking the nuclear submarine base with 100 people a day continuously for 365 days. But the strategy of bringing people from all walks of life to apply political pressure directly on the base, the police force and the politicians of Scotland has borne significant political fruit, pushing Trident opposition into a pivotal position right before the Scottish elections. It counts for a lot when the Scottish government's First Minister, Alex Salmond, tells the press: 'I want to get to a position where we can persuade the UK government to change its stance both on the replacement programme and on the general principle of maintaining a nuclear deterrent.' Faslane 365 contributed to bringing about this huge and challenging opportunity to make real progress on nuclear disarmament. If we succeed here, it will not just be for Scotland. A Trident turned out of Faslane will not easily be housed elsewhere and a UK without WMD will change the equation worldwide.

---

[15] For the full story, see Angie Zelter, *Trident on Trial: The Case for People's Disarmament*, Luath Press, 2001. Moxley's refutation is also good; see Charles Moxley, 'Lord Advocate's Reference the Unlawfulness of the United Kingdom's Policy of Nuclear Deterrence: The Invalidity of the Scottish High Court's Decision', *Disarmament Diplomacy*, 58, June 2001, Opinion and Analysis.

Environmentalists

EURIG SCANDRETT

The environmentalists' blockade took place on 26 April 2007, the anniversary of the explosive meltdown of the nuclear reactor in Chernobyl, Ukraine, near the border with Belarus. Twenty-one years ago on that day, a nuclear reaction went out of control while the safety system was temporarily switched off. Temperatures reached over 2,000°C, the fuel rods melted and the graphite covering the reactor ignited. With a violent explosion, the 1,000-tonne sealing cap on the reactor was blown off and radioactive fuel and fission products released into the air, contaminating neighbouring towns, through Ukraine and Belarus and spreading across Europe. The explosion released 100 times more radiation than the atom bombs dropped over Hiroshima and Nagasaki.[16]

Chernobyl is a terrible reminder of how dangerous nuclear material is to human life and health and the wider environment, a reminder that things can go wrong, and that when they do it can be devastating. Officially, 31 workers at the reactor died from the direct effect of the explosion, and the 45,000 inhabitants of the nearby town of Pripyat were evacuated. However, the number of deaths from the radiation which spread throughout Europe is expected to reach tens of thousands. The impact is still being experienced even in Scotland, where a number of sheep farms remain sufficiently contaminated that they are unable to sell their animals.

The idea for an environmentalists' blockade was initiated by a motion to the AGM of Friends of the Earth Scotland in May 2006. Friends of the Earth has a strong track record of opposition to nuclear power, and a presumption against nuclear weapons. Although many FOE members, activists and staff have been involved in anti-Trident campaigns, there hasn't been a focus on campaigning against nuclear weapons in recent years. However, with the prospect of unpopular new nuclear power stations in Scotland and the replacement decision for Trident, the time was ripe to make the connections between nuclear power and nuclear weapons explicit with an environmentalists' blockade. Eventually a small group of activists, mostly from Friends of the Earth and Greenpeace, got together to plan the event.

---

[16] www.foe-scotland.org.uk/pressreleases/277/.

Star of the blockade was Nellie, the 20-foot inflatable white elephant with a nuclear symbol attached, saying 'Say No to Nuclear Power: it's a white elephant'. Unfortunately the police wouldn't let Nellie anywhere near either of the gates to Faslane, clearly mistaking her for a Trojan horse, so she took up residence outside the Peace Camp, alerting passers-by to the connections between nuclear power and nuclear weapons. However, thanks to a team of committed volunteers, Nellie had produced a large clutch of daughters who accompanied the protesters down to the North Gate.

At the North Gate the protest took the form of a rally, with speeches from across a wide range of environmental groups. Duncan McLaren affirmed that Friends of the Earth Scotland was proud to add its voice to the opposition to nuclear weapons in Scotland, and to continue to campaign against replacement nuclear power plants. He said: 'In Scotland debate on nuclear weapons amongst the public, politicians and trade unions has been largely separate from that over nuclear power. But globally the two are joined at the hip. The lesson to be learned from the Chernobyl disaster is that the world needs fewer nuclear facilities, not more.'

Mandy Meikle from Greenpeace (Edinburgh Active Supporters Group) added: 'More than 40 years after the UK government signed an international treaty to eliminate nuclear weapons, Tony Blair is planning to reverse all that, and rush through plans to build new weapons – a replacement for Trident. These plans aren't going down well in Scotland, with most people opposed to wasting some £76 billion on Trident. This money should be invested in tackling climate change and building new infrastructure for our low-carbon future.'

The nuclear power industry has been promoting itself as a low carbon energy source which can be part of the solution to climate change, an argument which the then Prime Minister Tony Blair had fallen for. Many of the speakers at the rally referred to what a spurious argument that is. Gary Glass from the climate campaign group Rising Tide said that the group was firmly against nuclear power as a solution to climate change, partly because it isn't a solution compared to real policies to reduce energy consumption and shift to renewables, and partly because the nuclear legacy is as dangerous as a chaotic climate. Indeed, climate change makes the transport and storage of nuclear material especially risky as weather patterns become more extreme and unpredictable.

Leaving a legacy to future generations of carcinogenic toxicity is hardly an improvement on the droughts, diseases, floods, pests, hurricanes and crop failures which climate change will bring. As Dr Richard Dixon, Director of WWF Scotland said: 'Very few things are a bigger threat than climate change but a major exchange of nuclear weapons is certainly one of them. Scotland has the best renewable energy resources of any country in Europe, if any-one should be getting rid of all things nuclear and going for clean, green energy it is us.'

Dixon also emphasised that 'Given the inextricable historical link between nuclear weapons and nuclear power reactors it is very appropriate that we are at Faslane to remember the event of 21 years ago at Chernobyl.' The memory and ongoing struggle of the people directly affected by Chernobyl is being kept alive by the charity Chernobyl Children, which gives an oppor-tunity for children from Pripyat and other areas most directly affected by the radioactive explosion to get a break and a wee holiday in parts of the world which are less polluted – so far – such as Scotland.

26 April 2007 was the week before the election to the Scottish parliament, so one would think that politicians would have been falling over themselves to add their voices to the protests against unpopular nuclear weapons and power. Most political parties in Scotland have some form of policy against the replacement of Trident and a number of them are opposed to nuclear power. However, only one party accepted the invitation to speak at a rally

which connected the two: Stuart Collison of the Scottish Green Party, candidate for West of Scotland. As it turned out, the election was won, just, by the Scottish National Party, which is also opposed to both nuclear weapons and power, and with the support of the Greens the SNP formed a minority government. It remains to be seen what they can do about this while defence and energy policy remain at Westminster, even though many individual Labour and Liberal Democrat politicians are personally opposed.

Following the speeches and a wee bit of singing, we tucked into some delicious lunch from the Jeely Peace Café, for which we were extremely grateful. This provided a good bit of fuel for the symbolic die-in of the afternoon. On the sound of a siren, we all lay down in front of the gate for two minutes. When the siren stopped, an eerie silence hung in the air until the police started asking us to move. Those who chose to rose and moved out of the way but three of us stayed put, delaying the opening of the doors for a few more minutes until we were arrested and removed. Two of the three were arrested for the first time, although charges were later dropped.

So far this has been the story of the rally at the North Gate. There were actually two environmentalists' blockades on the same day. In a neat division of labour, the North Gate rally was the main focus for the environmental NGOs, including those whose charitable status or personal circumstances prevented risking arrest, while, independently, a group of autonomous direct action environmentalists closed down Coulport by erecting a tripod and staying there for several hours.

The emphasis at both protests was the connection between nuclear weapons and nuclear power. What is this connection and why emphasise it? At a certain superficial level, nuclear weapons and nuclear power are made from the same stuff, albeit in different forms. Naturally occurring uranium ore contains a mixture of three isotopes of uranium, U234, U235 and U238, along with a number of radioactive products of decay. More than 99 per cent of the uranium is U238, which is the least radioactive isotope, and only 0.7 per cent is the highly radioactive U235, the fissile material used to generate energy. Uranium ore is therefore processed to increase the proportion of U235. Uranium with a U235 concentration of three per cent ('low enriched uranium') is suitable for electricity generation, whereas weapons require a U235 concentration of 90 per cent ('high enriched uranium'). The remaining U238, or 'depleted uranium', is highly dense material which is used in military armour and weapons.

The environmental hazards of both weapons and power start with the mining of uranium. Brooks and Seth argue that 'In most countries, uranium mining has been the most hazardous step of nuclear materials production, both in terms of doses and in the number of people affected.'[17] Uranium miners are exposed to the radiological and chemical toxicity of uranium and its decay products through inhalation and ingestion, and through the accumulation of these substances in their tissues. High incidence of cancers of the bone and lung, kidney disease, tuberculosis and rheumatoid arthritis are found in uranium miners. The mine operations also affect local communities with the toxins remaining in the tailings.

These health impacts are an environmental injustice. 'The burden from the effects of uranium production, driven by a few countries seeking nuclear weapons and nuclear power has been disproportionately carried by indigenous, colonised and other dominated peoples. Approximately two-thirds of the United States' uranium deposits are on Native American land and almost a third of all mill tailings produced in the US from abandoned mill operations are on Navajo land. Northern Saskatchewan, home to some of the richest reserves, and where over 20 per cent of uranium in the world is mined, is inhabited by the Cree and Dene.'[18] Most of the UK's uranium comes from North America, Australia and Central and Southern Africa. UK company RioTinto mined uranium in apartheid South Africa and occupied Namibia. Even where mines are closed, the legacy of radioactivity and toxicity are bequeathed to the local communities, and the prospect of illegal uranium extraction ensures that the poorest risk their lives to supply a black market in radioactive materials.

Uranium is processed to increase the concentration of the fissile $U235$. Although the concentrations in low and high enriched uranium are very different, they are essentially achieved by the same process, and with the right technology it is possible to convert from one to the other. In the UK, the two forms of uranium are kept separate, although it is very difficult to verify this since the UK is reluctant to allow international inspection of its weapons.

The depleted uranium which is the waste product of enrichment continues to provide environmental and health damage. When used in weapons

---

[17] Robert Brooks and Anita Seth, 'The Uranium Burden', Institute for Energy and Environmental Research, *Energy & Security*, 4, 1998, www.ieer.org/ensec/no-4/umining.html.

[18] Ibid.

or armoury or field tests, depleted uranium can be inhaled or ingested where it is radioactively and chemically toxic and can cause genetic mutations, tumours, birth defects, neurological damage and cellular dysfunction.[19]

The connection between nuclear power and nuclear weapons is as much political as physical: the Nuclear Non-Proliferation Treaty is designed to keep the two separate. Nations are given assistance in developing nuclear power, so long as they agree not to develop or expand their nuclear weapons. This has the purpose, supposedly, of preventing the proliferation of nuclear weapons (and moving towards their reduction) while defending the right of nations to develop their own nuclear power. In fact the impact is to retrench the nuclear weapons capacity of the first group of states with nuclear weapons, while encouraging the proliferation of nuclear power.

Moreover, it does nothing to prevent the proliferation of nuclear weapons as non-nuclear states are attracted to the power which nuclear weapons preserve. Indeed, states which aspire to nuclear weapons are tempted to develop nuclear power as a halfway house, complete with technological support from the nuclear states. As soon as India had tested nuclear weapons, the US moved to negotiate a deal which would provide India with access to nuclear power technology. If the UK were really to fulfil its NPT obligations and negotiate in good faith to reduce its nuclear arsenal (including the non-replacement of Trident) then this would be destabilised by the presence of nuclear power, and therefore the capacity to convert low-grade uranium to high-grade. While the nuclear powers try to keep nuclear power and weapons separate, it is important therefore that campaigners keep them together.

It is true that nuclear weapons contain hazards which nuclear power does not, primarily the fact that nuclear weapons are deliberately explosively released in a way which kills and maims innocent civilians. The material which is stored and transported for nuclear weapons has considerably higher toxicity and greater instability than that required for nuclear power. Nuclear weapons are tested, and radioactive material is deliberately spread in a way that doesn't apply to nuclear power.

However, many of the dangers of nuclear material apply to both weapons and electricity generation. It would be a nonsense to oppose nuclear weapons and support nuclear power. The risk of Windscale or

---

[19] Lisa Ledwidge, 'Health Risks from Uranium May Be More Varied than Reflected', Institute for Energy and Environmental Research, 2005, www.envirosagainst war. org/know/read.php?itemid=2418.

Dounreay-style leaks, or of Chernobyl-style accidental explosion, applies equally to both kinds of nuclear facilities. And so too does the problem of decommissioning and storage of waste that remains highly toxic for many thousands of years.

But perhaps the biggest problem is that nuclear weapons are not fit for purpose even within their own terms. Having nuclear weapons today is a great threat and makes life more dangerous, and increases the risk which nuclear power stations bring. Trident and its like are designed for a cold war threat – a clear target with opposing ideology but comparable weapons. In the globalised world we live in, asymmetrically dominated by the US with an arsenal many times greater than any potential rival, the threat which faces Britain now is from the low-tech weapons of the terrorist. Nuclear weapons, their raw materials and waste become a terrorist target which would maximise the destruction caused by a mortar, grenade or suicide bomb. The same is true for nuclear power stations.

Trident and Tropical Fruit: Reversing the Race to the Bottom

ALISTAIR SMITH[20]

I wonder if it is the same people who think bananas and pineapples are produced in decent and safe conditions for human health that think nuclear submarines are safe and necessary. This may well seem like a random thought, but, for those of us who are trying to facilitate a transition to a world based on social and economic justice which leaves the natural environment in a healthy state for future generations, it is not as random as it may first appear.

In the world of tropical fruit produced for the richer consumers on the planet we speak of a 'race to the bottom', a race to produce and sell as much and as cheaply as possible. But 'cheap' in practice, in the current illogic of the world economy, means more environmental and social costs, costs that are not included in the price we pay at this end.

The race, now led by the world's giant supermarket chains and, in the

---

[20] Alistair Smith is International Coordinator of Banana Link, www.bananalink.org.uk.

Press Release – 27 March 2007 – Press Release

Trident IS Bananas!

16 banana activists were arrested today for blockading the North Gate of the Faslane Base. Forming three affinity groups the bananas used miniature arm locks and D-locks made of foil in their attempt to shut the base down. Assisted by three human supporters wearing Banana Support jackets, the banana blocks positioned themselves in front of the gates where they were immediately seized by eager police. Their banners read 'Trident is Bananas', 'Bananas say No Trident' and 'Make Banana Cake not War'.

The police were found to be hiding their grins as were passing drivers, as the supporters, a large French contingent who had just been let out of the police cells after their action the previous day, cheered and shouted *'Libere La Banane'*. The police lifted the bananas, lock-ons included, to the side of the road several times before carting them off to be processed in a police car. The supporters are currently ringing Dumbarton and Clyde-bank police stations to see where the bananas are being taken to and when they will be released. The police are finding it hard to decide which bananas are male and which female and are searching for a translator. The bananas legal support will check to make sure no strip searching goes on as these are peaceful and responsible bananas just trying to say that bananas also desire a nuclear free Scotland.

case of bananas and pineapples, five multinational fruit companies, is about finding production areas for industrial-scale tropical fruit plantations where wages are low, working hours can be illegally long and the bill for the damage to workers' health, water-courses, marine life or tropical soils does not have to be paid... at least not by the owners of the production or by the traders of cheap fruit sold in Tesco, WalMart, Aldi, Lidl or Carrefour.

The arms race, of which Trident is a very British symbol, is not just a race to the bottom – of the oceans in the case of nuclear submarines – in the literal sense, but also in terms of environmental, social and economic sustainability... just like the race to deliver tropical fruit to predatory retail buyers in Europe and North America.

The difference with the nuclear race to the bottom is that it is not subject to the same logic of keeping the price as low as possible. Trident has only one buyer and it is not a supermarket chain subject to consumer pressure like Tesco, Asda or Sainsbury's! We, the 'consumers' of Trident, can pressure the buyer with the argument that we don't want it, but in this case the buyer is not in the position of needing to resell at 59p per kilo (or whatever unsustainably low price you like) and satisfy customers and shareholders. Market forces, albeit driven by a cruel economistic (ill-)logic, do not apply.

The cost-price of Trident is not subject to consumer opinion or behaviour, it seems. The decision of the 'buyer' whether or not to pay the price of a new generation of 'racers to the ocean's bottom' is a decision of those who govern – where 'governing', as a former French prime minister (who died today)[21] just put it on the radio, is about 'prioritising the national interest'; but what *are* 'national interests' in a rapidly globalising world economy? This is precisely the 20th century thinking and language that has to change if we're to reach the 22nd century intact.

Campaigns about bananas, pineapples and Trident may not, at first glance, have much in common, but, as I've tried to argue, it's about what we – citizen-consumers of the world more and more united by the minute – want. More importantly, it's about what we need and about refusing to accept the illogics that are presented to us by government or supermarket buyers as the natural order.

As France's biggest non-nuclear cultural export, Manu Chao, puts it in his 2007 album *La Radiolina*: 'This world go crazy... it's no fatality!'

Cycling and Nuclear Protesting

SIMON GOULD[22]

Presumably people protest against nuclear weapons because they have the potential not only to kill vast numbers of people but also animals and the environment. Cars are the same except that their threat is realised daily. Not only do cars kill vast numbers of people and animals (100,000 foxes pa in the UK, for example), but they poison the environment and contribute hugely

---

[21] Raymond Barre died on 24 August 2007.

[22] Simon was one of 14 individual cyclists who came to Faslane on two cycle protests during Faslane 365.

to global warming. So obviously people who care about the environment (like anti-nuclear protesters) don't drive cars, because it's much simpler to address one's own polluting habits than to persuade the government to stop its nuclear disgracefulness. Well I assume that's true. Is it? If it's not and you who read this are anti-nuclear and still drive a car then give it up now. No need to hold debates. No need to discuss targets for reduction. Just give it up. Walking and cycling are decent ways to get about. 'It didn't take a war to fuel this bike.' The alternative for individual transport to walking and cycling is the car. Drivers' demand for petrol and biofuel is causing untold misery and death worldwide.

Naked Protest against Trident

KAT BARTON

Almost a month before the end of Faslane 365, I was part of the blockading group 'Cyclists from Everywhere'. Six months previously, a similar group of cyclists had blockaded the gates of Faslane and some of those involved felt they would like to repeat the experience before the year-long campaign came to an end.

So, on 5 September 2007, four of us – with our bicycles in tow – boarded a train from London to Helensburgh. Between us we were experienced in organising mass cycle protests via our involvement with the World Naked Bike Ride and other climate change bike rides, and it was for this reason that we had originally planned our trip up to Faslane to take the form of a mass cycle protest. However, as just one other cyclist – who we were meeting in Scotland – had committed to the action, we became aware that our small number would not lend well to a 'mass' cycle protest! Instead, realising that the common thread holding four out of five of us together was our involvement in the World Naked Bike Ride, we decided to do an entirely different kind of protest: a naked protest against Trident.

The World Naked Bike Ride is a unique environmental protest which seeks to highlight the vulnerability of cyclists on city streets at the same time as raising awareness about climate change in a fun and visible way. Having all experienced the power of nudity in protest, we felt that demonstrating naked outside the gates of Faslane would be a simple act of defiance, which we hoped would draw attention to the absurdity of nuclear weapons in a nonviolent and distinctly non-threatening manner.

We were all familiar with the sense of vulnerability that nakedness brings – a feeling that comes from being exposed and laid bare. But we also knew that this vulnerability does not make us powerless – far from it: by actively laying ourselves open in this way we are demonstrating that our power derives not from the clothes we wear, the look we espouse or any other mask we may hide behind. Nakedness, we felt, takes us to our very core: by removing the physical barriers between ourselves and others, it can serve to break down the political and social structures which position us in a particular place in relation to others. Devoid of artificial purveyors of power, our naked bodies – standing boldly outside the gates of Faslane – became in themselves extraordinarily powerful.

The sense of empowerment that we experienced that day, armed only with our naked bodies, lies in stark contrast to the feeling of false strength that comes from the use of force or indeed the threat of the use of force. Moreover, the power conveyed by our nakedness challenged the machismo of the nuclear weapons, thereby disempowering their phallic nature. For us, nuclear weapons represent naked aggression and can never bring peace because they are based on a fear of the other, rather than on respect and a willingness to engage with those with whom we disagree. By protesting naked and displaying ourselves in our natural, naked state, we felt we were laying bare our humanity and therefore enabling our opponent to view us as human beings.

True security does not come from being armed to the teeth with life-destroying weapons, nor even does it come from the ability to threaten the use of force. Security is built by creating trust between the parties involved, engendering respect and mutual understanding and ultimately by being able to view the 'other' as a human being. In this way, nudity can be the most powerful weapon of all as it exposes us for what we really are: human.

CHAPTER 3

A History of Scottish Anti-Nuclear Protest

HELEN STEVEN

IN 1983 MALCOLM SPAVEN wrote a book called *Fortress Scotland*[1]. Written as it was during the height of the cold war, the book outlined the strategic importance of Scotland and gave a detailed list of the huge number of important military facilities based all over Scotland. Although the strategic situation has changed, much of the military thinking has not, and the country could still be called 'Fortress Scotland'. The UK's nuclear capability of four Trident submarines is based at Faslane and Coulport on the Clyde; Glen Douglas is a vast underground store of ammunition; Cape Wrath is a NATO bombing range; St Kilda is still part of a missile testing range, and low-flying aircraft continually practise over Scottish air-space.

It might be thought that this is in keeping with Scotland's warrior tradition, and indeed Scottish regiments are in the front line in Iraq and Afghanistan. However, Scotland has a long history of radical anti-militarist activity. The great names of John McLean, Willie Gallacher and Hamish Henderson are still powerful in Scottish socialist memory and are undoubtedly some of the inspiration behind the peace movement in Scotland today. John McLean and Willie Gallacher spoke out at public meetings and mass open-air rallies opposing the First World War, and in 1915 John McLean was given a savage sentence of three years hard labour, which broke his health and led to his untimely death. The establishment was so threatened by the anti-war demonstrations and rent strikes, that in 1919 tanks were brought in to surround George Square in Glasgow. Understandably part of the legacy of dissent still lives on in the Scottish peace movement today, as shown by the 80,000 who marched in Glasgow against the Iraq War, and by the Edinburgh school children who occupied Edinburgh Castle in protest

---

[1] Malcolm Spaven, *Fortress Scotland – a Guide to the Military Presence*, Pluto, 1983.

against that war. Much of this protest has been sparked off by the use of Scotland as a base for weapons of mass destruction.

On 18 February 1961 *Proteus,* the US Polaris submarine depot ship, arrived in the Holy Loch on the west coast of Scotland as part of a joint British/US agreement to base nuclear weapons on the Clyde. The newly formed Campaign for Nuclear Disarmament held a demonstration in London with 4,000 people sitting down in protest outside the Ministry of Defence. But Scotland was the real focus of attention. Some 2,000 marchers set off from Aldermaston, some carrying their own canoes, and on reaching the Clyde they were soon joined by a veritable flotilla of small craft and canoes. The 'Glasgow Eskimos' became part of the Scottish legend. Action was lively, imaginative and good fun. Ardnadam Pier at Dunoon was effectively blocked and a peaceful raiding party attempted to board *Proteus*. They were repulsed with fire-hoses, but some did manage to attach themselves to the anchor chain and frogmen had to be brought in to arrest them. Over 300 people were arrested in the demonstrations.

And they sang. Not for down-to-earth Scots the solemn hymn-like words of the 'H-Bomb's Thunder', but parodies of cheeky Glasgow street songs. This one went to the tune of 'Three Craws':

Och, och, there's a monster in the Loch
A monster in the Loch
A monster in the Lo-o-o-o-ch
Och, och there's a monster in the Loch
But we dinna want Polaris.[2]

or to another well-known tune, 'Coming Round the Mountain':

Oh, the Yanks have jist drapped anchor at Dunoon,
And they've got a civic welcome frae the toon,
As they came up the measured mile,
Bonny Mary o' Argyle
Wis wearing spangled drawers below her goon.
Oh ye cannae spend a dollar when ye're deid
Naw, ye cannae spend a dollar when ye're deid,
Singing Ding Dong Dollar, everybody holler,
Ye cannae spend a dollar when ye're deid.

---

[2] This is still sung at anti-nuclear demonstrations with 'Trident' replacing 'Polaris'.

However the base on the Holy Loch was merely a foretaste of what was to come, as the Clyde estuary became the most horrifying nuclear base in Europe. Soon the old naval scrapyard at Faslane was to house Britain's own Polaris fleet of four submarines armed with nuclear weapons, and then a whole hillside in Glen Douglas, just near Loch Lomond, was hollowed into sinister underground bunkers to house half the ammunition for the north Atlantic fleet.

While CND in England was deeply divided over the issue of civil disobedience, this never presented such a problem in Scotland. One reason may have been the roots in the radical past, and certainly the movement was wide-based with strong support from the Trade Unions, and also stated anti-nuclear policies from political parties such as the Independent Labour Party, the Communist Party in Scotland and the Scottish National party. Janey and Norman Buchan write of this in *The CND Story*: 'From a very early stage it was apparent to us that the mobilisation of opinion in Scotland was more widely-based; more representative of the people in general, and therefore, in a word, more working class in character than the early days of CND elsewhere in Britain. In one sense the mix was the same – trade-union activists, academics, intellectuals – but the balance was different. And this was what gave strength and particular urgency to the struggle on the Clyde.'

Early on in the campaign there was clear recognition that the nuclear bases were major employers in an area of high unemployment and deprivation. Tom McAlpine, with backing from the Iona Community, set up a worker-run company based on the principles of Robert Owen – hence the name, Rowen Engineering. It made storage heaters and its aim was to provide alternative employment using the skills of the workers at Faslane. Although this important initiative only managed to last a few years, the question of alternative employment is now being seriously addressed by the STUC with encouragement from the Scottish government.

Movements and campaigning energy fluctuate and during the 70s the nuclear disarmament movement fell into decline, although in Scotland CND never quite went under and was doggedly maintained through the doldrums by such stalwarts as Alan Mackinnon and Ian Davison who kept the office going in Glasgow. Indeed from 1973 onwards a regular series of demonstrations significantly shifted the focus of activity from the US base at the Holy Loch to Faslane, home of the UK's own nuclear fleet. Eventually the US withdrew from the Holy Loch in 1992.

Another significant factor in the slow steady growth of awareness of the full horror of nuclear war was the showing of Peter Watkin's film *The War Game*. This stark black and white film showing a simulated nuclear attack over Kent was originally commissioned for the BBC in 1965, but subsequently banned because 'It could produce a wholly irrational response among many members of the audience'. Far from producing an irrational response, up and down the country it provoked the entirely rational response of outrage and horror and the impetus to become active against nuclear weapons. So, during the apparently quiet 1970s, anti-nuclear protest was never quite silenced.

By the end of the 70s Polaris was already becoming obsolete and rumours of renewal were around. This was the catalyst to galvanise action in Scotland once again, and in 1979 a few thousand marched from Helensburgh on the Clyde to Faslane, to launch a campaign 'against any possibility of Britain's immoral, expensive and suicidal involvement in the nuclear arms race being renewed'.

Perhaps predictably, the inevitable happened and on 15 July 1980 the Conservative government announced plans to replace Polaris with the Trident II D5 missile system. This new system would mean that each of the submarines would have the destructive potential of 2,500 Hiroshimas, an unthinkable escalation of nuclear horror. At the same time the UK government entered into an agreement with the US to allow Cruise missiles to be sited at Greenham Common in Berkshire. These two events spurred people to action as never before. In 1981 the famous Women's Peace Camp was established at Greenham and regular bus loads of women travelled from all over the UK. Buses left the women's centres in Glasgow, Dundee, Edinburgh and Aberdeen almost every Friday night, returning in time for work on Monday mornings. Many from Scotland were among the 30,000 joining hands around the nine-mile perimeter on 12 December 1982.

But it was often galling and most frustrating to speak with enthusiastic anti-nuclear protesters and try to persuade them to come up to Scotland and protest against the UK's own nuclear missiles at Faslane, only to have a response of 'Oh Scotland, that's far too far away.' It was time for Scotland to build up its own resistance to Trident.

In 1981 the March for the Future was organised, starting at Faslane and, over a period of two days, marching the 25 miles to Glasgow's Kelvingrove park. About 5,000 people took part with buses arriving from all over the UK. Faslane as a focus of resistance for Scotland was now firmly on the map.

Then in 1982 Keith Bovey and STUC member, Bill Speirs, returned from a visit to Stockholm where they had been inspired by a peace march. Maggi Sale was given the task of organising Peace March Scotland. The aim was to bring together the protests against nuclear power and nuclear weapons and to rally widespread support throughout Scotland. Over a period of 33 days a core group of 40 people travelled through Inverness, Aberdeen, Perth, Glasgow, Hamilton and Edinburgh gaining local support on the way and ending up with over 4,000 participants. All kinds of groups joined in; Women's Rural, Boy Scouts, Buddhist monks, unemployed young people. Even the police showed their support and on one occasion, when the group was scraping together their scant resources to buy some lunch, a police van drove up and began distributing bags of pies and bridies – and they even returned with apple pies for the vegetarian Buddhists. Often the marchers had camped along the way, and this and the courage of the women at Greenham Common,was the inspiration for the Peace Camp at Faslane.[3]

Travel along the A82 road from Helensburgh to Garelochhead and you cannot fail to see a motley huddle of brightly painted vans, caravans and buses parked precariously on the verge of the road. This is the Faslane Peace Camp, defiantly pitched as a controversial nub of visible protest directly opposite one of the access roads leading to the submarine base. For many people a significant date in the history of protest was the Embrace the Base action at Greenham in December 1982. It is interesting to note, however, that Faslane Peace Camp was actually started six months before that in June 1982. Bobby and Margaret Harrison, veteran campaigners who were to be seen at every possible march or demonstration, were among the prime movers, along with Les and Louise Robertson, and they were later joined by Jane Tallents. Over the years many people came and went, and Jane is now a key participant in all anti-Trident demonstrations, being a frequent supportive presence at the Helensburgh Court.

Over the 25 years of its existence the Peace Camp has remained as a constant symbol of protest and resistance. Always the centre of controversy, its mere right to exist has been disputed frequently. Dumbarton District Council granted planning permission while Strathclyde Regional Council who owned the land gave the camp a lease and charged a peppercorn rent of £1 a month; on the other hand Argyll and Bute Council has threatened eviction on many occasions, but still the Peace Camp outlasts them all.

---

[3] *Faslane, Diary of a Peace Camp* written by members of the Camp, Polygon, 1984.

It is hard to measure the effect of the Peace Camp over the years. Its very presence raises awareness of Trident. It is hard to pass by without taking in the messages on the banners. At every demonstration the camp has provided a rallying point, shelter, cups of tea, a toilet stop, and a challenging lifestyle. A constant stream of people of all ages and walks of life have come over the years to live in difficult conditions and put their ideals into action. Anarchy, debate, idealism, squalor, beauty and values all mingle by the smoky fireside. And it is not only peace protesters who can share their views there. Workers at the Base, police, and even naval personnel have all been faced with the challenge, and for some it has changed their lives.

Most important of all, the Camp provided a focus and stimulus for action for all the new peace groups that were springing up all over Scotland. Forth for Peace, Glasgow West CND, Stirling, Ullapool, Portree, Stornoway, the Highland Coalition, Tweedside Peace Group, the Orkney Dunsters, to name but a few. Then there were the various professional groups, Medical Campaign Against Nuclear Weapons (MCANWE), Physicians for Social Responsibility, Engineers for Peace, Journalists Against Nuclear Extermination (JANE), Scientists Against Nuclear Arms (SANA), All these were national groups, but had energetic Scottish branches.

Early in the 1980s an Australian paediatrician called Helen Caldicott started giving lectures in the US on the dangers of nuclear weapons. Her style was deadly serious, punchy and clinically factual. Building on the strong opposition to nuclear power, she would say, 'This is just the pimple on the pumpkin compared to all-out nuclear war'. She would then describe in medical detail what would happen to the human body in a nuclear exchange. She concluded by describing the effects of psychic numbing and urged her hearers to wake up and take action to save their children and future generations. The impact of her talks was devastating.

In Scotland a group of mothers, mostly linked to the Catholic Justice and Peace Commission, invited small groups of women to meet in houses up and down the country to watch videos of Helen Caldicott. The result was Parents for Survival. Focusing the concern of parents for their own children was immediately successful across a broad spectrum of society, hitherto uninvolved in the peace movement.

In 1986 Kay Caldwell of Parents for Survival came up with the ambitious plan of inviting people from all over Scotland to form a human chain right across the country from the Clyde to the Forth to show their opposition to nuclear weapons. It was a tall order, but the whole event was organised with almost military precision. People were detailed to organise a one mile stretch of the route. They were issued with detailed maps, legal briefings, registration forms and phone numbers. Picture the luckless organisers on a desolate stretch of moorland near Bo'ness, early in the morning, dressed up in hideously conspicuous day-glo bin-liners. Not a soul in sight! They were torn between disappointment and relief that none of their friends could see them dressed up in a bin-liner. Then the buses arrived, one after the other, and people poured out to join the chain. As they stretched out to join up with the next group, it looked rather like Michelangelo's God and Adam reaching out to touch. Helicopter photos showed the line weaving up hill and down dale, sometimes three deep right across Scotland. Well over 30,000 people joined in, many on their first-ever demo.

Perhaps inspired by this event, Paul Baker, a former monk turned peace campaigner, conceived the notion of writing a formal letter to the Queen. Arguing that the government was 'Her Majesty's', and that it was time she brought them into line over nuclear weapons, a letter was written and signatures collected publicly in Princes Street in Edinburgh. Heading the list were senior representatives of all the major church denominations in Scotland. A delegation then took the letter to the Queen at Balmoral. Meanwhile, Paul Baker, a Church of Scotland delegate and myself headed off to London to deliver a copy of the Balmoral Letter to every MP and to hand one in to the Prime Minister. Paul turned up wearing a somewhat monastic rig-out (hood and all), the Church of Scotland representative was wearing a flowing cape and we were led down the Mall by a piper in full Highland panoply. One of life's more embarrassing moments, but it thrilled the tourists.

The role of the churches in Scotland in taking a stand against nuclear weapons has always been somewhat different from their counterparts in England, in that they have almost always found unity. A Papal Encyclical *Gaudium et Spes* stated: 'Any act of war aimed indiscriminately at the destruction of entire cities or extensive areas along with their population is a crime against God and man himself. It merits unequivocal and unhesitating condemnation.'

The Catholic church in Scotland stated its anti-nuclear position clearly in a public statement written by the Bishops' Conference in 1982, saying that if it was immoral to use these weapons, it was also immoral to threaten their use. (This position has been re-stated in 2006 when all the Scottish Churches urged the government against the renewal of Trident.) The Justice and Peace Commission in Scotland actively encouraged local congregations to set up justice and peace groups and, although many were primarily concerned with issues of justice and world poverty, they soon perceived the links with nuclear policy and became active against nuclear weapons.

Perhaps in this instance a hierarchical system was an advantage. The Church of Scotland, has a more democratic process through its General Assembly and local presbyteries which makes it more difficult to reach a quick, united decision. In this process the role of the Iona Community was crucial.

The Iona Community is an ecumenical Christian community founded in 1938 by that formidable and remarkable character George Macleod.[4] Community members adhere to a five-point Rule, one of which is a commitment to working for justice and peace. Part of this states: 'We believe that the use or threatened use of nuclear and other weapons of mass destruction is theologically and morally indefensible and that opposition to their existence is an imperative of the Christian faith.' Year after year George Macleod, Roger Gray and other members of the Iona Community and those in sympathy would get up in the General Assembly of the Church of Scotland and propose resolutions against nuclear weapons. Year after year people stood outside the Assembly Hall on the Mound in Edinburgh with leaflets and banners. And year after year the vote went against them. Until the memorable Assembly of 1984 when George Macleod *didn't* speak, and his chief opponent *did* saying most movingly that he had been wrong all these years. The Assembly passed a motion saying that 'Nuclear weapons are contrary to the will of God'. The vigillers outside were totally amazed and couldn't believe their ears until a minister said rather wryly, 'Your banners say 'Pray for Peace'. Do you not believe it works?'

The Ecumenical Peace Team was formed to take these concerns forward, meeting regularly at Scottish Churches House in Dunblane with the support of ACTS (Action of Churches Together in Scotland). Church representatives were sent on peace delegations to the Soviet Union and Czechoslovakia and also to meet with high-ranking officials at NATO headquarters in Brussels. To some church members going to Communist states was highly questionable. After I had spoken to a church group about peace campaigning, a member of the audience stood up and said 'You couldn't say these kind of things in

---

4 George was awarded the Military Cross in the First World War, but after the war became an ardent pacifist.

the Soviet Union and not be locked up.' 'I have said these things and leafleted in Red Square,' I replied, 'and I wasn't locked up.' There was a pause and then she said, 'Well you should have been.' Some arguments you just can't win.

In the hiatus of opportunity at the end of the cold war, when global politics and defence priorities seemed to be undergoing a major shift, the Iona Community hosted a conference entitled 'Options for Defence; the Way Forward'. It was attended by an interesting cross-section of peace campaigners, church leaders and influential defence civil servants and retired generals. It was a remarkable week and for many it was the first time they had spoken frankly across what seemed a great divide. Somehow doing dishes together, cleaning the toilets, dancing the Dashing White Sergeant and sharing life stories creates unique possibilities for sharing and dialogue. Friendships and contacts were made there that paved the way for the three Rhu Consultations, the first of which was held in May 2002 when the Moderator of the Church of Scotland hosted meetings attended by very senior military and defence experts.

Soon all this protest began finding its way into the political corridors of power. Local authorities began to form 'nuclear free zones'. On 8 July 1981 Strathclyde Regional Council, whose area includes the submarine bases passed the following resolution: 'this council opposes the Atomic Missile Base at Coulport and demands the removal of all atomic weapons and bases in Strathclyde and Scotland.'

Such moves immediately gave access to council premises for meetings, council blessing for the planting of innumerable commemorative cherry trees, occasional funding for events, and some very classy receptions and dinners, but in fact when it came to actually being nuclear free, councils were fairly powerless. A blatant example of this is the transportation of nuclear warheads.

Warheads for Trident are serviced in Burghfield near Aldermaston in Oxfordshire. They are then transported in a menacing convoy of mammoth transporters, heavily guarded, under police escort, all the way to Coulport, travelling on major motorways and public roads, sometimes even going through major centres of population such as Glasgow or Stirling. Nukewatch was set up with an efficient early-warning system which reported the route of the convoy so that the opposition could be ready. Over all the years of convoys travelling every six weeks or so, hardly a single one has passed without its passage being noted and marked by protest. People have D-locked themselves by the neck to the axles; convoys have been pursued, ambushed, blockaded, and tied up; windscreens have been smeared with white paint. (Funny how reluctant the police were to arrest that one!) One picturesque action made the headlines by stopping the convoy right on the Scottish Border with a Saltire-waving blockade.

Such activities all helped to raise public awareness of the enormity of dangerous warheads travelling the length and breadth of the land. Stirling CND became an active focus of activity against the convoys, and representations have been made to the emergency services, the police, MPs and local authorities to flex their political muscles. At last this is paying dividends as both health and safety and transport are within the remit of the Scottish government, which can now make strong protest to Westminster.

Some campaigners felt that their energy should be directed towards political change and engaged in the political process in a variety of ways. In response to the rapid growth of CND, a counter-group was set up called Peace Through NATO, and many of their meetings were organised by the Conservative party. In Stirling a group of 15 women dressed themselves up to look suitably respectable and quietly infiltrated the meeting in the council offices. It was somewhat off-putting for them to be confronted by a platform bedecked with posters depicting Scotland encircled by a hammer and sickle formed out of a CND sign. However, undaunted, when it came to question time, all 15 women managed to embarrass by landing cogent questions until they were politely bundled out of the hall. Hardly surprising that subsequent meetings were not open to the general public.

Many people still pinned their hopes to the political party process. Murdoch Mackenzie is a Church of Scotland minister, who, at the drop of a hat, will open his briefcase and whip out – not the Bible – but a copy of Hansard, and reliably inform you how MP's voted on nuclear questions in parliament, and then help you draft a letter. On the Isle of Skye there was an optician called Roger Gray[5] who was an ardent peace campaigner. His optician's window in Portree didn't display samples of spectacles; it was full of peace posters and pamphlets, with an inconspicuous pair of specs in the corner – presumably to enable one to read the literature. He organised members of the Isle of Skye Peace Group to go round every household on the island collecting signatures for the World Disarmament Campaign to send to their MP. Anyone who knows Skye, will know what a huge island it

5 Helen Steven, *Roger – an extraordinary peace campaigner*, Wild Goose Publications, 1990.

is, what a distance they had to cover, and how remote some of the crofts and homesteads are. The task called for a high degree of dedication.

Vitally important as all such actions are, it soon became apparent that this was not enough. The huge demonstration in London of almost a quarter of a million people in 1982 was only mentioned in a small paragraph in the *Guardian*. A disappointed friend commented to me, 'From now on it has to be direct action'. All over Scotland groups were forming to learn the techniques of nonviolent direct action. Training programmes were set up at the Edinburgh Peace and Justice Centre, at Centrepeace in Glasgow, in the universities, at the Peace Camp, in the Abbey on Iona, and in the many local peace groups. In 1987 Peace House was established in central Scotland near Dunblane. This was a residential centre where people could come for study weekends and workshops as well as training in nonviolence. In its 12 years of existence over 10,000 people experienced the welcome of Peace House, and many still speak of it with warmth and affection. When it finally closed in 1999 the work continued in the Scottish Centre for Nonviolence in Dunblane. One of the aims of the Centre was to bring nonviolence into the mainstream of education. The Centre provided a module in nonviolence as part of a Masters Degree through the Centre for Human Ecology in Edinburgh. Although the Centre closed in 2007, the work is being continued energetically at the Edinburgh Peace and Justice Centre.

In these various courses participants studied the history of nonviolent protest and prepared for civil disobedience as a tactic. People learned how to resist nonviolently, how to cope with anger and aggression, and had legal briefings for arrest and court. They would challenge the immorality of Trident by putting their bodies on the line.

Actions were spontaneous, humorous and imaginative. One Christmas, protesters dressed up as Santa Claus tried to deliver sacks of goodies down the conning tower of a submarine. (How do you tell your children that Santa has been arrested?) Many had gained inspiration and confidence from times spent at Greenham Common and in 1983 an action was planned to have a peace presence at each of the 103 US or NATO linked bases in the UK. This immediately put Scotland on the map, and turned out to be an initiation for a some of the newly formed action groups. I was part of a group which had trained in Glasgow and we were keen and ready for action. Glen Douglas was the chosen site. Glen Douglas was a sinister place, where entire hillsides had been hollowed out to make huge underground ammunition bunkers. It was our first ever act of civil disobedience and, after a sleepless night listening to the barking of the guard-dogs, three of us managed to climb the fence and drop down inside the base to plant a 'Peace Rose' as a symbol of hope. When we were arrested, the police officer's comment was 'Regular bunch of gardeners, aren't you!' Hence the name, the Gareloch Horticulturists (the group is still active and about to celebrate its 25th birthday). The three of us were locked up in an empty ammunition shed, and the officer guarding us said dismissively 'You've failed to act at *all* the bases. There's no one at Macrihanish (a really remote base on the Mull of Kintyre)' We told him to check up, and sure enough three elderly women were found having a picnic on the runway. Confidence was indeed growing.

In April 1984, to mark the anniversary of the death of Martin Luther King, a mass trespass of the Faslane Base was organised. At a given time groups converged on the base, and each planned their own action. One person climbed up a crane, a sentry-box was occupied, football played on the Base's pitch, and of course, the Gareloch Horticulturists ('Hortis' for short) planted half a sack of potatoes. Altogether 47 were arrested and, as many refused to pay their fines, were given short prison sentences. For many this was their first experience of prison and marked a significant step in over-coming conventional fears and inhibitions.

For myself, as one of the potato planters, it was my first arrest, and I was most apprehensive about going to prison. How would the other women and the prison officers view a middle-class dilettante with all her naïve idealism? I needn't have worried. 'Oh, nuclear weapons – they're dreadful things' and 'You're doing this for all our children' were among some of the typical com-ments of the women, showing an innate understanding amongst the majority of ordinary folk of Scotland, and many of the prison officers were also openly sympathetic. This attitude is consistently reflected in opinion polls over the years showing strong opposition to Trident.

In 1985 an exciting new initiative was started in England and soon caught on in Scotland. It was called the Snowball Campaign[6]. The idea was simple and virtually unstoppable. Protesters would act in a highly symbolic Gandhian way by cutting one strand of security fence at a military base. They would write letters beforehand to the base commander, the police and the press explaining their action, and wait to be arrested. The action began

---

[6] Angie Zelter, *Snowball – the story of a Nonviolent Civil-Disobedience Campaign in Britain*, Gandhi-in-Action, New Delhi, India, 1990.

with three people at USAF Sculthorpe in Norfolk, then nine people, then 81 and then went on growing in numbers and taking place anywhere in the UK. Soon there were hundreds of people involved, many delighting in the simplicity, openness and companionship of the action. On the third Snowball action at Faslane, 11 local councillors turned up, dressed to the nines in striped suits with a flower in their buttonhole. The police stopped arresting, charges were not pressed and gradually the campaign lost momentum. A pity, because an army officer informed me later that they were really worried by the tactic, as leave had to be cancelled at all the bases on the weekend of a Snowball action, and that pressure would have been applied to stop a campaign that had the capacity to build an unstoppable campaign against Trident.[7] Perhaps it was too soon, or perhaps we lacked commitment – who knows?

All over Scotland creative ways of resisting the coming of Trident were being carried out. Regularly on International Women's Day at the beginning of March events would happen – a washing line of T-shirts with peace messages suddenly appeared inside the base at Glen Douglas; a naval loading crane at Glen Mallon became pink overnight (blushing with shame, perhaps?). In fact the police became so accustomed to a women's action near Glen Douglas, that they were quite put out when the women took action one year at Coulport instead. Grandmothers blockaded Faslane and then went to the main pedestrian areas in Glasgow and Edinburgh and collected hundreds of photographs of people's grandchildren which they then took to Westminster and presented to their MPs.

A group in Dalkeith cut up the Edinburgh telephone directory, pasted all the thousands of names onto a banner many metres long and then stood by the war memorial on 11 November with the banner saying 'The Dead of World War Three'. Wreaths of white poppies were laid at the Cenotaph in Glasgow, and a coffin carried round George Square. In the centre of Glasgow, Philip Taylor held a solitary vigil against Trident every Friday evening for 14 years.

One action was designed to show the sheer size and cost of Trident. 435ft of bright hazard tape was stretched the whole length of Sauchiehall Street, the main pedestrian precinct in Glasgow. Along its length people were stationed with placards comparing the cost of Trident with the number of schools

---

7 During the 14 stages of Snowball, which lasted just over three years, 2,796 people took part at 42 different bases in Britain. There were 2,419 arrests, most of which ended up in the courts.

and hospitals that could be built for the money, or quoting the killing capacity. To demonstrate the height of Trident, two people went to the top of a multi-storey car park and hoisted a banner one third the height of the conning tower. At its base passers-by could sign postcards to the government. As a finale 'Trident' was rolled-up to a flourishing trumpet accompaniment, and a procession went to the MOD offices in Glasgow where the main doors were super-glued shut and a notice put up saying 'Closed for business'.

One of the most scenic train journeys in Scotland is the West Highland Line from Glasgow to Oban, passing by Faslane, Coulport and Glen Douglas, all of which are clearly visible from the train. Obviously the tourists have to be leafleted occasionally about what they are actually seeing amidst the beautiful scenery.

In the cloisters of Iona Abbey some young people built a mock fall-out shelter, all to the ticking of a four-minute clock, and hundreds of tourists were given leaflets about the effects of a nuclear explosion. On one occasion a mock Trident submarine was carried into the Abbey and a service of lamentation held around it. Even at one-tenth the actual size it was huge enough to occupy the whole of the nave and half the choir stalls with its sinister bulk.

The real submarines themselves were to be based at Faslane on the Gare Loch, but the missiles were to be stored just over the hill at Coulport on Loch Long. This would mean excavating vast bunkers and extending the existing base to almost ten times its original size. Inevitably Coulport also became the focus for many actions. During the same weekend as Arms Across Scotland, a mass trespass, called Reclaim the Hills, took place and hundreds of people walked freely over MOD land. In the summer of 1985 a vigil was initiated. Every weekend for a period of six months a rota of different peace groups from all over Scotland would sleep over outside the main gate at Coulport and hand out leaflets to the workers at every change of shift. Each group made up its own leaflet highlighting a different aspect of Trident. I think it rained or snowed practically every weekend from June to December, but many conversations took place, and it was soon discovered that humour and songs are an effective way of getting the message across. The police were totally bemused by the number of groups participating. They would consult the previous week's notes and say, 'So you'll be Teachers for Peace.' 'Oh, no, we're Stirling CND – or Mothers for Peace, or Cat Lovers Against the Bomb, or Edinburgh Quakers, and so on.' It was chaos to try to organise, so it was really gratifying later to have a police officer say, 'You must be from that really well-organised group that does the vigil.' 'Yes, that's right!'

In spite of all our protests, the inevitable happened in 1992. At one level we had always known it was coming, but nothing can prepare one for the full horror of seeing that huge black monster being angled into position to invade our beautiful Scottish loch. As HMS *Vanguard* powered its way relentlessly up the Gare Loch past the Rhu Narrows to Faslane we were all there to greet it with our protest. Banners waving on the beach said 'Scotland says No'; crowds of reporters lined the banks, and a whole flotilla of floating craft of all descriptions were ready for launching. When the police told us that anyone taking to the water would be liable for arrest, a cheer went up and canoes, inflatables, rubber rings and even solitary swimmers all splashed in. We were brushed aside like stray bluebottles, and could only weep tears of helpless rage as Trident penetrated the sea-lochs of Scotland. It was our lowest moment, and singing 'We Shall Overcome' was well-nigh impossible.

And yet, even while the four submarines were being fitted out and deployed, momentous events that were to change the whole climate of opinion were already happening.

For many, many years a small group of dedicated campaigners – Keith Mothersson, Alan Wilkie, Christine Soane and others – had been working tirelessly to convince people of the illegality of Trident and all weapons of mass destruction under international law. Quoting the Geneva Conventions and Nuremberg, they made a totally convincing case, but many campaigners, while listening to their arguments, simply dismissed it as being a hopeless struggle that could never succeed in the legal establishment.

However, around the world the case was growing, and eventually with help from civil society groups around the world[8], the UN General Assembly managed to bring a request before the International Court of Justice sitting in the Hague to deliver a legal opinion on the legality of nuclear weapons. After considering the case for more than two years, in June 1996, the 15 judges delivered their opinion. Although couched in legal language, which can lend itself to argument and obfuscation, the basic ruling was absolutely clear. Because of the indiscriminate nature of nuclear weapons, their use

---

[8] Including INLAP (Institute for Law and Peace), the WCP (World Court Project), IALANA (International Association of Lawyers Against Nuclear Arms) and IPB (International Peace Bureau).

and threatened use would in all circumstances contravene international humanitarian law.

At long last one could stand up in court and argue the case from a strong legal basis, and many protesters did just that, but continually the courts disallowed any such defence, and it seemed impossible to make any headway. Until the advent of Trident Ploughshares.

Using the ICJ ruling that Trident is illegal under international law, Trident Ploughshares argued that the UK government was acting illegally and that therefore citizens had the right and duty to uphold the law by physically dismantling Trident and its related systems, safely, accountably and nonviolently.

On 8 August 1998 Trident Ploughshares was launched at the North Gate of Faslane, and from then on it was open season on Trident. Groups from all around the country and abroad signed the TP Pledge of Resistance, undertook training in nonviolence, and took action. The range and variety of activities was remarkable. People swam across the loch and under the defence boom right up to the sides and even the deck of the Trident submarines; two women, still dressed in their wetsuits, managed to climb into the conning tower of a submarine docked at Barrow-in-Furness; three Scandinavian protesters kept the gates of Coulport closed for hours simply by sitting astride the top of them singing songs; a yearly camp was established at Peaton Wood near Coulport, from where regular incursions were made to 'take back the land'; blockades with people locked-on to elaborate creations could keep the Base closed for hours. Scotland had become the focus at last for a wide international movement of direct action.

However, these events were still not in line with TP's intention of actually taking apart the Trident system. Then in June 1999 the opportunity came. On a glorious June evening, Angie Zelter, Ulla Röder and Ellen Moxley took a small inflatable dinghy out to a floating platform on Loch Goil where acoustic testing for Trident was conducted. To their amazement they found the facility totally unguarded and were able to climb in through an open window. They then proceeded to throw all the computers to the bottom of the Loch, leaving only the safety equipment and the drinking fountain untouched. Job done, they then sat down on deck with a picnic to watch the sunset and wait for arrest.

Then followed five months on remand in Cornton Vale Women's Prison until their trial in Greenock. The trial was a cliff-hanger. Perhaps the crucial moment was when Sheriff Gimblett decided to allow a defence under international law. At last the way was open for a full hearing of the ICJ arguments. Expert witnesses were called, advocates argued the case, and Angie presented her own defence brilliantly, with the result that, after four weeks, the 'Trident Three' were acquitted.

Suddenly the press, hitherto conspicuous by their absence, crowded round. Headlines like, 'How Four Middle Aged Ladies Sank UK Defence' and 'Outcry as sheriff rules nuclear weapons illegal' grabbed the front pages of the Scottish media. Perhaps the most interesting one was 'Trident case set to test Holyrood'. Defence was a matter reserved to the Westminster government, but the Scottish legal system is independent, and now Trident was illegal under Scottish law. This was a serious constitutional matter, and in effect the devolved Scottish parliament could have demanded the removal of Trident from Scottish waters. Obviously the UK government could not allow such a delicate situation to remain for long, and some months later questions were put to the Lord Advocate in what was known as the Lord Advocate's Reference (LAR). In a very strange hearing in the High Court in Edinburgh flaws were found (perhaps predictably) in the Sheriff's ruling, although senior legal experts insist that the fundamental principle of Trident's illegality remains, and the case of the Trident Three is still used as a case study in the legal schools[9]. As a sign of disgust at the result of the LAR some protesters chained themselves to the balcony of the Scottish parliament in the first act of civil protest in the new parliament.

In recognition of the huge impact Trident Ploughshares as a nonviolent campaign had made in the struggle against nuclear weapons, TP was awarded the Right Livelihood Award, sometimes known as the alternative Nobel Peace Prize, and Ellen, Angie and Ulla went to Stockholm to receive it on behalf of all those who had worked so tirelessly against Trident.

Inspired by the sheer energy and dynamism of Trident Ploughshares, Scottish CND joined with them to organise the Big Blockade in 2001, billed as the biggest blockade yet. It certainly was. Over 385 people were arrested, including clergy, MPs and an MEP. All the Glasgow police stations were filled to capacity and the courts took months to process all the cases.

Now the priority was to keep the pressure on and not allow the people of Scotland to lose sight of the fact that we have WMDs on our own

---

9 For the full story of the Loch Goil action, the legal arguments and Trident Ploughshares disarmament actions see Angie Zelter, *Trident on Trial – the case for people's disarmament,* Luath, 2001.

doorstep. The next idea was Faslane 365, a campaign to maintain a continuous blockade at Faslane every day for a year, with different groups from around the country being responsible for a 48 hour period. The idea soon caught on, and when the year ended on 1 October 2007 all were agreed that the event had been a huge success. Although not every day of the year was covered, a blockade was held on 189 days and 1,150 people had been arrested. But above all Faslane 365 was remarkable for the huge outpouring of creative talent and clever imaginative ideas. Academics held symposia and read solemn papers in front of the gates, an Oratorio was specially written and performed, full-scale choirs sang in harmony; Highland games and Ceilidhs were held; Welsh dragons and a 12ft-high wolf appeared at the gates; Buddhist chants, Quaker Meetings and Communion services were held – all kinds of appearances at the gates of Faslane throughout the year. Local newspapers up and down the country ran items on the activities of their own people, and the people of Scotland couldn't help but be intrigued.

During this momentous year of activity other important events were taking place. In May 2007 elections for the Scottish parliament were held and the Scottish National Party won by a narrow margin. The SNP policy on Trident was clear. 'We believe that nuclear weapons are the wrong choice for a successful Scotland. That's why we don't waste £25 billion on new weapons of mass destruction when it can be better spent in our schools, hospitals and other public services.'

Just a week after the new government opened, a motion was passed by a majority of 71 to 16 with 36 abstentions that the Scottish government was opposed to any replacement of Trident, and that they would work towards its removal from Scottish waters. On 22 October for the first time ever under the auspices of an anti-Trident Scottish government, a summit meeting was convened in Glasgow with representatives from the MOD, the STUC, church leaders, and MSPs along with peace activists,[10] to discuss the implications of a Scotland without Trident.

There is still a long road ahead, but could it be that we are beginning to see the possibility of a Trident-free Scotland and a nuclear weapon free world?

---

[10] Faslane 365, Trident Ploughshares, Nukewatch and Scottish CND all took part.

The SOCRAP Action

TANSY NEWMAN TURNER, LAVINIA CROSSLEY and EMMA BATEMAN

Tansy

Tuesday, 4 September, 1.30 am, Lavinia and I sat shivering, staring at a candle and listening to 'Seize the Day' 'With my hammer...', trying to arrange our nerves into a comfortable enough position to sleep. A couple of hours later, we had managed to rest briefly but were up again dressed in rather unattractive leggings and tight tops (in preparation for the razor wire) and fitted with belts carrying climbing devices specially designed for weld mesh fences.

The car journey to Faslane Naval Base was extremely tense, to make an understatement. I was struggling with panic, controlled only by keeping in mind the purpose of why we were doing it and the other climbers Emma and Lavinia were quiet, dealing with it in their own ways.

All too soon we reached the stretch of fence we had agreed on, leading into the high security zone of the base where the Trident Nuclear Submarines are docked. Lavinia leapt onto the fence (with a little rather inelegant pushing from Emma and I) fitting devices as she went. I followed as we became aware of an approaching Police Car. Lavinia and I pushed up into the razor wire picking our way carefully.

Shocked, the police seemed not to know how to react. One dangerously grabbed Lavinia's leg but soon let go. By this time I had slipped over the fence, through a handy little gap in the piled up coils of razor wire on the ground inside and had run off through the trees into the base, with the alarm system informing everyone 'Bandits, Bandits, Bandits in the Base'!

True to our aim, which was to investigate the great and terrible crime that is committed by our government by owning and permanently deploying on patrol hundreds of kilotons of nuclear arsenal, in violation of The Geneva Convention, The Nuremberg Principles, The Nuclear Non-Proliferation Treaty and the ICJ Advisory Opinion (1996) to name just a few, I headed off towards the submarine dock to see what I could find, only super-glueing myself to a gate when I heard a Police Van approaching. Lavinia remained on the top of the fence gathering as much information about the base from her privileged position as she could...

Lavinia

Sitting on top of the fence, in the middle of the night while most people were sleeping, I, along with Tansy and Emma, was continuing the pressure against Britain's nuclear weapons and the laws which protect them. With Tansy successfully inside the base, Emma was shouting encouraging words to me as I hung our banner on the fence.

The sun had now risen, Emma had been arrested and it felt like I had been up on top of the fence for some time. As another team of police arrived (this time very determined to get me down), I happily continued my protest. The police discussed the charge I would face as they looked up at me on the fence: The Serious and Organised Crime and Police Act. A law brought in to 'protect' the base or 'deter' terrorists, yet I believe will be used only to deter peaceful protests against the illegal weapons within. As the police discussed ways of cutting the fence to retrieve me, I decided I did not want the unnecessary destruction of a perfectly good and climbable fence, so I climbed down into the base. After scurrying under the razor wire I was grabbed by two police officers and gently walked into the base.

The next 24 hours I spent alone in a cell, reflecting on what we had done and thinking about the court case which lay ahead. I contemplated my reasons for acting, my small act of defiance against the state and these weapons. My belief in our actions brought me on to the fence and into the cell, as they have before. My belief to act outside the 'legal' channels as well as within them has been determined after years of writing to MPs, signing petitions, protesting outside bases and marching with thousands of others and yet feeling ignored.

I feel Britain's nuclear weapons system is a senseless way of creating fear, devastation and destruction, the norms of our society should be a reflection of our society. I do not feel the weapons are a reflection of the beliefs and morals I and most other people follow in their lives.

Emma

In the car flowing over the hills in dark quiet, the adrenalin rides my veins. I am stepping through a comfortable poem in my mind – a focus to distract from the riotous rattle of fear underneath which gradually tunes to a hum of 'if this is how it feels confronting a fence, what is it like in a war trench waiting for the 'go!' cry.'

We arrive, jump out and I run the wrong way. I am fortunate; Tansy and

Lavinia are sharp, they find the spot and get to work. I am to help Lavinia up the fence. I mentally tighten to this tiny job; I can do this. Lavinia hauls herself up and sits on my head. We are not at our most elegant. Time splits; Lavinia seems to sit for ages, but the sound of the police car rises in an instant. Lavinia pulls herself up the fence, Tansy skims after her. The car stops. I am caught by the voice of the policeman, my hesitation a reflex to his shout. In small defiance I unhook the climbing device near my hand, stretch up and place it under Lavinia's flailing foot.

The police woman who holds me is angry. She tries to keep my head turned away from the fence to stop me watching, but this effort stops her seeing too and she can't keep it up. She wants to look. I get bolder, urging Lavinia and Tansy onwards and upwards. At first the police woman tells me to shut up, but as we are drawn together into the tension of the girls scaling the fence, and the trap of razor wire drama, in the end I believe she quietly, secretly wants them to get over too.

In the police cell a friendly pc chats. She says Lavinia and Tansy look very young. Am I certain they are over 18? I sense she feels they are too young for this kind of thing – it's OK for us older ones to struggle with nuclear weapons, but youth shouldn't be troubled by such thoughts. I suggest to her that being young and pretty will not shield them from a nuclear blast, and that their generation might have to pay in every way for the foolish Trident replacement conceived by us, their elders. If they don't have the right to try and prevent that, who has? She looks crestfallen.

As I lay in my cell comfortably shattered, the day rewinds in my mind and I run the moment I paused at the policeman's shout. I imagine myself leaping at the fence and grabbing the top in triumph. Because time was swaying unsteadily I don't know if the gap between the shout and the grasp on my arm was large or small, but I decide next time, yes next time, I will not stop at 'stop!'

And Finally... From Us All

Our action was to demonstrate our continuing rage at Britain's hypocrisy in owning nuclear weapons and show solidarity for those who have suffered, lost loved ones and homes due to horrific nuclear attacks and accidents. We acted in hope that a future free from these atrocious inventions really is possible and we face our charges without fear because of the strength we gain from the wonderful support we receive and our conviction in the wrong that nuclear weapons embody.

A Night Challenging SOCPA

JOAN MEREDITH

Irene and I were part of the team that challenged the SOCPA[11] law, as part of Faslane 365, on 5 September 2007 by trying to enter the Faslane and Coulport bases. We were the support for the group who were to cut through the Faslane fence and get into the base.[12] The first attempt took place at 11am but had to be abandoned because the petrol driven saw failed. After the saw was re-checked we tried again at 8pm at the same place but the saw failed again. We went back to our meeting place and decided on another plan for the evening at Coulport.

By this time there were only three of us left. We took the 10.15pm bus to Coulport and eventually alighted near the beach. We walked along and made our way to the loch until we saw a police car trailing slowly along on the road before stopping. We hurried into a hedge and sat there until the police finally went. Keeping close to the hedge we made our way nearer the base until we were near the fence which sticks out into the sea. Al said we would have to sit and wait till round about midnight so that the tide was right out and we could paddle round the end of the fence. When he judged the time was right we moved closer to the fence. The going was rough and I found it difficult stumbling over the slippery rocks and stones. However, it was a fine night and quite warm.

When we got to the fence we waited until Al got round and came level with us on the other side of the fence and we knew it was safe to follow him. We had taken off our footwear and rolled up our trousers. Holding the fence we both walked round the end of it and caught up with him. Then a really difficult climb up the rocks from the beach took quite a long time. The other two waited for me well into the shadows because we were afraid we would be easily seen in the bright lights. We hurried off and eventually came

---

[11] Serious Organised Crime and Police Act 2005 (SOCPA) which makes it a crime to enter various military sites.

[12] Three women had already climbed into Faslane over the fences very early that same morning. They were later charged with SOCPA. Three others had cycled into the base and were charged with breach of the peace. They were all part of the same SOCRAP SOCIAP (Serious Organised Crime Investigation and Prevention) Team.

to a building right on the edge of the cliff. The perimeter fence followed us right round on our right.

Al knew exactly where the fence could be cut while Irene and I waited. Once through the fence and the razor wire we continued until we found ourselves at the gate near the jetty where the submarines berth. We were amazed that no one had found us yet. We were very tired and feeling a little nonplussed at how easy it had all been. Al decided at this point that he was going back but Irene and me decided to continue. We thought we were sure to find someone if we went towards a well-lit building a little further on past the jetty. There was no one. We walked up into the middle of the building complex looking hopefully into the rooms blazing with light. Still there was no one.

By now Irene was wishing we had gone back with Al. We went right back to the hole in the fence and crawled through and hurried back to the sentry box near the fence. I was afraid that the tide would be too far in and although Irene was willing to try I felt I would rather be arrested than risk drowning. Anyway, I was sure the guard in the box would arrest us if we went there. Irene agreed that it would be difficult to go around the fence and I went to find the MOD guard. I couldn't believe it; there was no one there. Always at the Trident Ploughshares Coulport camps someone had been on duty there. So, reluctantly we walked all the way back along the fence to the hole, climbed through and back to the brilliantly lit buildings by the jetty. No one was around. Back we went into the complex, we walked towards the main gate, past what used to be the holding blocks, past the telephone box. I told Irene that if there was anyone at all on duty we would find police in the duty block at the main gate and I knew in which direction that was. By this time we were so tired we were closely linking arms and trudging along. We could see the main gate with lights on in the sentry block. We were in the lorry park and could see the bus shelter. I thought if the worst came to the worst we could sit down there and perhaps smuggle ourselves out in a lorry when the morning shift started.

By then we were near enough to the duty block to see a policeman inside standing at the window. He appeared to be phoning someone. I was sure he had seen us and we would be arrested at last. But no! He came out, walked across to something and went back in. I was waving frantically. I couldn't believe it when he went back in. Then he appeared to pick up the phone again and as he did so he turned and looked out of the window and saw us. I could swear his hair stood up on end. He came out, looked across at us as we were waving and went back in. Then he and a second young policeman came out, caps on, machine guns over their shoulders. They just stood there and waited for us to approach them. I felt they were the ones who were afraid.

They asked us if we knew we were on unauthorised property. We assured them that we did. What were we doing there? We said we were lost. How had we got in? No comment was our reply. The older one went in to call whoever was in charge. We answered no comment when asked for our names. Irene sat down on the kerb and I sat down on a concrete flower pot and leaned against the bush planted there. We were so tired. We must have been walking about inside the base for at least two hours. I thought we might have been invited inside and given a chair. After what seemed a long wait MOD staff appeared with lots of vans. Someone who appeared to be in charge started to question us. They were anxious to know how on earth we had got in. The man in charge was very brusque when we stuck to no comment; whipped round and said 'You know you are silly women – you're just two silly women?' how dare he say that in the middle of all that waste? Billions spent on weapons of mass destruction for what? Certainly not for the security of ordinary people if two old women can get in. Silly men, I think.

More police arrived, one with a dog. They discussed what they would do. They wanted to know how we had cut the fence. They were amazed that we appeared to be quite dry and had no cutting tools of any kind. The man in charge had disappeared in a temper. Another more patient man took over. Two arresting police, one man and one woman, arrived. They were all talking together. Then it became clear that they were going to arrest us. I gave the statement of intent to them. Then we were searched and processed. Everybody was beginning to relax. I had a conversation with the younger of the two police with the guns, about different accents. Then another one talked about teaching the deaf. The arresting policeman told me that his father lived in Brayton Selby where I had lived when my daughter was born. All the time they discussed what they were going to do and decided the perimeter fence must be inspected and some went off with the dog. The more patient man asked me to tell him whether or not there were more people inside the fence. I said I could only say that as far as I knew there was no one else but I couldn't take responsibility if more were found. Then they said they were taking us down to Faslane. I discovered I hadn't got the book that Eric had lent me to read in the police station. We had been given chairs outside by this time. I jumped up and the arresting policeman went back into the office with me. 'What's it called?' he said. '*Bloody Hell*', I replied. 'That just about sums up tonight', he said.

At last Irene and I climbed into the back of one of the cage-like vans. It was the first time in my 78 years that I had ever ridden in one. It is very unpleasant, more suited to carrying dogs than people.

Once down in Faslane we were treated like long lost friends. We were searched and our belongings bagged up. They asked what they could do for us and I asked for a warm blanket. They had put the heating on and I wrapped myself up and gratefully lay down on the bench. I was soon called to have my finger prints taken by someone who had never done it before, and needed help and had my photo taken with my crime number by Ian who congratulated himself on taking a good one. I declined to look at it – it was about 4.00am. Not the best time for photographs. I went back briefly into the duty office. The young policewoman asked me how old I was. I wearily told her I was 77 saying that by the same time next week I would be a year older. I was finally allowed back into the cell and tried to sleep. I had asked if I could have something to drink. I was promised a cup of tea. The duty sergeant came a little later to apologise because they had no milk. I assured him anything would do – we were unexpected visitors. He brought the tea and I was grateful that it was in a cup and not a polystyrene beaker. When he came to collect the cup he told me that we were going to be released and taken to the Peace Camp. I was so relieved. I was dreading having to go to court feeling so very tired. But he apologised because it would be half an hour before he could arrange it because of all the paper work that needed to be completed. I told him not to worry, to take his time and do whatever he needed to do. In about half an hour I was called to the duty desk. He was such a pleasant young man. He was at pains to point out that we were being released because of him. He had told the Procurator Fiscal that that was what he was going to do. Breaching the by-laws was only a minor offence and we were not to appear in court that morning. If we were arrested again though we would be straight into court. We would be receiving a letter from the PF at some future time.

It was so good to see our friends and supporters again and to drop exhausted into bed. It was 7am.

CHAPTER 4

International Security, Law and Abolition of Nuclear Weapons

REBECCA JOHNSON

ON 21 FEBRUARY 2007, just three weeks before the UK parliament's vote on Trident, Tony Blair responded to a question from a Labour MP, Chris Mullin, by saying that 'the non-proliferation treaty... makes it absolutely clear that Britain has the right to possess nuclear weapons'. Mullin had referred to comments from the Director General of the International Atomic Energy Agency (IAEA), Dr Mohamed ElBaradei, that 'Britain could not modernise its Trident missile system and then credibly tell countries such as Iran that they do not need nuclear weapons?'[1]

Whether through ignorance or intention to deceive MPs, Blair's combative despatch-box reply misrepresented the 1968 Non-Proliferation Treaty (NPT). With 189 states parties, the NPT provides the baseline for the non-proliferation and disarmament regime. Far from conferring any right to possess nuclear weapons, the Treaty actually requires Britain and the other nuclear weapon possessors to eliminate their nuclear arsenals. Blair's dishonesty about Britain's obligations was symptomatic of the government's whole approach to deploying and renewing Trident, seen also in the fraudulent use of information in the run-up to the war on Iraq and in the so-called 'war on terror'. If the government had shown more respect for international law and had chosen

---

[1] Question from Chris Mullin MP, Prime Minister's Questions, 21 February 2007, Hansard. The verbatim exchange was as follows: '**Chris Mullin (Lab)**: What is my right hon. friend's response to Mohamed ElBaradei of the International Atomic Energy Agency, who said recently that Britain could not modernise its Trident missile system and then credibly tell countries such as Iran that they do not need nuclear weapons?

The Prime Minister: I should remind my hon. friend of the Non-Proliferation Treaty, which makes it absolutely clear that Britain has the right to possess nuclear weapons. As Mohamed ElBaradei is the custodian of that treaty's implementation, I think it would be a good idea for him to act accordingly.'

to implement its own obligations under the NPT rather than carry on nuclear business as usual, Faslane 365 would not have been necessary.

Though Faslane 365's strategy was to make Trident undeployable in Scotland, we appealed also to international groups, campaigners and law-makers to come to Faslane and help us uphold the law. Clearly, whether nuclear weapons are replaced, modernised or eliminated affects not only Britain's national security and place in the world. There are also far-reaching repercussions for international law and security, including strengthening the implementation of treaties and global efforts to prevent proliferation and war.

These links were made visible on the blockades by activists and banners from as far away as Japan, Australia and the United States, and from nearer neighbours in Europe and Scandinavia. European and Dutch parliamentarians were arrested together with Members of the Scottish parliament. An American teacher and advisor to the United Nations on disarmament education celebrated her 40th birthday at Faslane with a transatlantic group of friends. A former UN Assistant Secretary-General and professor of international development was arrested with his wife – an internationally renowned professor of human evolution – and their two daughters in a blockade that included professors and students from Sweden, Germany, the United States and Japan as well as Scotland, England and Wales. Eminent diplomats and Nobel prize winners signed statements of support. On another occasion a Nobel peace laureate was arrested after locking arms and blocking the base for over an hour with her group from Ireland.

One story – out of many – serves to illustrate the connections. On 25 July a group of elderly Japanese women and the son of a Nagasaki atomic bomb survivor (Hibakusha) laid paper peace cranes in front of the North Gate and sat down, singing in gentle voices, 'Furusato no machi yakare' (the time our town was burnt up). We sang for them, 'Five minutes to midnight', an update of a Greenham song.[2] Some more Japanese Hibakusha linked arms

---

[2] On January 17, 2007, Professor Stephen Hawking moved the hands of the Doomsday Clock two minutes closer to midnight, signalling deepening concern about the prospects for international security and survival, particularly in relation to nuclear weapons and climate change. The Doomsday Clock was initiated in 1947 by the *Bulletin of the Atomic Scientists*, which used the metaphor of midnight to represent nuclear catastrophe. Since then, the *Bulletin* has charted nuclear developments and security trends and provided warnings and information to raise awareness so that humanity can take the necessary steps to avoid destroying ourselves.

through bamboo tubes with younger activists. One held a banner calling on the UK government to take the lead in moving the world towards the abolition of nuclear weapons. Five of the Japanese protesters and a Swedish-Finnish member of the steering group were arrested and held overnight in Clydebank police cells. After being charged with 'breach of the peace' under a law dating back 600 years, one, Masahiko Moriguchi said, 'How can they call our peaceful sitting down 'disturbing the peace'? Don't they realise how terrible these nuclear weapons are? With them, there is no peace.' Mr Moriguchi was seven years old when his home in Nagasaki was incinerated on 9 August 1945. His parents and sisters died of radiation sickness and cancer in the early years following the nuclear destruction of their home. His brother and his son travelled with him to Faslane to join in the protests.

It was important for Faslane 365 to be internationalist because nuclear weapons are a global danger and we must all take responsibility for building international security and law and holding governments accountable. Of course, the nuclear problem also has specific regional complexities, not only for Scotland but in areas of potential conflict like the Middle East, South Asia and North-East Asia. In Europe, NATO continues to deploy hundreds of US nuclear weapons as relics of the cold war, and Britain, France and Russia continue to parade their possession of nuclear weapons as if it was an emblem of leadership granting them status above their neighbours.

In a world where real security threats are global, like climate change, or transboundary, such as terrorism and trafficking in arms, drugs and people, the Trident decision has shown that the UK government is stuck in a time warp, still evoking the out-dated demands of 'national security' and 'nuclear deterrence'. International *human* security is neither dependent on nor upheld by nuclear weapons. On the contrary, 182 countries joined the NPT as non-nuclear weapon states because their leaders recognised that nuclear weapons were a security problem, not an asset. If detonated by accident or intention, the effects of nuclear weapons would be serious and far reaching. Where not destroyed, cities and large areas of the world would need to be practically quarantined. Agriculture, transportation, trade and commerce would be hard hit, causing widespread economic misery and hunger. Even if nuclear bombs are never used in war, they carry heavy costs. The raw materials and technologies pose dangers of radiation release, leakage, pollution and accidents. Mining uranium, and developing, testing, manufacturing, maintaining and guarding nuclear weapons create unnecessary hazards and absorb not just money but human energies and talents, with lives put at risk at every level.

Shared understanding of the catastrophic consequences of nuclear weapon use underpin the moral and legal obligations to pursue and accomplish nuclear disarmament. They are recognised not only in the NPT, but the United Nations, the International Court of Justice and a panoply of other humanitarian laws and agreements.

Whatever his reasons, it is a serious matter for the UK Prime Minister to lie to the House of Commons about Britain's legal obligations, especially as he also gratuitously insulted the head of the UN's nuclear watchdog. Though the Foreign Office moved swiftly to explain that the government's White Paper does not say that Britain has a right to nuclear weapons under the NPT, the incident begs some serious questions. Did Blair genuinely believe that the NPT gave Britain and certain others the right to have nuclear weapons, and did his decision on renewing Trident rest on this mistaken belief? His confidence in repudiating the concerns raised by Dr ElBaradei probably persuaded other MPs to ignore expert legal advice that renewing Trident would breach the Treaty and undermine the nonproliferation regime. Would the decision have been different if MPs had been truthfully informed about Britain's commitments under international law?

Why Blair Was Wrong

It is not surprising that Blair reacted defensively to Dr ElBaradei's criticism of Trident renewal. The Prime Minister was bent on getting as many Labour MPs as possible to suspend their judgement and consciences and vote in favour of procuring the next generation of Trident in a few weeks time, so needed to bat away any suggestion that Britain would be acting contrary to its international treaty commitments. The government had also claimed that the Foreign Office had explained the decision to replace Trident and that Britain's allies and treaty partners 'understood', implying that there was no problem. Blair was no doubt rattled to receive such open criticism of Trident renewal from the head of the IAEA, responsible for safeguards under the NPT. As discussed below, more criticism was voiced at the NPT's Preparatory Committee meeting (PrepCom) held in Vienna in May 2007.

It is important to get the facts right. Nowhere does the NPT state or even imply that Britain – or any of the five defined nuclear weapon states – has a right to possess nuclear weapons. On the contrary, Britain is required by Article VI of the NPT 'to pursue negotiations in good faith on effective measures relating to cessation of the nuclear arms race at an early date and to nuclear disarmament, and on a treaty on general and complete disarmament under strict and effective international control.'

The term 'nuclear weapon state' was defined in the text because it was necessary to recognise the status quo in order for the NPT to govern differential obligations: non-nuclear weapon states were required not to seek to acquire nuclear weapons, and the nuclear weapon states were required not to supply or trade in nuclear weapon technologies or components and to pursue nuclear disarmament. As defined, a nuclear weapon state was one that had manufactured and exploded a nuclear device prior to 1 January 1967 – with no reference to any kind of right to possess the weapons in perpetuity. The only time the concept of 'right' is employed in the Treaty is in Article IV, which reflects the 'atoms for peace' dreams of the 1950s and '60s in referring to the 'inalienable right of all the Parties to the Treaty to develop research, production and use of nuclear energy for peaceful purposes...' Yet Blair has been one of the first to complain when Iran or other developing countries quote Article IV to justify their uranium enrichment or nuclear energy programmes. This Article IV 'right' constitutes the NPT's deepest flaw. Nuclear energy never fulfilled its proponents' early hopes: it is not cheap, safe or clean. On the contrary, it is dangerous for the environment and provides the technologies and materials for nuclear weapons.

To understand why the NPT defined some states as nuclear weapon states it is necessary to look back at its genesis in the 1960s, at the height of the cold war arms race when nuclear technology was being embraced as a wondrous resource and cure-all for everything from energy generation to medicine and agriculture. At the same time, the Cuban Missile crisis and other near-fatal miscalculations between the two superpowers had brought nuclear armageddon terrifyingly close and exposed the profound dangers for the world if a nuclear free-for-all resulted in many more nuclear-armed nations, thereby multiplying the risks of nuclear accident, miscalculation and use. Though Ireland had initiated the idea for a nonproliferation treaty, the superpowers took it over and remodelled the text to suit their own interests, hoping to halt the horizontal spread of nuclear weapons while keeping their own. This was not acceptable to non-nuclear countries, which insisted on introducing disarmament by the nuclear powers into the nonproliferation equation. They queried the dominant powers' position that the problem was not the weapons, but their spread, with its concomitant assumption that nuclear weapons were essential for some countries' security and deterrence, but too dangerous or unsuitable for others to develop.

While agreeing that unbridled proliferation would be bad for international security and could increase the risks of nuclear accident or war, the non-nuclear weapon states pointed out that for them to renounce weapons of such awesome power for the foreseeable future only made sense in terms of national security if the foreseeable goal was the complete elimination of those weapons from the face of the Earth.

In a world of sovereign nation states, it would not be possible to sustain over time a regime built on differential rights regarding the strategic-military equipment states could have. Though people can see weapons as profoundly immoral, in 'realpolitik', governments could not be expected to forego forever a weapon system that others – rivals or allies – kept for themselves in perpetuity. So the non-nuclear states insisted on a disarmament obligation, and the nuclear superpowers ensured that the language was as weak and woolly as they could get away with. The non-nuclear countries also insisted that the NPT should initially be of only 25 years duration, with a provision for collectively deciding whether and how it should continue after that.

The cold war had ended by the time the NPT came up for renewal, in 1995. Strategic and political relations and expectations were undergoing profound change worldwide. As the concept of human rights was developed to incorporate principles of non-discrimination and universality, weapons – including nuclear weapons – were perceived either as the right of no one or the right of everyone. Because of the poor record of the NPT in curbing vertical proliferation (thousands were added to the major stockpiles at the height of the nuclear arms race), and with serious concerns by states in the Middle East that the nuclear programme of Israel, a non-party, was untouchable while NPT parties in the region were constrained and inspected, the extension of the NPT was not achieved easily. The decision to indefinitely extend the Treaty was not a stand-alone agreement, but bound together with negotiated decisions containing Principles and Objectives for Nuclear Non-Proliferation and Disarmament and on Strengthening the Treaty. Immediately after this package was agreed by consensus, NPT parties also adopted a Resolution on the Middle East which called, among other things, for a zone free of WMD in the region.

The Post-1995 NPT has Stronger Disarmament Obligations than the 1968 NPT

Without these three decisions and the resolution, it is unlikely that the NPT would have been extended indefinitely. Certainly, it could not have been extended by consensus, which was important for maintaining collective 'ownership' of the non-proliferation regime, regarded as essential for its sustainability and credibility into the future. The consequence of this, as international lawyers have attested, is that the NPT now in force is the Treaty as extended in May 1995.

Though the Treaty was not formally amended, the way in which the extension decision was adopted only after the two decisions on Principles and Objectives and on strengthening the review process had been adopted without a vote, means that they are an integral part of the legal obligation and meaning of the NPT.[3] In other words, the post-1995 NPT, which is now in operation, is not the same as the original NPT that entered into force in 1970. With regard to disarmament in particular, the obligations are stronger and more specific. Harking back to the Article VI language of 1968 and arguing that it contains no deadlines misses this crucial point – by itself, that 1968 treaty would not have survived to 2007.

In the summer of 1996, the International Court of Justice (ICJ), responding to requests from the UN General Assembly and World Health Organization, delivered an important Advisory Opinion on the use and threat of use of nuclear weapons. This spelled out the Court's unanimous assessment that 'There exists an obligation to pursue in good faith and bring to a conclusion negotiations leading to nuclear disarmament in all its aspects under strict and effective international control.'[4]

The Court also established that the use of nuclear weapons would 'generally be contrary to the rules of international law applicable in armed conflict and in particular the principles and rules of humanitarian law', though they could not definitively agree whether 'the use of nuclear weapons would be lawful or unlawful in an extreme circumstance of self-defence in which the very survival of a state would be at stake'.[5]

---

3 The Resolution on the Middle East has different, more contingent status, as it was a resolution rather than a decision, and adopted after the Treaty had been extended.

4 Decision F, International Court of Justice Reports 1996, p 225. [Reported for 8 July 1996, General List No. 95]. The full decision, documentation and dissenting decisions also formed the Annex to 'Advisory Opinion of the International Court of Justice on the legality of the threat or use of nuclear weapons', Note by the Secretary-General, United Nations General Assembly A/51/218, October 15, 1996 pp 36–37.

5 Decision E, International Court of Justice Reports 1996, op. cit.

The ICJ drew from Article VI of the NPT, but gave it additional legal force and urgency, first by emphasising that the obligation is not only to negotiate in good faith, but to bring the negotiations to conclusion, and secondly, by not making nuclear disarmament contingent on general and complete disarmament, a linkage that some nuclear weapon states have relied on to justify keeping their nuclear arsenals. A month later, in August 1996, the Canberra Commission on the Elimination of Nuclear Weapons published its report, which recommended several disarmament steps and demolished the idea that the doctrine of nuclear deterrence could be made relevant in the post cold-war-security environment.

The first Review Conference of the NPT following the 1995 extension took place in May 2000, in the shadow of conflictual relations among key states.[6] However, it counfounded expectations of failure when representatives of 187 countries gave consensus to a very substantial final document containing agreements that covered a range of measures, from deploring the 1998 nuclear tests by India and Pakistan to diplomatic language on Iraqi non-compliance. It reaffirmed the goals of the Resolution on the Middle East, emphasised the importance of the strengthened IAEA safeguards, and mentioned for the first time environmental and safety concerns around issues such as the transshipment of radioactive materials and the nuclear fuel cycle. Most importantly, the states parties endorsed an 'unequivocal undertaking by the nuclear weapon states to accomplish the total elimination of their nuclear arsenals', as part of a 13-step plan of action for the implementation of Article VI.[7]

Other steps included: entry into force of the Comprehensive Test Ban Treaty (CTBT); conclusion of a fissile materials production treaty (fissban); moratoria both on testing and on production of plutonium and highly-enriched uranium (HEU), pending entry into force of those treaties; deeper unilateral and bilateral US-Russian reductions in nuclear forces; transparency (i.e. the provision of more open information on nuclear capabilities and the implementation of disarmament agreements); reductions in non-strategic

---

6   For a detailed examination of the political context and choices before the Sixth Review Conference, see Rebecca Johnson, *Non-Proliferation Treaty: Challenging Times*, ACRONYM 13, The Acronym Institute, London, February 2000.

7   2000 Review Conference of the Parties to the Treaty on the Non-Proliferation of Nuclear Weapons, Final Document, adopted May 20, 2000, New York, NPT/CONF.2000/28 (Part I).

(tactical) nuclear weapons; concrete measures to reduce the operational status of nuclear weapons (diplomatic euphemism for taking the weapons off alert); diminishing the role of nuclear weapons in security policies (understood to mean abandoning the potential first-use of nuclear weapons that underpins NATO and Russian nuclear doctrine and deterrence); the principle of irreversibility to be applied to nuclear arms control; five power disarmament approaches; and further initiatives to put fissile materials (declared 'excess') permanently under safeguards.

Britain's International Legal Obligations to Disarm

On three occasions during 2004–6, eminent British and international lawyers[8] gave authoritative Advice that the consensus decisions and agreements adopted by NPT states parties in 1995 and 2000 have become part of the legal meaning and interpretation of the Treaty. They argued that Article VI contained legal obligations, consistent with Articles I, II and III, and that strict observance with the letter and the spirit of the NPT is required of all its parties including the nuclear weapon states. This, they said, applies to the disarmament obligation no less than the non-transference and non-acquisition obligations.[9]

---

[8] Rabinder Singh QC and Professor Christine Chinkin (Matrix Chambers and London School of Economics) and Philippe Sands QC were consulted by different clients and gave different but consistent Advice regarding the NPT and the British government's proposed renewal of its nuclear cooperation pact with the United States (the Mutual Defence Agreement, originally signed in 1958 and renewed several times thereafter) and procurement of a further nuclear weapon system as a follow-on to Trident. See www.acronym.org.uk

[9] Under Article I, the defined nuclear weapon states have a set of obligations '*not to transfer to any recipient whatsoever nuclear weapons or other nuclear explosive devices or control over such weapons or explosive devices directly, or indirectly; and not in any way to assist, encourage, or induce any non-nuclear-weapon State to manufacture or otherwise acquire nuclear weapons or other nuclear explosive devices, or control over such weapons or explosive devices.*' This paralleled the Article II obligation on states joining the Treaty as non-nuclear weapon states '*not to receive the transfer from any transferor whatsoever of nuclear weapons or other nuclear explosive devices or of control over such weapons or explosive devices directly, or indirectly; not to manufacture or otherwise acquire nuclear weapons or other nuclear explosive devices; and not to seek or receive any assistance in the manufacture of nuclear weapons or other nuclear explosive devices.*'

Rabinder Singh QC and Professor Christine Chinkin (Matrix Chambers and London School of Economics) asserted in the first Advice (2004) that 'The importance of Article VI to the objects and purposes of the NPT is shown both by the negotiation history of the NPT and by the reaffirmation of its significance by the 2000 Review Conference. The Review Conference also emphasised that strict observance of the NPT is required, that is observance with both the letter and spirit of its articles.' [para 36] In relation to the specific principles and steps negotiated by states parties and agreed in 1995 and 2000, 'A Declaration of a Review Conference such as that adopted by consensus [in 1995 or 2000] would fall within the wording of article 31 (3) (a) [of the Vienna Convention on the Law of Treaties (VCLT)] and is thus an appropriate source of interpretation of the obligations of the NPT.' [para 20][10]

Following on from this interpretation in a further Advice in 2005, Singh and Chinkin concluded that:

- The use of the Trident system would breach customary international law, in particular because it would infringe the 'intransgressible' requirement that a distinction must be drawn between combatants and non-combatants.

- Article VI is a provision 'essential to the accomplishment of the object or purpose of the treaty'.

- The replacement of Trident is likely to constitute a breach of Article VI of NPT; and

- Such a breach would be a material breach of that treaty.[11]

In particular, they underscored, 'Enhancing nuclear weapons systems... is, in our view, not conducive to entering into negotiations for disarmament as required by the NPT, article VI and evinces no intention to 'bring to a conclusion negotiations leading to nuclear disarmament in all its aspects'. It is

---

[10] Rabinder Singh QC and Prof. Christine Chinkin (LSE), *Mutual Defence Agreement And The Nuclear Non-Proliferation Treaty*, Matrix Chambers, London, 20 July 2004. Discussion and full text of the legal advice can be found at www.acronym. org.uk/dd78.

[11] Rabinder Singh QC and Professor Christine Chinkin, *The Maintenance and Possible Replacement of the Trident Nuclear Missile System*, Joint Opinion, Matrix Chambers, published by Peacerights, 19 December 2005.

difficult to see how unilateral (or bilateral) action that pre-empts any possibility of an outcome of disarmament can be defined as pursuing negotiations in good faith and to bring them to a conclusion and is, in our view, thereby in violation of the NPT, Article VI obligation.'[12]

Although there is no treaty that explicitly and universally prohibits the use and acquisition of nuclear weapons, there are other laws that apply, including the UN Charter and the law of armed conflict. The fundamental rules of humanitarian law constitute 'intransgressible principles of international customary law'.[13] According to international humanitarian law, states that use force must do so with discrimination i.e. not make civilians the object of attack. Nor should states cause unnecessary suffering. Even with regard to *combatants,* states are prohibited from causing harm greater than that which is 'absolutely unavoidable to achieve legitimate military objectives'.

Though the United States and Britain say they recognise the applicability of the rules of proportionality, discrimination, moderation, and civilian immunity, their nuclear policies violate these rules.[14] The doctrine of nuclear deterrence as practised by the United Kingdom, for example, relies on continuous at sea patrols by at least one submarine armed with up to 48 nuclear weapons. The reason given for this is that potential adversaries should take into account that the UK is ready and able to use nuclear weapons at any time. Hence the deployment of Trident constitutes both an ever-present threat and, some would argue, a 'use' of nuclear weapons similar to the use a robber makes of a gun when brandishing it in a bank, even if the gun is never actually fired. Moreover, having concluded that the use of nuclear weapons would generally breach international and humanitarian

---

[12] Ibid.

[13] ICJ Report, op. cit., para 79.

[14] Charles J. Moxley, Jr, *Nuclear Weapons and International Law in the Post Cold War World,* Austin & Winfield, 2000. Moxley specifically raised concerns that the continued pursuit of nuclear deterrence policies introduces 'significant risk factors with implications both for security and for compliance with the principles and obligations in the international, US and British legal systems: the danger of precipitating a nuclear war; the fostering of an arms race; the fostering of nuclear proliferation; the risks of terrorism; the risks of human and equipment failure; risks of testing, production, storage and disposal of nuclear weapons materials; the risk of the degradation of conventional weapons capability; jeopardy to rule of law; and overriding risk factors as to the likelihood that the unlikely will occur'.

law, the ICJ also confirmed that 'it is unlawful to threaten to do that which it is unlawful to do.[15]

It is on this basis that nonviolent activists disrupting the Faslane base to prevent the deployment of Trident argue that our actions are undertaken to uphold international law.

Trident Renewal Condemned Internationally

The international context in which Tony Blair sought to modernise and renew Britain's nuclear weapons is utterly different from that of the cold war, when Mrs Thatcher over-ruled her navy chiefs to saddle Britain with Trident first time round.[16] The priority security imperative is to find collective ways to mitigate and survive the effects of global warming and climate change. Within that context, most countries also put emphasis on the importance of reducing nuclear dangers and preventing WMD capabilities from falling into the hands of anyone who might use them (labelled 'terrorists'). The failure of the 2005 NPT Review Conference was deeply troubling, and it was widely recognised that a primary reason for this failure was the repudiation by some of the nuclear powers – most notably the United States – of disarmament commitments agreed by the 2000 Review Conference.[17]

In January 2007, as nations prepared to meet in Vienna for the Preparatory Committee meeting (PrepCom) for the next NPT Review Conference, scheduled for 2010, a group of eminent US diplomats including former Secretaries of State and Defense Henry Kissinger, George Shultz and William Perry and

---

[15] Moxley, op. cit.

[16] The First Sea Lord, Sir Henry Leach, dismissed Trident in 1979 as 'a cuckoo in the [naval] nest'. See Eric J. Grove, *Vanguard to Trident: British Naval Policy since World War Two*, Bodley Head, London, 1987, pp 347–354.

[17] Rebecca Johnson, 'Politics and Protection: Why the 2005 NPT Review Conference Failed', *Disarmament Diplomacy 80* (Autumn 2005), pp 3–32; and Sergio Duarte, 'A President's Assessment of the 2005 NPT Review Conference', *Disarmament Diplomacy 81* (Winter 2005), pp 3–5. For further information on the 2000 NPT Review Conference, see Rebecca Johnson, 'The 2000 NPT Review Conference: A Delicate, Hard-Won Compromise', *Disarmament Diplomacy 46* (May 2000), pp 2–21; and Rebecca Johnson, 'Towards Nuclear Disarmament' in W. Huntley, K. Mizumoto and M. Kurosawa (eds.), *Nuclear Disarmament in the Twenty-First Century*, Hiroshima Peace Institute, 2004.

the former Chair of the Senate Foreign Relations Committee, Sam Nunn (co-architect of the Nunn-Lugar Cooperative Threat Reduction initiative) published an influential editorial in the *Wall Street Journal*. This bipartisan group called for a 'solid consensus' to reverse reliance on nuclear weapons globally. They argued for the United States and other nuclear weapon possessors to wake up and realise that 'the world is now on the precipice of a new and dangerous nuclear era', which will be 'more precarious, psychologically disorienting, and economically even more costly than was cold war deterrence'. Quoting Ronald Reagan, that nuclear weapons should be abolished because they are 'totally irrational, totally inhumane, good for nothing but killing, possibly destructive of life on Earth and civilization', the writers called for nuclear weapons to be devalued and the NPT's goal of a world free of nuclear weapons to be pursued in earnest, starting with a series of practical unilateral, plurilateral and multilateral steps.[18]

No one could possibly accuse Kissinger and Shultz et al of being 'soft on defence', the label that certain politicians seem to fear most. Even if they once thought nuclear weapons useful, they now recognise them to be a major security problem, more likely to provoke proliferation and use by others than to deter. Indeed, they addressed the UK justification for renewing Trident head on, noting: 'Deterrence continues to be a relevant consideration for many states with regard to threats from other states. But reliance on nuclear weapons for this purpose is becoming increasingly hazardous and decreasingly effective.'[19]

Britain has long presented itself as upholding and strengthening the NPT. From the 1998 Strategic Defence Review to Margaret Beckett's speech before leaving office in June 2007, the Labour government has emphasised its 'commitment to a world free of nuclear weapons'.[20] But while in statements and conferences – at home and abroad – British representatives portray the UK as taking the lead internationally in non-proliferation and nuclear disarmament

---

[18] George P. Shultz, William J. Perry, Henry A. Kissinger, Sam Nunn and others, 'A World Free of Nuclear Weapons', *Wall Street Journal*, New York, January 4, 2007.

[19] The writers may have been too tactful to refer explicitly to the UK debate over Trident, but the timing and tenor of the op-ed were intended to give pause for thought at a critical juncture in Britain's decision-making.

[20] Margaret Beckett, Secretary of State for Foreign and Commonwealth Affairs, *Speech to the Carnegie Endowment of International Peace Non-Proliferation Conference*, Washington DC, June 25, 2007.

actions, other countries see Britain embedding its nuclear weapon possession and preparing to procure the next generation of nuclear weapons, thereby obstructing and impeding efforts to get meaningful progress towards devaluing and genuinely eliminating nuclear arsenals.

Although many governments toned down or generalised their public criticisms, the UK's plans to build a new generation of Trident was deplored by many countries. At the 2007 Preparatory Committee meeting for the NPT, for example, Ireland, speaking on behalf of the New Agenda Coalition of non-nuclear states, objected that the 'replacement or modernization of nuclear weapons' ran 'counter to the agreement reached at the 2000 Review Conference ... to eliminate these weapons'. A statement on behalf of over 110 non-aligned states parties, was clear where the primary responsibilities lay: 'The nuclear weapon states and those states remaining outside the NPT continue to develop and modernise their nuclear arsenals, threatening international peace and security. We must all call for an end to this madness and seek the elimination and ban on all forms of nuclear weapons and testing as well as the rejection of the doctrine of deterrence.'[21] South Africa was even more explicit in its condemnation, saying: 'We were disappointed to learn about the decision of the UK on the Trident to maintain its nuclear deterrent. This could have been a landmark decision for others to follow, which could have provided the necessary impetus to a disarmament process that desperately needs to be reinvigorated.'[22]

The UK's response to these criticisms was to declare that the vote in March was only 'to begin the concept and design work required to make possible a replacement for our current submarine fleet' together with a decision 'to participate in a programme to extend the life of the Trident D5 missile system'. This, said Ambassador John Duncan, 'does not mean that we have taken an irreversible decision that commits us irrevocably to possessing nuclear weapons in 40 or 50 years' time.' He then stated, 'Any suggestion that the UK is further developing its nuclear weapons is a misunderstanding. The UK is

---

[21] Norma Goicochea Estenoz, Ambassador of Cuba on behalf of the Group of Non-Aligned States Parties to the NPT, statement in General Debate, First Preparatory Meeting of States Parties to the NPT, Vienna, 30 April 2007.

[22] Abdul Samad Minty, Special Representative for Disarmament for South Africa, General Debate and Cluster 1 Statements, First Preparatory Meeting of States Parties to the NPT, Vienna, 30 April 2007.

retaining *not* modernising its deterrent. There is *no* change in the capabilities of the system, *no* move to produce more useable weapons and *no* change in nuclear posture or doctrine. The UK's nuclear weapon system will *not* be designed for war-fighting use in military campaigns. It is a strategic deterrent that we would only ever contemplate using in extreme circumstances or self defence.'[23]

Such assertions were belied by the evidence and by documents from civil society. Nongovernmental publications about Trident renewal, including an open letter from the heads of Scotland's Catholic and Protestant Churches, Cardinal Keith Patrick O'Brien and the Right Reverend Alan D. McDonald, were distributed to all delegations, reminding them of Scottish opposition to Trident and civil society protests against Trident deployment at Faslane. The Scottish Church leaders' letter stated, 'We consider these weapons of mass destruction to be immoral, inhumane, and contrary to the teachings of all the world's major faiths. Nuclear dangers and human insecurity will increase if nuclear weapons continue to be treated by some countries as a currency of power or as if they were an indispensable part of defence for the foreseeable future.' The letter quoted from the 2006 General Assembly of the Church of Scotland that: 'To replace Trident would represent a further announcement to the world that safety and security can only be achieved by threatening mass destruction; this is to encourage others to believe the same, and thus to hasten proliferation.' Urging the British government 'to take this historic opportunity to devalue these 'weapons of terror' and renounce its plans to renew Trident', the letter emphasised that: 'Such a step would strengthen the NPT and underline that its core obligation is not just to reduce nuclear arsenals, but to eliminate them. We believe that, instead of perpetuating nuclear proliferation, Britain could show real leadership and humanity.'

Despite the UK diplomats' efforts to portray Britain's procurement of the next generation of Trident as a done deal (and as merely a step to replace the submarine platforms), civil society promoted considerable discussion about the UK debate and developments at Faslane and Aldermaston. NPT delegations showed particular interest in how the Scottish elections of 3 May might affect UK nuclear policy. Many were also outraged when informed in a press

---

[23] 'UK working paper on disarmament', NPT/CONF.2010/PC.I/WP.59. Emphasis in the original.

release that nuclear warheads had been transported across Edinburgh on the penultimate day of the NPT meeting.[24]

The working paper produced by the Chair of the 2007 PrepCom, Ambassador Yukiya Amano, put on the record: 'Concern and disappointment were voiced about plans to replace or modernise nuclear weapons and their means of delivery or platform, the increased role of nuclear weapons in strategic and military doctrines, and the possibility of lowering the threshold for the use of nuclear weapons.' In case anyone was in any doubt about which plans were causing such concern and disappointment, paragraph 12 explicitly noted that 'In response to those concerns addressed to the United States and the United Kingdom, they provided their clarifications and explanations on their efforts towards nuclear disarmament...'[25]

To Strengthen Security and the NPT, Nuclear Weapons Should Be Explicitly Outlawed

Although it is increasingly acknowledged that the use – and therefore threat and deployment – of nuclear weapons cannot be carried out without violating international and humanitarian law, nuclear weapons are not comprehensively banned by treaty as biological and chemical weapons are. In June 2006, the Report of the international WMD Commission was published. Chaired by Dr Hans Blix and comprising 14 high level representatives from key states, the Commission characterised all WMD as 'weapons of terror' and employed the concepts of 'outlawing' nuclear weapons and 'freeing the world of nuclear, biological and chemical arms'. It stated: 'Weapons of mass destruction cannot be uninvented. But they can be outlawed, as biological and chemical weapons have been, and their use made unthinkable. Compliance, verification and enforcement rules can, with the requisite will, be effectively applied. And with that will, even the eventual elimination of nuclear weapons is not beyond the world's reach.'[26]

This approach recognises that what prevents the nuclear genie from being put back into its bottle is not the existence of nuclear knowledge, but

---

[24] Whether intentionally or merely tactlessly, the warheads were taken on the Edinburgh by-pass just one day after the new Scottish parliament – committed to getting rid of Trident – had been sworn in at the Holyrood parliament.

[25] 'Chairman's Working Paper', NPT/CONF2010/PC.I/WP.78

[26] *Weapons of Terror: Freeing the world of nuclear, biological and chemical arms*, Report of the WMD Commission, Stockholm, June 2006, p 17.

the high value still accorded to nuclear weapons, particularly by states that have them. While it is true that the basic knowledge cannot be 'unlearned', the plutonium and highly-enriched uranium that make the nuclear explosions are not found in nature and so can be controlled, removed and kept out of circulation. Containing sophisticated nuclear technologies would present fewer hurdles than for chemical and biological weapons, both of which have been prohibited, despite the ubiquity and commercial applications of many of their raw materials. Proliferation and 'breakout' would be much less likely under conditions of nuclear abolition than they are in today's contested world of 'haves' and 'have-nots'. Recognising that the practical steps of verified disablement, dismantlement and irreversible denuclearisation and disarmament will take time and resources, the WMD Commission emphasised outlawing nuclear weapons as a first step because this can be brought about through political and legislative action, such as a UN Security Council resolution, following the precedent set by UNSCR 1540. Or it could be accomplished as part of a process of multilateral negotiations, as with the treaties that prohibited biological and chemical weapons and nuclear testing.

National and International Security Imperatives

Real world security requires humanity to prevent war and pay attention to our use of resources and impact on the environment. Even within the narrower agenda of governments that emphasise preventing nuclear terrorism, blackmail, threats, accidental and environmental dangers and nuclear weapons use, practical approaches dictate not the current world of nuclear haves and have-nots, but a non-discriminatory regime that prohibits and abolishes nuclear weapons for everyone. It is the outdated ideologies of nuclear weapon states like Britain that get in the way of the most effective approaches for reducing nuclear dangers and stemming proliferation. Current UK defence policies divert attention and resources away from dealing collectively with the real threats that face humanity and our planet.

There is an inherent contradiction when non-proliferation and prevention of nuclear terrorism are divorced from disarmament: one has to divide the world into good and bad, responsible and irresponsible, safe and dangerous, ally and rogue. These categories do not exist so neatly in the real world and are quixotically dependent on the politics and perspectives of different governments and actors at different times. Such naïve divisions are not a strong or effective basis for sustainable security or for dealing effectively with nuclear threats.

A non-proliferation policy without disarmament may be enforced in the short term by major powers using political and military coercion. History shows that though such approaches may work in the short term, they are counterproductive over the long term. They suffer from the contradiction that when the nuclear states seek to modernise or enhance capabilities they are actually emphasising the military utility, status or security value they themselves attach to nuclear weapons. This defeats non-proliferation efforts by making the weapons appear desirable, especially for weak leaders and terrorists seeking status, deterrence or power projection.

Far from disarmers being unrealistic, it is the nuclear addicts who fail to understand the real, complex, multinational world that is concerned about state and non-state acquisition of nuclear weapons and fears and threats of potential use. Following the landmark 1996 ICJ Advisory Opinion, a growing number of states and civil society organisations – from doctors and lawyers to scientists and mayors – have been advocating a nuclear weapons convention. Though specific campaigns or networks have tended to rise and fade in cycles, the demand for a nuclear weapon convention has grown ever stronger. Most recently, the International Campaign to Abolish Nuclear Weapons (ICAN) was launched at the NPT PrepCom in Vienna, with publication of *Securing our Survival: The Case for a Nuclear Weapons Convention*.[27] This book outlines the steps to achieve a nuclear weapon convention that would codify the NPT's disarmament obligations in a clearer, unequivocally legally-binding prohibition of the possession, development, transfer and use of nuclear weapons, with specific steps and a timetable for eliminating existing arsenals and building confidence and greater security through legislative and verification mechanisms. This may not be the way it happens in the end, but it is important to understand that throughout the world the pressure to abolish nuclear weapons completely is picking up pace. Britain's decision to renew Trident sits like a confused dinosaur, impeding progress and lacking all sense and intelligence about future security and survival.

---

[27] *Securing our Survival: The Case for a Nuclear Weapons Convention*, May 2007. http://www.icanw.org/securing-our-survival

Globalised Resistance

PETTER JOELSON and ANNA SANNE GÖRANSSON

Petter

In December 2001, I had left the sinking ship of the Swedish Ploughshare movement, got out of touch with peace activism, and didn't think very much about my Trident Ploughshares pledge from 1998 to disarm the Trident system. That was when I found out that Ulla Röder, Angie Zelter and Ellen Moxley would come to Stockholm, my home town at the time, to receive the Right Livelihood Award for Trident Ploughshares. So, I and a couple of friends organised a public meeting at the Cultural House in Stockholm with the three, and did our best to put the word around about it. I and my friend Anna also asked the women how we would go about organising peace actions in Sweden. Angie's answer was clear – come to the blockades at Faslane and learn how to do it! So that's what we did, and from nothing we got 30 people to go there and blockade Faslane the following February. And after that, we have kept coming back.

The network Ofog (mischief) that came out of that blockade in 2002 has since then been doing regular actions at Faslane, joined the Bomspotting actions against NATO nukes in Belgium a few times and inspected Star Wars bases in England and Norway. We have gone against the trend of the rest of the Swedish peace movements declining membership and dependency on state funding. With no money but lots of passion, we have time after time managed to get people to travel across Europe to visit various military bases and police cells.

But it takes time and effort to keep a group alive, and two years ago there was a time when we never had more than three people at our meetings and didn't really know what to do next. That's when we heard about the new crazy idea from our friends in the UK: a year long blockade at Faslane! This was exactly the kind of push Ofog needed to get back on its feet. We worked on it for almost a year, and managed to repeat our success from 2002 and get 30 people to cross the sea to Scotland.

Our problem since 2002 had been that we never really got our act together to do civil disobedience in Sweden. Maybe we were taken care of too well in Scotland, maybe the organising there was too good and we were afraid not to be able to do the same thing ourselves? I don't want to blame people for being perfect, but the Faslane 365 experience when we actually had to do it ourselves, with a security net from out Scottish hosts, really changed things for us. Our really effective two hour blockade, that made the cutting team break their gear on our imported Swedish steel tubes, made us realise something: We can do this ourselves now!

It was only after our first 365 blockade that Ofog had the confidence to do it at home too. In May, we met the biggest NATO exercise in the Baltic Sea in modern times with paint, wet suits, a canoe and dinghies. And the next month we had a wonderful peace camp at Sweden's prime weapons supplier to the occupation of Iraq, BAE-Systems Bofors. It was a real success with 50 people camping, blockades, inspections and lots of other creative actions. The Swedish police had far less experience than their Scottish colleagues and our steel tubes, the same sort as we used at Faslane, really made them sweat.

So I really can't overestimate the importance that the resistance at Faslane made for us. We thank all the people who have made it possible for us to get to know the Scottish fences, roads and waters closer. And we will keep coming back until Faslane is just a story that we can tell our grandchildren. That said, we certainly hope for you British people to visit our lovely Swedish weapon companies and police stations in the future. To succeed, I think that our solidarity and resistance has to be at least as globalised as the military industrial complex.

Anna

I remember very well, five years ago, the meeting with Ulla, Angie and Ellen in Stockholm. I remember the swelling inside as I heard them speak and understood the possibilities. A small hotel vestibule and the world growing wider around me. What we wanted to try in Sweden was not only possible but in full swing already, somewhere else.

The advice we got was: Come, watch, learn, participate. Good advice. I still think learning by doing is the best way. We really don't need to know all that much to act. We need to realise what we actually know – draw the conclusions – and act upon them! To some this is old news, to us it was fresh and hot from the oven. We did not need to be experts or professionals, our own views and thoughts were valid. This was big, like a bracing medicine to apathy that you want to intoxicate a world with!

And the more you do, the more your want to know, the more you learn, the more you want to share, the more you want to do, the more... and it goes on like that.

In Sweden activists and society as a whole is very divided into age categories. 23 year olds with 23 year olds and 50 year olds with 50 year olds etc. Evidently we lose much capacity that way. In Scotland we were met by grey-haired activists or just plain grown ups, or people who brought their kids along or people who brought their grandparents. Suddenly much more was possible, because we would not have a span of five years to do things, but a lifetime! That opens the perspective and changes the possibilities and the strategies. And we had all these great personalities to learn from and share and plan with. Ideas are all good, but there is no better example to inspire you than the right-in-front-of-you-alive-one.

We were hooked and delighted and came and participated year after year. We came in contact with other direct action groups and joined actions at NATO headquarters in Brussels and the US nuclear base at Kleine Bruggel in Belgium. We went to protests against nuclear weapons testing in France. We arranged camps at US spybases in Norway. We investigated, gathered knowledge, climbed fences – and spread the word. Action-trainings and informations were held in Swedish schools, pensioners associations, women's organisations, social forums and open meetings.

The Ofog women went to Menwith Hill and filmed the inspiring ladies there. They told us her story that we kept gasping at. Why did no one tell us before?! Greenham Common is common land now. Grass where there were missiles. And our history books tell us that kings and presidents rule, tell us that wars inevitably 'happen'. But we learnt about what actually happened in South Africa during apartheid, in the '50s in the United States, in India in the '40s, about women fighting for their right to vote in the '20s, about slavery ending. It was not the rulers nor the warring rulers who made that kind of change come about. By joining the Faslane blockades, and all that followed, was to understand that we can make history.

To me these kinds of actions are not about not conforming to evident madness. They are incomprehensible horrors that we are dealing with. For that reason, it needs to be fun at the same time. Not constantly laughing but often. People die, and people live poorly or stripped of self-determination because of these monster-bases. So our methods are the opposite – rich in music, colours, dance, rage, passion, laughter, dignity. Joy, respect and justice cannot be put on hold while we try to fix things. Things have to be fixed by joy, justice and respect. It's fun, long-term and direct, because anything else would be crazy.

Finnish Tripods

MIIRA RAUHAMÄKI

In 1996 there were a small group of Finns who were very interested in non-violent actions against nuclear weapons and who were also connected with Aseistakieltäytyjäliitto (AKL – Union of Conscientious Objectors of Finland). Some of these activists moved to Ghent, Belgium, to start working with anti-nuclear activists there and by the beginning of Trident Ploughshares – in the autumn of 1998 – Finnish activists came to Faslane both from Finland and from Belgium. Two of the Finns, living in Belgium – Katri Silvonen and Hanna Järvinen – swam to the Trident base and spent a month in Cornton Vale Prison awaiting trial and got huge amounts of media attention in Finland. AKL sent out information about these events and also organised support actions in front of the British embassy in Finland.

In the Spring of 1999, AKL mobilised a bus full of people to join the peace walk from The Haague to Brussels. Small groups of Finns also joined in the Trident Ploughshares actions in Faslane in 2000. There was a lot of media coverage in Finland, when Finnish Elisa Silvennoinen and Swedish Petter Joelson swam to a Trident submarine in 2002. Then in 2003 AKL organised its first bus trip to Faslane. 50 Finns joined, of whom 30 got arrested at the Really Big Blockade. The year after AKL organised a minibus (about only half a dozen people) to the Ploughshares camp. In 2005 some Finns joined the G8-demos at Faslane.

Then in the Autumn of 2005 Swedish Ofog asked AKL to join what they jokingly termed a 'Blocking Tournament Sweden v. Finland', as part of the Faslane 365 campaign which would start the year after. So, in 2006 there were around 30 people travelling to Scotland with the bus that AKL organised. And the Finns managed to block the road near the South Gate of Faslane base for almost three hours. The policemen were totally surprised, as some Finns came from Glasgow, dragging the police after them and some Finns had stayed at the peace camp and without any police nearby had set up their tripod in the middle of the road. This was at the same time as the Swedish activists blocked the North Gate. Media coverage was again great in Finland, and the action got onto the main TV news as well.

A year later AKL once more organised a bus to Faslane with around 25 Finns and 10 Swedes, to join in the final action – the Big Blockade of Faslane 365. Swedes stayed at the camp near Coulport and Finns at the peace camp near Faslane. The Finns and Swedes decided to mainly work separately. Once more, on 1 October 2007, the Finns managed, with great luck, to block the road near South Gate, exactly the same spot as the year before! Again the police were really surprised to find the tripod standing in the middle of the road. There was also a sit-in blockade near the Finnish tripod, where people tubed their arms together. It took almost three hours for the police to arrest these 12 Finns. One Finn joined the Swedish blockade at the North Gate at the same time and got arrested there. One Dutchman living in Finland also tried to swim to the base the same night, but police only told him to swim back! The following morning an international block of six people stopped the traffic at the South Gate for a couple of hours. Two Finns joined that as well.

Many have asked why we Finns travel that far to join the Faslane campaigning. Maybe different activists have different answers, but one reason probably combines them all: nuclear disasters influence the whole planet, not just the country they are are situated in and launched from. So it is our issue as well.

Bamboo and Crane Blockade

TOYOSHIMA KOUICHI

When I was told about Faslane 365 by Angie Zelter in the autumn of 2005, I was delighted that we could have an opportunity to take part in such an efficient and interesting activity to abolish nuclear weapons. After an unsuccessful effort to persuade major anti-nuke organizations in Japan to take part in it, I personally organised a committee to gather people to go to Scotland.

Thanks to the work by Rebecca Johnson at the anti-nuclear rally in Nagasaki in October 2006,[28] several hibakushas (survivors of Hiroshima and Nagasaki) in Nagasaki offered to go. Finally 12 people came to Scotland: three former school teachers, a former director of the Peace Promotion Office of Nagasaki City, a young man who specialised in physical anthropology, a woman who runs a small language school, a housewife, a fashion designer,

---

[28] The 3rd Nagasaki Global Citizens' Assembly for the Elimination of Nuclear Weapons. October 21–23, 2006, in Nagasaki City.

two professors, a retired professor, and a graduate student. The first four are from Nagasaki and are all Hibakushas. Rebecca, Anna-Linnea and Adam, of the Faslane 365 steering group, joined us in Scotland to make it all possible. We arrived at the North Gate about 10am on 25 July 2007 and began our series of actions by displaying pictures of the aftermath of the A-bombing on the perimeter barriers of Faslane Naval Base. Prof. Miyoshi, who brought these picture panels all the way with him, spoke about them to a policeman who listened seriously to his explanation. Meanwhile a ceremony was improvised by Moriguchi Mitsugi, from Nagasaki, where drops of 'water of peace' were poured on the hands of all the people gathered there. The water had been bottled by him at the Peace Fountain near 'ground zero' at Nagasaki.

We began the blockade by putting paper cranes[29] on the entrance to the gate. Four women and a young man then sat behind them, singing a song 'We will never allow another atom bomb to fall'[30]. While the police were taking care of the cranes, another five people, separated in two groups, dashed into the gate entrance with three bamboo tubes under their arms. The first group successfully locked their hands through the bamboo and the police then had to work at cutting the bamboo and arresting the blockaders.

It was a weekday afternoon and the traffic through the gate was quite busy. We blocked the gate for some tens of minutes. Four Japanese and Anna-Linnea were taken to a Strathclyde Police Station. Since we had been well briefed about the friendliness of the police, we were almost relaxed and enjoyed the arrest experience. Ueyama Kohei, a graduate student from Hiroshima, asked a young policeman which soccer team he liked. I personally enjoyed a silent and peaceful night in the police cell.

Most of us risked arrest on this action. We believed that it is essential in order to highlight the illegality of nuclear weapons. We had to pose the question to everyone: which is illegal, the WMD, or blockading the WMD?

Bringing bamboo tubes was somewhat bothersome but fully rewarded by getting the appellation 'Bamboo Block'. In addition, Sadako's cranes have grown from cranes for prayer to cranes of action. The presence of many local Quaker people not only encouraged us but also were an indispensable human shield to hide our bamboos from the police. All of us enjoyed the action very much and were also empowered by the action.

---

[29] Paper crane folding originated from Sadako, a young girl who made hundreds of paper cranes in her hospital bed to pray for her recovery from the A-bomb illness.

[30] http://unionsong.com/u236.html

Seeds of Change: Japanese Youth from the Peace Boat

HAZUKI YASUHARA

When you live in a country where speaking your mind and taking direct action on issues can lead to social exclusion rather than social applause, it takes a lot of courage and soul-searching to join the year-long Blockade at Faslane. On 28 July 2007, however, 19 young people from Japan gathered up their courage and took part in the Blockade along with a Hibakusha (an A-bomb survivor from Hiroshima) and members of BANG! (Ban All Nukes generation), a European youth network for nuclear disarmament. Faslane 365 was the first chance for the students to witness nonviolent direct action and even to see a demonstration.

Nineteen Japanese participants, mostly in their early 20s, joined the Peace Boat's[31] 58th Global Voyage and took a course entitled 'The Nuclear Age and Us', which was part of an intensive on- board peace education program called 'Global University'. The course asked students to question the very idea and possibility of living in the world with the ever present threat of nuclear weapons and fear of contamination from radioactive material. A study tour to the UK to visit the blockade at Faslane and then to go onto Sellafield reprocessing plant formed a key part of the course. Although these 19 students had an initial interest in the topic, most of them had little knowledge of the issues related to nuclear weapons or nuclear energy. Some

---

[31] Peace Boat is an international non-governmental and non-profit organization based in Japan and founded in 1983 by a group of Japanese students in response to disputes in North-East Asia over the representation of history. Peace Boat carries out educational programs on board a large passenger ship with global voyages lasting three months. Its main activities focus around peace, human rights and sustainable development and around 1,000 participants visit 15–20 different countries on each voyage. Peace Boat provides a venue for participants to engage with people affected by issues our world faces today. These experiences build face to face connections and allow participants to gain a better understanding of what is happening in the world and the realities of the people they meet, in turn motivating them to play an active role in bringing about social change. http://www.peaceboat.org/english

had heard stories from Hibakushas before or visited Hiroshima on school trips, but for most students, atomic bombs were something in the past, not something related to their own present and future.

Their journey started on board when they met the guest speakers for the program, Mr Michimasa Hirata, a 71 year old Hibakusha from Hiroshima and Ms Manami Suzuki, an expert from Greenpeace Japan on nuclear issues. Mr Hirata confessed after finishing the program that he had been somewhat skeptical at first about working with young students as many youths in Japan do not even know when the two atomic bombs were dropped on Hiroshima and Nagasaki. The program attempted to reconnect Japanese youths with nuclear issues by introducing them to the global movement and meeting people engaged in the issue, allowing them to form their own ideas, motivations, and connections. Passionate lectures and talks from the two guest speakers inspired a surprising level of enthusiasm amongst the students. For nine intensive days before their visit to Faslane, the students felt doubt, anger, sadness and confusion as they struggled with information that was new and shocking to them.

Despite a deeper understanding of the issues, they were still unsure about joining the blockade. For all of the students, it was a big step to 'take action'. One student opened the discussion saying that she did not feel comfortable expressing opinions on something that she did not know enough about. Even when the students agreed that nuclear weapons should be abolished, some felt afraid of taking part in a demonstration, an action not widely accepted within their own Japanese society. Others doubted that an action of this kind would make any difference. But the day before leaving the boat, they agreed that each should participate in any way that felt comfortable to them, whether it was walking around the gate, bearing witness or taking action to support those who were blockading for the first time.

There was a big change among the students when they met with the BANg! youths for the first time in a Glasgow youth hostel, a day before the blockade. The lively energy of the BANg members, combined with the Global University students' curiosity and excitement, were enough for students to instantly associate themselves with the youths who were around their own age, about to take action for their beliefs. Answering the question asking why they were participating in the blockade, one BANg! member said simply that he did not want nuclear weapons in his future. Others expressed their belief that far from breaking the law, they were in fact upholding international law, which indicates the illegality of nuclear weapons.

Meeting the members of Faslane 365 and BANg! was very empowering and inspirational for Global University students. One student was impressed by the simplicity of one of the BANg! member's reasons for taking action which opened his mind to possibilities for what he could do back in Japan. Finding fellow youths who were so clear in their mind and explicit in their will to demand what they wanted for their own future, the Global University students felt a huge encouragement. At the same time, they came to realise what it means to be young Japanese people living at this time – at the end of the program, back on the ship, presenting what they had learned and experienced to the other Peace Boat participants, the students described themselves as 'the last generation' to be able to learn directly from Hibakushas. Thus they had the responsibility to ensure that all nuclear weapons are abolished and transmit Hibakushas' message to the world and following generations. They declared excitedly to the other few hundred participants on board; 'We can make a difference, we can be a change and bring an end to nuclear weapons!'

The students, now back in Japan and separated from each other, but inspired by their experiences at Faslane and the strong tie they built with Mr. Hirata, have started to take action themselves, spreading the positive energy and message to their friends and widening their network. They wrote a 'youth appeal' and presented it to Sergio Duarte, High Representative of the Office for Disarmament Affairs (ODA) at the United Nations and people of New York at a Peace ceremony on Nagasaki Day. As the Faslane 365 blockades reached its climax on 1 October, the students made their own action and presented their appeal to the British Embassy in Tokyo. The students are now involved in the anti-nuclear movement with actions to stop Rokkasho reprocessing plant in the north of Japan. The seeds of change and empowerment which they received at Faslane are growing in each of the students, making each one of them a builder of peace on their own ground.

CHAPTER 5

What the Hell Do You Need Training For?

ANNA-LINNEA RUNDBERG

'Training?! What the hell do you need training for? When I first went to Greenham there was nobody there training us in what to do – we just did it!' Helen John, 2007

THE WORD 'TRAINING' IS often associated with someone telling you 'what to do' and then 'how to do it'. When you have completed the session you are supposed to be able to say 'I have been trained in this' and so you should know what to expect and how to behave.

In some ways this is true also for the trainings offered within the Faslane 365 network: if you lie down in the road you will most probably be arrested, unless you do it carelessly in which case you might get run over instead. In this sense it's true that the facilitator is telling you what to expect and how your behaviour might influence the situation. But the training is much more than just passing on information. It is about exploring your personal hopes, fears and responses in the context of taking direct action against nuclear weapons. It is also about group building, doing an action together with people you might not have known before but who you are now preparing to link arms with because you have common ground in the cause. And it is about planning and plotting. Coming up with a theme for your action. A lock-on device. A message. A banner. A song. A place to stay. Something to eat. And a way to get there. And back. Then tell the press about it. And deal with court cases. Maybe future actions. How anyone could ever tell you that 'this is the way to do it' beats me – you have to figure it out for yourself. The facilitators are there to ease the process, ask the questions and bring you updated factual information. The rest is up to the group. So let's drop the word 'training' and from here on we are talking about workshops. Nonviolent direct action workshops.

Why Workshops in Direct Action?

Taking direct action can be scary. It is scary because it involves the risk of arrest and getting arrested might affect your studies or your job or you just don't like the thought of being locked up for a night. It is scary because you could meet people who will be very cross for not getting in to work or who are trying to take their kids to school but can't because you are lying in the way. You might be worried about not knowing enough about the place, how to get there or that you will somehow cock up and fail the rest of the group. The police that are on shift might be of a particularly grumpy kind, your mum has sworn never to talk to you again if she sees you on telly with your arm down some tube or you might be afraid that if this doesn't change things – what the hell do we do? In the case of nuclear bombs we are ultimately challenging the state and its ways of defining security. This in itself can be scary. One thing that usually helps in these situations is meeting others who have or are going to do something similar and talk it over with them. Taking part in a workshop can help clarify what it is you are trying to achieve and how you will do it. It can also give you an opportunity to clarify your own fears and accepting them as well as trying to find solutions or ways of dealing with them.

Workshops are also good in terms of group building, action planning and getting to know each other. During Faslane 365 almost all the workshops were done with groups that had decided that they would go to Faslane as a unit. However, the workshops were often the first time the whole group met. What I as a facilitator noticed was that it really kickstarted the practical preparations around the action as well as planning regarding travel arrangements, accommodation, food and media work. In other words, the workshops proved useful simply in the number of questions that were raised and needed answering before the action could happen. And since most of the people who in some fashion were going to take part in the action were there for the workshop various tasks, roles, practical decisions and so forth could often be decided there and then. As well as when the group should meet next.

Workshops are also valuable in terms of planning and practising a specific action, be that blockading, fence-cutting, civilian inspections or office occupations. Going through who will be doing what, when, and preferably also how, is vital for a successful affinity group action. When it comes to blockading it can be said that timing is of great importance, especially if the gate or roundabout is crammed with yellow jackets (police). Sometimes you get lucky in your timing, sometimes not, but it can be said that people who have practised their lock-on or their song or their cycling together before the day of action more often get into position than those who haven't. Having said this things can still go pear-shaped even if you have practised launching from the back of that rental van a hundred times before the real thing. And while we are at the topic of launching from vans in heavily policed areas, here is a little tip: before you head off to the blockade or action it is good to have decided on a person who will make the call whether to go for it or wait depending on what the situation on the ground looks like, just in case there isn't enough time for quick consensus decision making. If this person sits at the front they will have a good over-view of what is happening and if they decide the coast is clear enough they just shout: 'Go, now!' and usually the chaos that then emerges gives at least a few in the group time to establish themselves in a blockade.

In short, a workshop is preparation. And unless you have very large numbers of disobedient people all in rain gear, linking arms and sponta-neously sharing sandwiches in front of all the gates of Faslane at the same time, you will need some preparation in order to disrupt the bomb deploy-ment with the numbers you've got.

How Were All the Workshops Organised?

In the beginning was the Mad Plan. It was mad because it was so big and because we thought it just might work. The initial number of people for each of the 365 days and groups was 100, a nice round number that would sustain the blockades until the next group came along and took over. However, I realised fairly early on that this might in theory prove a bit of a challenge in terms of offering workshops for everybody. Had everyone wanted to take part in a workshop we would have found ourselves providing workshops for 36,500 persons in roughly one year. Naïve as it may seem now, it was with this in mind that I set out to try to find direct action facilitators around the country who would be willing to help. The fact that we were talking about preparing roughly 10,000 more people than the entire popu-lation of my home country for some reason didn't put me off[1].

The word went out that lots of facilitators were needed and soon we

---

[1] I live in the Aaland Islands.

had a list of 15–20 people who could be called on when groups 'booked' a workshop. The worry was always that there wouldn't be enough facilitators to take on all the requests, but with hindsight that didn't turn out to be a problem. Most of the workshops happened during weekends and usually we would try to find folk who could run workshops in the area where the group came from, to cut down on the travelling and to strengthen local connections. This was however not always possible even with the wide geographical spread of direct action facilitators in the UK.

Facilitators involved in networks such as Turning The Tide, Trident Ploughshares and Seeds For Change have been involved both in developing the agenda for and running the workshops. People with backgrounds in Peace Brigades International and other networks that use similar techniques and exercises in their workshops have lent the project their time and facilitated direct action workshops. The cross-over with networks that are not primarily direct action oriented has been fruitful in many ways, for my own part it's been particularly interesting to see nonviolent communication used as a tool in dealing with potentially tense situations during actions.

In April 2007, halfway through the year, I organised a two-day 'training for trainers' facilitated by folk from Seeds For Change specifically to increase the pool of trainers for Faslane 365. At the end of it a handful of new, eager facilitators became involved and have since the end of the project gone on to continue facilitating workshops that are direct action oriented. The hope has always been that Faslane 365 would draw in new people who would continue to do stuff also after the campaign finished, and I feel that as far as the workshop running is concerned that has been achieved.

Any type of full-day workshop becomes more bearable for all parties if there are at least two facilitators. We worked on a co-facilitation model that meant that usually two people would share the facilitation, break the pace up a bit and make it more interesting for the participants as well as more sustainable for the facilitators. However, sometimes it just wasn't possible and a couple of times someone had to facilitate a workshop on their own. In any case, the work of every single facilitator that has been involved in whatever way in the Faslane 365 campaign is highly valued.

While we didn't end up running workshops for 36,500 people I reckon we did between 60-70 workshops altogether. A rough estimate of the average number of participants in each workshop would be between 15–20, and so the number of people who have taken part in direct action preparations of this kind would be somewhere over 1,000.

What Did the Workshops Cover?

The typical direct action workshop would start with a fairly detailed intro-duction where the facilitators and participants would introduce themselves and give an idea about what the expectations were but what was possible to cover in the time allocated. Having a group agreement decided upon at the beginning of the workshop can be a useful tool to refer back to and this often covered things like respect, equality, time keeping and confidentiality. Practical arrangements and any special needs were also announced at the beginning of the session, as well as an agenda check, breaks and finishing time. Pretty basic things really, but without them there would have been more assumptions and confusion.

Next we usually had a paired listening exercise where we talked about what inspires us to take action and what is our motivation. Questions like 'why nonviolent direct action?' and 'why us, why now and what do we want to achieve?' were as much ice-breakers as pin-pointing why people were there. After this we usually went through the nonviolence guidelines, discussed them and clarified any questions about them:

We are committed to always acting in a way that causes no harm to our-selves or others. We ask that everyone taking part in Faslane 365 respect and follow these guidelines:

- Our attitude will be one of sincerity and respect towards the people we encounter.
- We will not engage in physical violence or verbal abuse toward any individual.
- We will carry no weapons.
- We will not bring or use alcohol or drugs other than for medical purposes.
- We will clear the blockade to allow emergency vehicles in or out of the base and then resume the blockade afterwards.

A very useful tool that visually as well as verbally can be used to quickly divide people into groups or start a discussion is an exercise usually referred to as the Spectrum Line. The way it was most often used in the Faslane 365 workshops was a nonviolence spectrum line, where one end of the room would be 'nonviolent' and the other 'violent' and in between a sort of barometer that the participants would move along depending on what they thought about the various statements that were read out to them. For example, the facilitator would say: 'Making lock-ons that contain sharp bits of metal that can shatter in order to make it more difficult for the police to cut you out – do you think it is violent or nonviolent?' and people would move along the scale according to what they thought. One of the points of this exercise, in this setting, was to draw out more general themes of controllability, escalation, tension and atmosphere as well as perception, and with this in mind the co-facilitator often took on the role of the devil's advocate. The exercise was also useful as a way for the participants to get to know what others in the group thought of different scenarios and what sort of action that group would be comfortable with.

Next we talked a bit about affinity groups and what the benefits in organising in such a way could be. So starting from a more individual perspective where we explored why we want to take direct action and what our own position is on various scenarios we now moved into what we can do together, as a group, and what kind of support we might need to do it. Using an exercise referred to as 'I'd do that if...' the participants would in pairs go through scenarios like: 'I'd run an information stall in town about Faslane 365 if...' and 'I'd sit in the road and link arms with others if...' and talk about what they would need in order to do that particular thing. At the end of this exercise the participants would have a list of specific tasks that would make the action easier or more comfortable to do, and what usually emerged from it was that all the support work such as legal support or media work or driving would actually be the tough bit – not the lying down in the gateway.

No direct action workshop is complete without a little practice of 'going floppy', basic blockading techniques, being carried away and some fashion tips. Various ways to link arms, sitting or lying down together or locking on to each other was also something the workshop included, and this section of the workshop usually took on a life of its own – which was great fun. A certain vicar in West Yorkshire apparently came up with the idea of supergluing the hands of the blockaders together after one of these sessions, a hugely successful tactic the first three or four times it was performed. After this the cutting team had come up with the ultimate solvent: hot water and soap. But they did spend a good few hours massaging hands the first time a neat pile of glued-together Yorkshire folks blockaded the base for two and a half hours.

How we respond in stressed situations or when things get heated is useful to know. It is also useful to 'be in the shoes of the other side' and feel how your behaviour impacts the mood. The purpose of the hassle lines is exactly that: to find out how we react while being 'hassled' by someone, may it be a sensationalist journalist, an arrogant police officer, a worried parent or an angry employee. How does having eye contact with someone change the atmosphere? How do you bring a very loud person back to a normal voice level simply by adjusting your own tone of voice? When do we engage and when is it better not to? All these are questions that come up during the hassle line exercise. There are no rights or wrongs, but being aware of your own responses and maybe applying some nonviolent communication tools could make your communication with any of the above mentioned people more effective.

Quick consensus decision making was also part of the agenda. Actions sometimes require very fast decisions, and they can be difficult. One important thing to remember however, is that no decision at all is usually the worst decision. Sometimes it can be good to take 10 seconds or so after the situation has been summarised and just think, quietly, what should we do? This gives more quiet time for people who are more reflective in their way of thinking and can sometimes change the outcome of the decision. It also helps if the people in the affinity group know each other well and if the communication is clear and to the point. Interesting questions to ask a group after a completed decision making process are: was it a quality decision? Did the group follow the process successfully? If not, why? Personally I also think talking about the limits of consensus decision making is useful, and could save future headaches when it feels it's not working.

Towards the end of the day we usually went through the legal briefing and what happens when you get arrested. Sometimes there would be time for a role play, but more often the legal briefing would be done in a Question and Answer session, with written handouts for the participants to take home with them. Interestingly, at the start of the workshop while discussing the expectations for the session, the legal section was the most commonly requested. Basically: 'What happens when I get arrested and how will it affect my job/studies/sex life?'

The workshop usually ended with an evaluation and a look at what the next steps for that group were. With some groups this was a very brief session, with others a lengthy discussion of how the practicalities were going to be taken care of. Sometimes a different meeting was called for the next steps to be sorted out.

The agenda was always based on a common draft but was adapted based on the facilitators, the time available and the group's requirements.

Lessons Learnt From the Big Blockade

'Why aren't people getting into the road?! Haven't these people been trained?' A member of Seize the Day, 1 October 2007

During the year of actions at Faslane most groups came with a well-rehearsed plan and found themselves in a situation where their group was the entire action at that moment in time. By contrast, the Big Blockade was a mass action, with many dozens of groups striking all at once. Add a large number of 'non-arrestables' and you might think you have all the chaos and confusion you would ever need to get into the road. However, this wasn't really the case.

There is a difference between working with just your own affinity group and the same group functioning effectively in a mass action. What I felt was missing from the Big Blockade was a lack of awareness among the groups of the importance and the methods of taking and holding space in that sort of situation. I also felt the non-arrestables weren't making the most of the many opportunities that came up during the day, especially when the police were starting to pen people in. We had the entire main gateway to claim, the roads leading into it, as well as South Gate and the other minor gates towards Garelochhead. There were between 700 and 800 people present. We could have been a lot more mobile and given arrestable affinity groups more 'surges' to launch from had this been encouraged during the workshops leading up to the Big Blockade.

A lot of people went straight up to the North Gate on the pavement, which effectively meant walking into a pen. And then they thought 'where do I want to be?' A lot of folk also hung around the buses further down, which didn't really help the crowd surge into the road in front of the gates. I know it is a lot to ask from people who really can't or don't want to get arrested to potentially risk arrest and go with the crowd into the road, but had we all done it, at once, we would have taken that gate and we would have been there for a bit longer before the police would have herded all the non-arrestables out of the way. We should have just been a bit more disobedient. And unpredictable, from the police's point of view.

For future mass actions of this type I would make sure the trainings included more on awareness of space and ways of claiming and keeping space, as well as on the differences between a mass action and an isolated affinity group action and what this means also for doing collective support for each other. In addition to this it is also important that the crowd is alert to various 'hidden' messages that could be songs, slogans or flag waving, and when the signal is given a 'surge' could happen and people could get into the road and stay there. Not all the people in the surge would end up staying in the road, although that could also be a possibility.

Having said all this I am still impressed with the way lots of smaller groups made it into the road during the Big Blockade. There was a magic hour or two in the late morning, just after the sun had broken through the mist, where various lock-ons and blockades kept relieving each other every 10 minutes or so, and the gateway was pretty much shut the whole time. In other words, there was just enough disruption not to allow the gate to open. And the affinity group model worked, it really worked the way the entire year had been envisaged to work: many, small, effective, continuous actions, all relieving each other, making it impossible for the base to function.

Why I Went to Faslane

ROGER LLOYD PACK

The name of Faslane has been a scar on my brain, for some time now. In the same way that the upgrading of Trident has been referred to as 'son of Trident' (how obscene, the attempt to anthropomorphise this weapon of destruction, by making it seem lovable and human), then its predecessor, Polaris, could be deemed to have been 'father' of Trident, and that's the weapon whose name dominated my consciousness as a young man when I walked on the early CND protest marches from Aldermaston to London. Polaris used to live in Holy Loch (another obscene juxtaposition of names). But I'd never been there, to Holy Loch or Faslane. I only had a blurred image of what Faslane might be like, so when Angie Zelter, the inspiration behind it, asked me to go up there and attend the Power of the Word group as part of the year long Faslane 365 Blockades, I decided it was time to pay a visit.

Faslane is a naval base on the upper reaches of the Clyde, 40 minutes north of Glasgow. I went up with a couple of friends on the Monday night to attend a workshop relating to the following day of action. As it happens I had already decided not to blockade the entrance and get myself arrested, but learning the practicalities of civil disobedience and peaceful direct action was helpful and instructive. There were a modest few of us, eight or nine in all, including Angie and the highly qualified Rebecca Johnson, a poet, two singers, a representative from the Ghandi Peace Foundation, and myself and friends. We would be joined on the day by a couple of dozen more seasoned campaigners. We were instructed in our legal rights, the likely response of the police (generally low key and intermittently sympathetic), and shown various rope holds and lock-on techniques to make the action more effective. We also did some role playing, setting up improvised confrontations between police, protesters, Faslane workers, and members of the public, so that I felt as if I was engaging in some familiar theatrical enterprise.

We stayed the night in Glasgow and took the 8.25 train to Helensburgh, and connecting bus to the North Gate for the 10am commencement of the demonstration, passing the 25 year old peace camp of highly coloured caravans on the way.

Two or three years ago I visited Auschwitz concentration camp, another centre of mass destruction. The effect on me was oddly grounding, as if witnessing the actual place somehow enabled me to properly acknowledge what had taken place there. The reality, however terrible, can never be as bad as what one might imagine. It's hard to explain, but it felt better to have been there. I felt the same about Faslane. And though its entrance gates were as ugly and as scary as you like, the place was, at the same time, curiously mundane. Three small country roads lead to a sort of central concourse, the fourth side of which opens up to the barbed wired entrance of the base.

When we arrived, there was a disparate group of people clustered round the tea urn, and another group on the opposite side attending to the PA system, criss crossing in front of the entrance, which was lined on either side by about a dozen policemen and women of different ages and persuasion, all wearing yellow jackets. Four more vans arrived during the next half hour so that there were, in fact, more police officers than protesters, changing shifts every hour or so. (This was the second Power of the Word protest of the 365 campaign, which possibly accounted for the low turnout.)

We entertained them and each other for about three hours, until lunch. Allan Cameron and Gerry Loose read some of their poems, A.L. Kennedy did a very funny stand up routine about the lies used to justify the nuclear deterrent, Theo Simon, from the folk group 'Seize the Day', sang some of his own songs, as did several other singer song writers, including a version of Dylan's 'Masters of War' by Paul Baird. I performed a Joni Mitchell song with Rebecca Thorn, John Rowley spoke on behalf of the Ghandi Foundation and Sean Legassick read a poem about Hiroshima. The actual power of the word was diminished by an erratic elderly gentleman, overlooked by Care in the Community, who kept up a ceaseless march across the gates for about two hours chanting 'No Peace without Justice', on behalf of the personal tribulations of a female friend of his ('Not that I like her. I don't. She's a pain but what woman isn't. But fair's fair'). And then, at one o'clock, we broke for lunch. So did the police.

After lunch Leon Rosselson started singing and at a pre-arranged signal, it being Angie's birthday, a cake was produced, and as we sang Happy Birthday, four of our company, with this diversion, rushed to the gates and lay down on the ground in front of them, blocking the entrance, to be joined by Angie (of course. It was her birthday, after all, and what more appropriate way of spending it). The police moved in quickly and respectfully to remove the protesters, taking them off to a nearby centre to be processed, and then taken to the local police station, where they were released later that evening without charge. (Very few people, in fact, are charged, only persistent offenders).

After the event three of us were taken on a tour of the beautiful local highlands. We could see, from the other side of the loch, the vast grey hangar, suspended above the water, where Trident comes in for maintenance. We were shown where the warheads are stored, conveniently stacked up a sheer rock cliff in case of accident, to 'minimise the damage'. There's a small village across the loch from the storehouse but 'there's only a few dozen people living there and most of them are old'. The MOD has constructed a custom built straight road to transport the warheads to the base, with special roundabouts that the lorries can drive straight through.

The thing is, Trident is going to cost upwards of 76 billion pounds. That's 76 with one hell of a lot of noughts after it. We could do an awful lot of good with that money, rather than spend it on something that is highly dangerous and can never be used. (I've never understood, by the way, why we have to have enough weapons to blow the world up many times over. Surely once would be enough?) New schools and hospitals, for example, care for the weak, the ill and the elderly, like the afore mentioned gentleman. We could combat climate change and global poverty, where the real danger lies. We would have the moral authority to encourage other nations to stop developing nuclear weapons. Just now there is an alarming escalation of hostile words and a return to the days of the cold war, as a result of the US wanting to construct a protective shield over Poland. Whatever Europe feels it owes America for their help in the Second World War I'd like to think that debt has been re-paid many times over by now. And if Britain thinks it's worth bigging itself up by owning deadly weapons, do we really think any the less of countries that don't have them? Sixty five per cent of the country doesn't want Trident. Many politicians don't. Even a lot of the civil service. It appears that we're trapped in outdated patterns of the past.

I cling on to a sliver of hope, however. The First Minister of Scotland and his party are opposed to Trident. It is conceivable, with enough support, that they could outlaw it (never mind that its already illegal).

Treatment Not Trident: Why Nuclear Disarmament Is a Health Professionals' Issue

DR LESLEY MORRISON

Rather than taking part in the Faslane blockade, should we not have been at home taking care of our patients?

By being at Faslane we were taking care of our patients. General Medical Council guidelines exhort us to protect the public health, and Trident is a major threat to the public health. As doctors, nurses and other health professionals we are trained in the care of sick and unwell people, but our responsibility also extends to their preventive health care which was the reason that, in 1985, International Physicians for the Prevention of Nuclear War (IPPNW) was established and went on to be awarded the Nobel Peace Prize. Its British affiliate, Medical Campaign Against Nuclear Weapons, is now known as Medact, Medical Action for Global Security[2], and works to educate and inform about the connection between disarmament, development and the environment.

Very rightly, the public's concern about climate change and its effect on the environment is growing; we are in a crisis situation. What tends to get forgotten, or conveniently ignored, is that nuclear disarmament and our ability to respond to climate change are inextricably linked. Resources, funding and expertise, which are desperately needed to develop carbon technology and alternative energy sources, are being wasted on nuclear weapons. They are, for many, the elephant in the room, the massive threat

---

[2] www.medact.org

that they have become accustomed to and no longer see. Younger people, who have grown up with Trident in the Clyde and a political acceptance of the nuclear 'deterrent', do not identify with them as their issue. In preparation for our presence at Faslane, I spoke to groups of socially conscious and concerned medical students about Trident. For most, it did not seem to be an issue of their generation; it was passé. The shocking thing to me was the sea of blank faces when I quoted Bruce Kent. 'Does anyone know who Bruce Kent is?' Not one hand. So there's our challenge; to make Trident, and its removal, urgent and essential for the new generation of health professionals.

There are medical students who do understand. A group of 20 IPPNW students from all round the world were with us when we returned to Faslane on 1 October 2007. From Ecuador, Nepal and the Philippines, they had firsthand experience of poverty and grossly expensive international militarism. They were joined by others from Europe, Russia and the US who understood the effects that their governments' polices were having on other countries, as well as their own.

Despite criticism and cynicism about the health service and doctors, surveys still show that the public trusts doctors and listens to what they say. Which is why we believe that we have a duty to speak out. Not in consulting rooms, and not in any way which would interfere with patient care, but in public, as concerned citizens with relevant knowledge and understanding. The British Medical Association, on behalf of doctors, began speaking out in 1983 when it published 'The medical effects of nuclear weapons', drawing attention to the health effects of radiation and nuclear weapons. 'When the bomb falls, don't call for the doctor', there's no point, we won't be able to do anything, was MCANW's message. 'Prevention is better than cure'.

Often we found, giving talks, that the gross numbers and statistics, were meaningless for people, they could not connect with them. Numbers of weapons, numbers of kilotons, were abstract. But tell them that, if a one kiloton bomb, a very small nuclear bomb, falls in the heart of their community, everyone within a 600m radius will be killed, your child at school down the road will be immediately dead and your other child at school slightly farther away will suffer the excruciating pain of second degree burns, and it begins to seem real. The other, and very important part of the message, was that our country having nuclear weapons made it much more likely that we would be subject to attack. The most important part of the message was that, as in any anxiety and fear inducing situation, the most effective way of responding to the fear, and avoiding the paralysis of denial or depression, is to take action. 'He never made a greater mistake than he who did nothing because he thought he could only do a little'.

Encouraging people to see themselves as active partners in health care makes sound sense. Our banners at Faslane said, 'Treatment not Trident', 'Health not nuclear holocaust' and we distributed prescriptions for the prevention of nuclear war, 'Dialogue for disarmament; take as often as possible'. We had deliberately chosen Burns Night for our protest on the banks of the beautiful Scottish loch. Burns is the poet whose strong sentiments about social justice and internationalism are expressed in the powerful words, 'For a' that an' a' that, It's coming yet for a' that, That man to man the world o'er, Shall brithers be for a' that'. We arrived at the North Gate to the sound of the bagpipes, sang Burns songs, danced, toasted the haggis and then presented it to the police officer in charge. In brief conversations, it seemed that many of the police on duty were clearly sympathetic to our views and understood why, as health professionals, Trident is our business. The press present also understood. Many of us were interviewed and got the opportunity to draw attention to Medact's publication, 'Britain's new nuclear weapons: illegal, indiscriminate and catastrophic for health'. We explained that as doctors we spend our professional lives encouraging people to express their concerns about their health. The major decision to replace Trident, which would so dramatically and adversely affect the health of millions, was been taken without any opportunity for proper parliamentary or public debate. Our aim in making this public statement was to encourage people to express their concerns, to make their voices heard in the democratic process. Radio Scotland carried a long piece on the six o'clock news and our mission to make use of all of our various local papers and radio stations resulted in widespread coverage in the general, medical and nursing press.

What was the response from patients and colleagues? My first patient when I returned to work, a veteran of police custody, was impressed, 'We've got something in common, doctor'. Comments were generally very positive; 'Well done on taking a stand', 'Thanks for doing that for us'. I accepted any comments offered but did not engage in discussion. The 10 minutes was for them to discuss their current health concerns. Of course, any patient who disagreed with my stance would be less likely to say so. Any who were offended or felt they could not continue with me as their GP could change to another GP, although this would undoubtedly be difficult in a single-handed rural practice. Response from colleagues varied; an article in the *BMJ* attracted positive feedback, most of my GP partners chose to say nothing, one stated strongly that he felt my actions were inappropriate and might bring discredit to the practice. His fears were unfounded and his view very much a minority one.

Fundamentally, the issue is one of freedom of speech. As doctors we are privy to information about individuals and families which we would never divulge in public. Because we have a public profile in our communities and people are likely to be interested in what we say on issues of social justice, should that mean that we cannot say it? Like any other citizen, or taxpayer, or patient, we have the right to express our views. We have a right to expect that they will be listened to. And we hope that they will be.

CHAPTER 6

We Fought the Law... and the Law Ran and Hid

ADAM CONWAY

ONE OF THE ATTRACTIONS of the idea of Faslane 365 for me (apart from the obvious need and desire to step up the pressure on Trident) was that it would force us to really, properly decentralise and spread both the load and the skills and knowledge of all the support roles. Much campaigning, especially the direct-action end of it, is largely decentralised and actions at Faslane over recent years were no different. Nonetheless, mass actions had always required the key support roles to be organised centrally. This was certainly true of legal support – a role people often think needs more expertise than it does. Faslane 365, however, would be different. Even had we wanted to (and trust me, we didn't!), we did not have the resources to organise legal support every day for a year. Groups would have to provide their own legal support.

That didn't mean we were going to throw everyone on their own entirely. We, collectively, have a lot of experience of blockading Faslane and of the potential consequences, legal process, etc. With Faslane 365 actively trying – and, as it turned out, succeeding – to encourage people who hadn't taken this kind of action before to take that step we had to provide some support and information. One of the biggest barriers to people taking on any sort of legal support role is the impression that one has to be an expert on the law so our primary aim was to provide people with the tools and information necessary, including legal briefings, to provide legal support to their own groups.

To this end there *was* a group centrally called the Legal Working Group (LWG), to distinguish it from the legal support teams within each blockading group. The role of the Legal Working Group was to provide information and support to these Legal Support teams, not to provide direct legal support ourselves. Of course, there were occasions when one or both[1] members of

---

[1] There were only two of us.

the LWG were ourselves involved in a blockading group and took on a legal support role. However, there were also occasions when both members of the LWG were involved in the same blockading group and were both arrestable – and the people doing legal support that day just had to manage.

So what do I mean when I refer to legal support. Obviously telling people about the law – possible charges, process, etc. is part of it. But, as I've said, you don't really need to know any law to do legal support – we produced the briefings covering the legal bit so the legal support teams just had to distribute them and make sure people had read them. On the day, the biggest role of the LST is simply keeping track of who's where and making sure everyone's released. There's no legal knowledge required here, it's just keeping track of information. After that, supporting people through court cases. Again, we provided briefings and answered detailed questions (to the best of our ability). The support we looked to the LST to provide was again distributing info and providing practical and emotional support to people facing the courts.

Neither member of the LWG are lawyers nor do we have any formal legal training. We are simply activists with a fair amount of experience of the courts ourselves and a lot of experience of supporting people through them and generally of providing legal support. Our legal knowledge comes partly from research and a lot from experience. And the two don't always match – we frequently have to say 'Well in theory the law/procedure is this, but in practice they're most likely to do that!' I would also say that the fact that someone *does* have legal training doesn't necessarily mean they get either the law or the procedure correct. Of course, we do know some solicitors who we've worked with before who we can recommend to people and one was always on call if she was needed.

Over the years, we have developed a particular style, or system, for Legal Support at mass actions at Faslane. While much of our approach is fairly standard for any form of legal support, some aspects aren't appropriate in some other situations. For example, there are some actions where you wouldn't even try and get everyone to fill in a registration form in advance. However, it does work well at Faslane (and for small to medium sized group actions) so the system we recommended was essentially the one we've developed for Big Blockades, with a few minor amendments.

One of the first things the steering group did, months before the start of the actual blockades, was to produce the initial version of the resource pack. The LWG worked on the basic legal briefings that went into that – what charges to expect if you blockade Faslane, what the arrest process is, etc. At this point we knew what the likely charges were, and how the police and the base had responded to one-day Big Blockades and other actions, but we didn't really know how they'd respond to Faslane 365. The whole concept was, quite deliberately, an escalation in terms of the practical disruption of the base and, we hoped, the political impact. Thus we looked at all the possible options we could think of. These ranged from simply a continuation of the Big Blockade tactics up to various attempts to ban protests entirely, such as if the MOD had sought some kind of Interdict.[2]

Our next job was to write the briefings on how to do legal support. If you haven't already worked it out, one thing that became apparent as the project went on was we seemed to have a slightly compulsive need to write briefings on everything. However, we were trying to equip the LSTs as best as possible. While we obviously didn't want to overload people, a big part of legal support is providing reassurance and giving people the confidence to take action, knowing that they know what they're getting into and that someone is watching their back. We wanted to both equip people for that and empower them, so they felt confident taking on a legal support role. The solution we eventually came up with was to produce four sets of briefings: the basic legal briefings (which we hoped everyone[3] would read), the court resources (for people who were actually prosecuted as they went through the courts), the 'how to do legal support' stuff (for the LSTs who wanted them) and then a set we called the 'break glass' briefings, because they were only for emergency situations. This covered things like powers the police might try and use but weren't likely to through to what to do if someone who had been arrested got ill and went to hospital.

However, while the legal briefings were essentially just updates and rewrites of things we'd written many times before, the 'how to do legal support'

---

2   For readers more familiar with English legal terms than Scottish, an Interdict is the Scottish equivalent of an Injunction. In other words, it's a court order preventing people from doing something. Nothing like this approach has been used at Faslane so far, so we have less experience with it but we remain convinced this would have been unwarranted and challengeable. However, we had to consider all possible reactions.

3   Or at least everyone relevant. There were a couple everyone should read, then a couple of others for specific groups (young people (and their parents!) and internationals) who might have specific concerns.

briefings proved a bit harder. We realised that we'd never actually written this down before. We'd done briefings for Legal Observers, who are the people on the ground making notes of what happens, who's arrested, etc. But the rest we'd always shown people as they were helping do it. After many attempts we finally wrote the briefings. A couple of weeks later, I attended a film screening in Glasgow. Several films were shown including a film made by a Glasgow-based activist film collective called Camcorder Guerillas about the 2004 Big Blockade. This included a short interview with Jane Tallents who was one of the people doing legal support that day (and now half of the LWG). In less than a minute, and off the cuff, she summed up what the 'office end' of legal support does in a way we'd been struggling to do on paper for weeks!

The blockades themselves started on 1 October 2006. Back in March of 2005, both members of the LWG had been part of an action outside the Scottish parliament during which they and eight friends had locked themselves inside a specially built model Trident submarine across the road. All 10 of them were fined £300 each. Neither of us had paid these fines, which had eventually been transferred to our local Sheriff Court in Dumbarton. We both got cited to come to court on 20 September 2006 for the unpaid fines. As you can imagine, the timing could have been better. If we refused to pay then we might get Supervised Attendance (unpaid work, a bit like Community Service) or we might get sent to prison. £300 would have meant a 14 day sentence which would have meant serving seven days. While ordinarily both of us would have been quite prepared to go to prison, we would only have been released on 27 September, with the blockades starting on 1 October. We considered asking for Supervised Attendance. We even considered agreeing to pay the fine. Even when we got to court, we were still uncertain what we'd do. Jane was called first. She explained where the fine came from. She explained how the High Court had told us to seek a political solution, and that this was our way of doing it. She held up a photo in *The Herald* newspaper from a few days earlier of the Long Walk for Peace (from Faslane to the Scottish parliament) arriving with church leaders at its head, explaining that they were simply asking the parliament the same thing we were. The Sheriff said he understood, but the fine was imposed elsewhere and his job was just to enforce it. However, he said he wanted to think about it and that he'd recall the case at the end of the day and that if she stayed in the court building until then he'd take that into account! Jane said she was happy to do that, except that she knew they shut the building and threw everyone out for an hour over lunch. He said he'd recall the case before then.

I was up next. He took one look at the paperwork, he said 'Is this the same situation?' and I said 'yes'. He said that the same applied and I sat down. We sat through some more cases until the court adjourned. At this point we went downstairs (we were only told to stay within the building) where there is a little tea room for the court. We got a cup of tea and worked on a few of the more unlikely legal briefings, which we still had to finish. We then went back up to the court room and waited for our cases to be called again. When they were we confirmed that we'd stayed within the building and the Sheriff said that he considered that to be a restriction on our liberty, however slight, and to be a form of punishment. Then he remitted (dropped) the fine and told us were were free to go!

The other safety net we wanted to put in place, for the legal support teams in the blockading groups was some way for them to contact us for advice if something unexpected came up. At the same time, neither of us wanted to be on call 24 hours a day for a year! The solution we came up with was to get a mobile phone and a new number, which we gave out as the contact number for the LWG, both for advice in advance and if something unexpected came up during the blockade. We then took turns having this phone, which meant that whichever one of us had it was on call 24 hours a day but it also meant that after a few days we could hand it over to the other one and get a rest. It also meant that I knew, if the landline or my own mobile rang when I was asleep or in the middle of something I could ignore it and ring back later, but if the 'bat phone' rang, you jumped to answer it. This sounded fine in theory, but to our surprise also turned out to be a very effective way of managing it in practice!

The Blockades Begin

So, with the briefings we could think of in advance written and with all the possible reactions and responses still up in the air, we finally got to the first blockade. 1 October was a Sunday, so that day was mainly used for gathering and preparing, with most people preferring to wait until Monday morning, when it was busier, to actually sit in front of the gates. Some of the Greenham Women, in keeping with that history, wanted to spend the night camped by the North Gate. Most of them were opposite the gate, on the other side of the road. However, a couple of them decided to camp right next to the fence. This turned out to be the first interaction with the police. The layout of the road just there is that there's a roundabout, with four exits: three roads and the North Gate. There's a pavement, then a motor-way style crash barrier, a yard or two of grass (with some big rocks on it[4]) then the fence. It was on this patch of grass, a bit down from the gate, that some of the women decided to camp. The MOD Police (MDP) objected and told them to move. The initial response was along the lines of 'Under what power can you make us move?' and the cops reply something like 'I don't know. I was just told to tell you to move. I'll go and ask the boss.' They went away to ask and we got our first call to the LWG phone line, asking what powers they might try and use. The ownership of this strip of land is unclear, although we expected the MOD to claim it. However, we couldn't see any law they could use to force them to move. There are new criminal trespass powers covering a number of bases including Faslane. This is under the Serious Organised Crime and Police Act, which we initially abbreviated as SOCPA but which the MDP, at least in Scotland, refer to as SOCAP. On hearing this we decided to use the 'CR' rather than just 'C' for 'crime'... SOCRAP. However, the area covered by this law is not defined by a map, or by land ownership, but by a written description as 'the area inside the outer perimeter ... fences'. There are also by-laws covering Faslane, but while they do include a map and can only apply on MOD land the primary definition is again written, and is the same as the criminal trespass power above. We confirmed this and the women waited to see what power the police came up with. Shortly later the police returned with their claimed reason. We got a text message from the LST for the Greenham Women: 'They say SOCAP, we say SOCRAP'. The two women in question stayed and spent the night camped right next to the fence.

The next morning, a number of women sat in the road in front of the North Gate. They were arrested and charged with a Breach of the Peace.

---

4   As the year wore on, the number of big rocks kept increasing. I think officially these rocks are supposed to be there to stop people ramming through the fence with a vehicle. However, the MOD responded to people peacefully gathering on this grassy area next to the gate. This area filled both a protest role, with many colourful and visible presences and also a welfare role, with hot drinks and shelter frequently based here. After spending countless hours in the local courts hearing people being told that there was no need to block the road because you could make your protest by standing at the side of the road with a banner it was ironic, to say the least, that the MOD responded to this campaign by seeking to reduce the space available to stand next to the North Gate with banners!

This was expected. They were held overnight and told they would be taken to court the next morning. This wasn't quite the usual pattern for actions at Faslane but was one of the possibilities we'd considered. The police in Scotland do have the power to hold you to the next working day in order to take you to court. They can also release you (either on a commitment to come to court on a specified day, or without any paperwork) but they can't[5] put any bail conditions on you. Only the courts can do that. The ongoing nature of Faslane 365 did make us wonder if they would take more people to court and put them on bail to try and stop them going back. What was somewhat more unexpected, however, was that no one was taken to court the next day! Around lunchtime the following day, all the women arrested the day before were released from the Police Office. On their release they were handed a letter from the Procurator Fiscal[6] saying, in essence, that he believed you were guilty as sin and he could prosecute if he wanted to, but he wasn't going to this time. Oh, but don't do it again! If you do it again he 'might' prosecute you next time. In practice, it seemed most people only got prosecuted on their third or fourth arrest.

A couple of weeks later, I set off to drive down to Northern England to do a workshop and bring some folk back. I stopped in Dumbarton, about 10 miles away, to fill up with petrol and get a sandwich. As I was about to leave someone knocked on the window and pointed out the stream of petrol pouring from my petrol tank and onto the ground. I called for a tow. I think I knew, from phone calls either before or shortly after the tow arrived that, as part of the action that day, the Bristol group had stopped their minibus on the roundabout outside the North Gate and several people had jumped out and blocked the gateway. I think at that point I knew the van had been moved to the side and the driver was talking to the police, but no one knew if he'd been arrested.[7] I did know that the company who turned up to tow my car back to Helensburgh were the same ones who had the police towing contract since we'd just written a briefing on getting vehicles back if they were taken by the police. I think you've guessed where this is going – halfway back to Helensburgh the driver gets a call on his mobile. All I hear

---

5   At the time of writing at least!

6   The prosecutor in Scotland.

7   Seize the Day had done the same thing the day before and their driver had been talked to by the cops but not arrested.

is something like: 'So what size van?... So do I just go to the North Gate or where?... I'll be there in about 20 minutes'. I surreptitiously texted Jane to tell her the van had been impounded. I think the legal support team from the south-west group were a bit taken aback when their call to the LWG phone to say that their van had been impounded got the response 'yes, we know'! The problem was the van had the whole group's luggage in it – including the people who hadn't been arrested. We arrived back in Helensburgh and Jane met us with the paperwork about the car. Between us we tried to keep the driver talking as long as possible, to give the folk at the base time to persuade the police to give them their bags back. It turns out that one of the people whose bag was on the bus had a heart condition and his medication was in his bag. Rather than being a problem this turned out to be the solution – one of the others was a cardiac nurse. She found the senior police officer who when faced with 'I am a cardiac nurse, this man is a cardiac patient, his medication is in that van, this is what you are going to do...' quickly arranged for everyone to get their bags off the van before it was towed away.

To Prosecute or Not to Prosecute

This pattern quickly became established. Unless there was something different about the action (say, anchoring an icebreaker against the boom around the Trident area[8]) most people didn't get prosecuted the first or even the second time. There didn't appear to be any account taken of your previous record, either at Faslane or elsewhere – it was just the number of prosecutions as part of Faslane 365 which counted. (Indeed there was an occasion when three members of the Faslane 365 steering group, on a day off, went for a walk on a beautiful Scottish hillside with a visiting friend from the US. The hillside in question did happen to be adjacent to RNAD Coulport, the sister base to Faslane, where the warheads are stored when they aren't on the submarines. This hillside is owned by the MOD but leased to local farmers. The by-laws covering it don't say you can't be there, but do make it an offence not to leave when a cop tells you to. Eventually, the MOD police found them and told them to leave. They agreed, but there was some debate about the route by which they left (a grey area in the by-laws) which ended when one of the MDP got overexcited and started arresting people. The three members

---

[8] Like the Greenpeace ship *Arctic Sunrise* did.

of the Faslane 365 steering group[9] present were arrested, taken to Faslane and processed and then released after a couple of hours, on the grounds that it was 'nothing to do with Faslane 365'!)

Over the whole year we had 1150 arrests and only 75 prosecutions[10]. There was only one group where all the arrestees were prosecuted first time, and that was 12 folk from Coventry in February. We're still not totally clear why this group was treated differently. They were the first group after we got up to 500 arrests, so they could have been the Procurator Fiscal (PF) testing the water, wanting to add a little bit of uncertainty to see what happened. Or maybe it was a visiting PF who didn't know the policy. Or maybe the PF had a really bad experience in Coventry once. We don't know. What we do know, is that it was quite clear there was a policy in operation: hold people overnight then release them the next day with the 'you've been a bad boy/girl – don't do it again!' letter from the PF and only actually prosecute on the third or fourth arrest.

Now a lot of people were quite annoyed about this policy. For some people, the main thing is the action itself, and the court process is an annoyance to be got through. For some, the court process, explaining why it was the right thing to do and challenging the legal system and the state in that fashion are a very important part of the action. Indeed, two of the women who'd been part of the Greenham Women group that kicked off the Faslane 365 blockades were so annoyed that they went to Edinburgh on 11 November 2006 and covered the side of the High Court building in painted slogans about this abuse of the legal system. They became the first people to go to prison as a result of Faslane 365 actions, receiving 40 and 44 day sentences while the courts are still seeking – vainly, knowing the two women in question – to recover £1,500 compensation from each of them.

Some people, however, were quite happy to do an overnight stint in a police cell if it meant not having to bother with court cases, etc. You could either look at it as an outrageous abuse of the legal process, or as a 'free' blockade. Or as both!

---

9 But not our American friend. Initially there were only three cops, so they arrested one person each. By the time back-up arrived they had calmed down and no one saw the need to arrest anyone else!

10 This number could rise very slightly, as we haven't yet had the plea hearing (first calling) of all the folk getting prosecuted for their part in the Big Blockade. But it won't rise significantly. I feel confident saying the final number of prosecutions will be significantly less than 10 per cent of the arrests.

In principle, it is a clear abuse of the system. The European Convention on Human Rights (ECHR) says, in Article 5, that 'No one shall be deprived of his liberty save in the following cases'. Of the cases listed, the only one which can apply when the police arrest someone for allegedly committing an offence (but which they haven't yet gone to court for) is 'the lawful arrest or detention of a person effected for the purpose of bringing him before the competent legal authority on reasonable suspicion of having committed an offence or when it is reasonably considered necessary to prevent his committing an offence or fleeing after having done so'. Well, there's no question of fleeing – we're sitting in the road and trying to stay there! And, in their terms, we've already committed the offence by sitting down so the only bit left is 'for the purpose of bringing him before the competent legal authority'. So if they're not planning to take us to court, they shouldn't be holding us. The preventative bit *might* allow the initial arrest but the detention overnight can only be justified if the police are actually doing it in order to take you to court. It is true that people were often told they were being held in order to be taken to court the next day. However, the police were often honest enough to tell both the people themselves and their legal support teams that in all probability they would be released the next day with the usual warning letters.

The reason this abuse of the system was possible, and the reason it was so difficult to challenge, was that you had two separate bodies making two separate decisions but the combined effect of those decisions was punishment without trial, albeit only for one[11] night. The way it works is this: you're arrested and the police have to decide what to do with you. They can release

---

[11] The police can hold you to the next working day so someone arrested on a Friday can in theory be held until Monday. In practice, most people arrested on a Friday or Saturday were released either that day or the next day. The only ones held all weekend were: Tim the cyclist, who was the first person to be arrested twice during Faslane 365, the second time (on a Friday) accidentally for cycling too slowly around the roundabout; the entire crew of the Greenpeace ship *Arctic Sunrise*; and one person from one of the Trident Ploughshares actions who was offered release on an Undertaking to come back to court but refused to sign it. The latter was released, without signing an undertaking or going to court, on Monday morning but was eventually cited to court. Tim got a second warning letter. The captain of the *Arctic Sunrise* was taken to court on Monday and released on bail, but the rest of the crew were released on the Monday without going to court.

you without any paperwork[12], they can ask you to sign an Undertaking agreeing to come to court on a certain day or they can hold you for court the next day. But the police in Scotland can't initiate a prosecution themselves. If you're held, they send a report to the PF who has to decide whether or not to prosecute. The fact the police held you for court doesn't mean he has to, it's his decision. He can tell the police to release you or he can take you to court. In our cases, the police claimed to have decided to hold us for court the next day. The next morning the PF looks at the reports and decides not to prosecute but to release with a silly little warning letter. Each of them are allowed to make that decision, and there are cases, where both sides were genuine in their approach and where they wasn't any alternative[13]. The problem comes when it becomes an established policy since the cumulative effect is certainly not compatible with the spirit, at least, of the ECHR.

The police, when challenged on this at both junior and senior levels, claimed simply to be following the standard policy they followed for any arrest, as laid out in the Lord Advocates Guidelines[14]. However, in an article[15] published by the MOD Police in January 2008, it was revealed that there was a joint planning team, involving the MDP, Strathclyde Policy and PF, months before Faslane 365 started (no great surprise). More damningly, Chief Inspector Jim Gillen, the Deputy Senior Police Officer at Faslane says in the same article: *'The prosecution policy adopted from the outset by the Fiscal, supported by both the MDP and Strathclyde Police at a strategic level,*

---

[12] This doesn't prevent you from still being prosecuted since a report is sent to the PF who then decides whether or not to prosecute. If he wants to prosecute, he sends a citation by registered post.

[13] When someone is arrested, as we often were, at 7am one would have thought the PF could consider it that day, rather than waiting until the next morning!

[14] When asked why they were holding us for court, rather than releasing us after a few hours (as had been standard practice for previous Faslane protests) the response was that this was an ongoing, yearlong action and one of the criteria was the risk of re-offending. They didn't explain why, during previous prolonged events (such as the annual two week TP camps), they had still usually released people that day.

[15] 'MOD Police respond to Faslane 365 – a year of protest' published on 9 January 2008 in the 'Defence News' section of the MOD website. Available at http://www.mod.uk/DefenceInternet/DefenceNews/EstateAndEnvironment/ModPolice RespondToFaslane365AYearOfProtest.htm.

is now being considered as 'best practice' throughout Scotland for similar events.' We did look into a legal challenge to this policy once it became established, although the technical legal obstacles, in part outlined above, are not inconsiderable. However, the deciding factor, at least for myself (who would in many ways have enjoyed doing it) was that it would probably take years to get a result – certainly Faslane 365 would be over before the legal process – and I'd rather focus on disrupting work at Faslane. If someone had come forward really wanting to take this on we would have supported them but it wasn't something we had enough energy to take on ourselves. That said, in the light of the quote above we may get more opportunities in the future.

While the legality of holding people overnight, in the face of an established policy of non-prosecution, is at best debatable, holding people while the Fiscal sends a silly little warning letter over is not debatable – it's clearly illegal. What I mean is this: the cops are allowed to hold people for court and the PF is allowed to decide not to prosecute. However, once he has decided that, the police no longer have any grounds for holding you at all. They probably do have a certain administrative leeway – they have to do the paperwork, make sure you've got all your stuff back, etc. and if there's several folk in the same position it could be half an hour before they're all out. However, there were several occasions when the police informed either the arrestees themselves or their legal support team (who rang up asking when they'd be out) that they would be getting released with a warning but they were waiting for the PF to send over the letters first. This could take two or more hours (or, in the case of the Nordic group, six to eight hours because the PF decided he needed to get the letters translated first!). These letters are not part of any formal legal process – they're from the prosecutor not any judicial authority. The fact they say they think you're guilty as sin and have the evidence to prove it is meaningless – it's just the PF's opinion. He's entitled to that opinion, and to express it to you, but it has no formal legal status. In fact, the only formal legal status the letter has is that it drops the charges. In legal terms, it's a 'not guilty' letter, despite the paragraph about how guilty you are! There is nothing in the ECHR which allows detention of someone in order to serve a letter on them telling them that they're not guilty of a crime! If the PF wants to write pointless warning letters to people, he can send them in the post![16]

---

[16] And on occasion – such as folk released at the weekend or when the Fiscal's computers were down – he did.

As I said, while most of us recognised that it was an abuse of the legal process, opinion within the people coming to Faslane was divided as to whether they would have preferred to be prosecuted or not. I can understand, at a pragmatic level, why the PF didn't want to prosecute very many of us: most of us plead Not Guilty even though we're freely admitting to having sat in the road; we're a difficult bunch, who make a fuss about other related rights such as accessible courts and access to witness statements; and he has hundreds of person-hours of his Fiscal's time tied up arguing International Law and basic morality in a District Court. All that and he knows that at the end of the day it doesn't stop us! We do it, get convicted and come right back and do it again. (Indeed, in our experience, the act of standing in a forum like a court defending your actions, why it was the right thing to do, why it was necessary, the urgent need to do something to get rid of these horrible, evil weapons can be something which really commits people to the cause.) That said, I still think it's a cop-out. If they think that we're breaking the law they should have taken us all to court.

Breach of the Peace

The usual charge for blockaders is almost always 'Breach of the Peace'. This is said with a straight face by the police as they arrest us and prosecuted without any acknowledgement of the irony it entails. Indeed, in July 2007 I saw several policemen pick a number of Japanese gentlemen off the road, take them to the side and solemnly and straight-faced charge them with having committed a 'breach of the peace' for sitting peacefully in the road. One of them was a survivor of the atomic bombing of Nagasaki in 1945, who had come all the way from Japan to peacefully protest the ongoing possession and deployment of our nuclear weapons. It never ceases to amaze me how the police can arrest and charge such people with 'breach of the peace'.

It's not even like what we do falls within the definition of Breach of the Peace (BOP) in Scots Law anyway. Or at least, not in my opinion. Breach of the Peace is supposed to be something which causes alarm to ordinary people and threatens serious disturbance to the community. Now, if you accept the Faslane base as part of the community (which I find difficult while it continues to service nuclear weapons) then we were quite openly trying to seriously disturb it. However, I've lost count of the number of times when even all the police witnesses have said that no one was alarmed and the atmosphere was peaceful and friendly and the defendant has still been convicted. It is true that the High Court has upheld some of those convictions on appeal but it also recently upheld some acquittals in similar circumstances. The only way I can reconcile the most recent High Court judgment on BOP with the earlier ones is to say that the judge is allowed to find either way in a number of cases!

I should probably mention here that Scots Law is a separate legal system from English Law[17] and the English offence of Obstruction of the Highway doesn't exist up here. However, we do have much more interesting names for the offences in Scotland: Wilful and Reckless Conduct, Malicious Mischief (our equivalent of Criminal Damage) and so on.

Court Cases

The court support side of Faslane 365 turned out somewhat differently from how we had anticipated it would. In large part this was due to far fewer people being prosecuted than we expected. There was almost no need for any immediate court support and very few people were actually taken to court the day after their action. The captain of the *Arctic Sunrise*, the Greenpeace ship which anchored across the boom at Faslane was but because they used the more serious criminal process[18], the first hearing was held in private so we couldn't get into court. The *Arctic Sunrise* herself was still in MOD Police custody at this point[19] so quite a crowd of supporters greeted him on his release, with a banner saying 'You can't sink a rainbow – and you can't lock up the *Sunrise!*' The only other people actually taken to court the next day were the people who got into Faslane as Serious Organised Crime Inspectors in September 2007 and the women who redecorated the High Court in Edinburgh. A few others were transferred from

---

[17] In particular, the concept called 'Breach of the Peace' in English Law is totally different from the offence of 'Breach of the Peace' in Scots Law.

[18] In Scottish legal jargon, they used the 'petition procedure' which allows them a year to keep investigating before they have to issue a final charge. This usually leads to a jury trial, but we don't yet know if they are going to actually follow through with a charge or not.

[19] When they finally released the ship, the rumour is that the MOD Pilot who guided it out of Faslane got to chose the music as he did so and chose The Clash's 'I Fought the Law'.

the Police Offices[20] to the court cells but then released without actually appearing in court.

Both members of the LWG lived in Helensburgh at the time, and there were a number of other people based locally who were happy to help with court support. However, both in principle, since the support was supposed to be decentralised, and in practice if they took hundreds to court, we had hoped the blockading groups would do a lot of their own court support. We had always planned to keep track of the names of all the people prosecuted, so we could pass information from the people who had been in court to those who's cases had been called in their absence but we had hoped not to have to go to every case ourselves. In the end, there were remarkably few prosecutions and quite a number of them were for actions which we had been the Legal Support for, either because we were involved in the blockading group anyway or because it was the Big Blockade on 1 October 2007. The principle worked to an extent but wasn't fully tested.

We did keep track of all the prosecutions, for the reasons given above. We kept a note of the number of arrests for each blockading group, as reported by their LST[21] and the names of all those prosecuted. We designed our own database system, with a (secure) web interface written for the purpose to allow us both to keep track of the court cases together.

Helensburgh District Court is an experience like no other. It's technically part of the Scottish courts system but it does have it's own peculiarities. In fact, we discovered, when a new PF challenged it, that is has a special dispensation from the Sheriff Principal that, unlike most summary courts in Scotland, it doesn't have to set Intermediate Diets[22] (pre-trial hearings) if it doesn't want to. Anyway, the only thing we could say with total certainty going into the year was that Helensburgh District Court would find new ways to be weird and random – and it didn't disappoint.

A classic example was a recent case of one of the women from Coventry. After the police evidence she chose to give evidence and went into the witness box. She said some of what she wanted to say but when she started

---

[20] The Scots use the word office for the English word station when referring to police stations/offices.

[21] For statistical reasons.

[22] Any hearing in a court case in Scotland, at least at this level, is referred to as a 'diet'.

going into legal argument the clerk suggested that should be done later, not as evidence[23] and she stopped and sat down again. At this point the Justice of the Peace (JP) announced that he found her guilty. Both the PF and the clerk tried to explain that he couldn't do that yet – both sides still had to sum-up and present their legal arguments – but he insisted. This left the PF with little option but to announce that she was no longer seeking a conviction, and the defendant was acquitted! The JP left grumbling about the waste of time and still unaware that he'd wasted it! The defendant had indeed had her time wasted as she had previously had to travel all the way up from Coventry in November only to discover the trial had been adjourned at the Intermediate (which she was excused from having to attend) but the court had forgotten to write and tell her!

Other incidents have included the court setting a date (after much deliberation) for the continuation of a part-heard trial without realising the date in question was a Sunday and the JP getting so frustrated by the confusion being caused by the PF's lack of knowledge of the roads around the base that he grabbed a piece of paper, sketched a map and told the witness just to mark where the accused had been sitting. One person arrived at court to find that charges arising from two separate blockades had been joined into one case. She objected, successfully, and the charges were split into two cases. At the Intermediate Diet (which she was excused from) the PF said to 'treat the cases as not called'. He later claimed this meant that the cases fell and the trials could not go ahead[24]. A couple of months later, the same person was served with a new complaint for the same two charges, again joined into one case. This time the PF wanted to push it to a full 'diet of debate'[25] so he could argue the cases shouldn't be split. Whether they were, and whether he could have resurrected these charges in these circumstances, is now unknown as recently she was informed by letter that the cases had been dismissed.

---

[23] You have two main opportunities to speak: you can give evidence, which should be factual and you can sum-up which is where you put the legal argument.

[24] I remain unconvinced of this. While the PF is the only person who can call the cases initially, I believe that the *court* had set trial diets and the court had ordained the accused to appear at those trials. As such, I believe only the court can discharge the trial diets. We were awaiting to see what the court thought of this and other points when the legal argument was to be heard only to be told that both cases were being dismissed!

[25] A hearing just for legal argument.

Disclosure

One issue which appears to be going backwards, at least temporarily, is the issue of disclosing witness statements to the accused. We believe that you have a right, as part of the Right to a Fair Trial in the ECHR, to be given a copy of the statements made to the police by the Crown witnesses before the trial, to help you prepare your case.

Historically this had not been a problem in practice in this area. The PFS in Dumbarton had claimed that technically they didn't have to give them to us if we represented ourselves and that they only made them available to defence solicitors as a professional courtesy but in practice they had given us them as well. Both members of the LWG had been involved in a case in Edinburgh in 2005 when the PFS there had refused to give them to us on the grounds that we were representing ourselves. We had challenged this before the courts, relying in part on a Scottish Privy Council decision (at that point only two months old) that such disclosure was a Right, not a professional courtesy and in part on a European Court of Human Rights case, from France, which dealt specifically with the issue of self-represented accused. A date was set for the legal argument but a week before the argument was heard the PF backed down and supplied the statements. We were involved in supporting some cases in Ayr in 2006 where the same thing happened. But we hadn't had a problem in Dumbarton.

Then, in the Autumn of 2007, Dumbarton suddenly started refusing to supply statements to self-represented accused. So far, they also have backed down when really challenged and we are writing to the Area PF and the Lord Advocate to try and stop them being so daft. It gives the impression that they will back down when challenged properly so as to avoid a judgment against them but will continue to withhold disclosure when they can get away with it.

Getting Our Property Back

One similar issue we had a problem with in the first few months of Faslane 365 was about getting all our property back. When you are arrested all your property is taken from you. It is split into two piles: your personal property is taken with you to the police office and returned to you on release but anything considered potential evidence for the court case is kept as a production. For actions at Faslane this all goes to Dumbarton Police Office. In our cases the stuff kept as productions is often only the remains of the, now dismembered, lock-on tubes which are actually of no further use to us anyway. However, there are sometimes locks or tubes which you didn't manage to get locked on with, or something like a banner which you want back. We've even found that having a few cut-up tubes can be useful for workshops, as people can practice with them and see how they are cut-out.

As mentioned above, the only legal significance of the PFs warning letter is that the charges are dropped. So, folk who were held overnight then released with these letters started asking for their productions back – if the charges are dropped then there is not a court case for it to be a production for. The first few were successful then the Productions Office at Dumbarton started telling people that the PF had told him that anything taken from someone blockading Faslane had been used in the commission of a crime and should be destroyed. Again, this was something we had some experience with. The LWG had, in a former life, been jointly convicted of Malicious Mischief for constructing an unauthorised entrance in the fence around RNAD Coulport. Our boltcroppers had been a production in the court case. After the case we asked for them back and were told that they had been used in the commission of an offence and would be destroyed. After exchanging a few letters (I think sometimes that Dumbarton PFs office lose every other letter you send them) about how they needed a court order to do that and they'd missed their chance by not applying for a forfeiture order at the trial, we got them back.

Well, if we can get them back after being convicted, we can certainly get them back when the charges are dropped. If the charges against all the people involved in an incident are dropped then in law, technically, there was no crime committed – or, at least, those people didn't commit one. Again, the PFs backed down and admitted people could have their stuff back. The Productions Officer is supposed to write to people and given them two months to claim their property before he destroys it – he doesn't always seem to get people's full addresses but nevertheless people can now get their stuff if they want (which they don't always).

In similar fashion to the Disclosure issue above, this could be malice and an attempt to deprive people of their rights if you can get away with it but back down if challenged. Or it could be incompetence, rushed or badly thought out work. Whichever, it does not reflect well on the PF's office.

Looking Forward

As I write this, the legal aspect of Faslane 365 is far from over. Less than half the court cases have actually finished – some haven't even started yet and we already have trials set until at least May 2008. Even after that, there will be further hearings for those who don't pay their fines (myself included). I have already identified that the Disclosure issue needs more work, some of which we will do, some may be done by others. If the policy of punishment without trial continues, it will eventually be challenged, although probably not as part of Faslane 365.

The process of supporting people doing legal support for Faslane 365 was an interesting one. Many things worked quite well, some can be improved. Of course, any new project would need to design its own structures for that context, but all the briefings we did are on the website and can be reused by others if they feel they are appropriate. We may, at some point, consolidate much of this with the work we've done with other campaigns and for the G8 into a more comprehensive resource on Scots Law for activists.

Finally, although not technically part of Faslane 365, I can't help but ponder the intriguing possibility that the tables may yet, soon, be turned in Scotland and the real criminals at Faslane may yet face the courts. There was a Bill tabled in the last session of the Scottish parliament, during Faslane 365, which aims to prevent crimes such as targeting, servicing and facilitating the use of weapons of mass destruction in Scotland. In other words, much of what Faslane does would finally be explicitly[26] recognised as criminal acts under Scots Law. This Bill was still in its initial stages when the parliament dissolved for the elections but is expected to be brought back at some point during this parliament. We don't yet know if it will pass of course, though we hope so given the strongly anti-nuclear sentiment in Scotland. If it does, the UK government will challenge it in the courts so it will be some years, even on the most optimistic analysis, before it could actually become law. In many ways its political impact could be achieved through those processes before it becomes law and no case under it may even be needed. Nevertheless, as someone who has spent a lot of time studying and discussing the

---

[26] I would argue much of this is already covered by the 'Acts Ancillary to War Crimes' offence in the International Criminal Court (Scotland) Act but that interpretation is disputed. This Bill is much more explicit.

possible interpretations of the various laws they use against us, it was a slightly surreal but very encouraging feeling when I found myself discussing possible laws that could finally be actually used against the bomb.

Rise Up Singing

PENNY STONE

'I believe that I am upholding international law, and that this is my duty as a citizen of this country, and of the world.'

To hear myself saying this was a great relief, as I had deliberately not prepared a statement to make when the charges 'breach of the peace' were brought against me at Faslane Nuclear Base. I was relieved that what came out was both logical and correct. We had been singing through ceaseless rain for many hours, with good humour, and with deep concern, assisted by our old friends the midges. Songsheets disintegrated in our hands, and we kept singing. This continued all day with different choirs and song leaders teaching us new songs, and munching through some old favourites, such as 'War Machine', that are sadly still relevant today. It was one of those days when you just have to give in to being drenched, and enjoy it all the better for it.

As a group, we moved into the road singing 'Freedom come all ye' and continued to sing as some of us sat down. As a unified whole, we turned our backs on the beautiful countryside that holds our weapons of genocide, faced the gates of Faslane, and kept singing. We reinforced for ourselves that we will use our personal resources not for destruction, but for constructive means, by creating living, working music together as a community. We sang for ourselves and each other, and we sang for the police, the military, and the wider community, that they may hear our message and feel both the pain and hope that we express.

Those standing in the road moved away to the relative 'safety' of the pavement, and those of us sitting in the road remained. And still we sang.

I didn't really notice being arrested on a very conscious level. We were singing 'Bin the Bomb', and I looked past the gates, and was very aware of being one of many voices, of being part of a choir. I met eye to eye with my arresting officers as I was carried away, singing with all of my force. One by one my friends joined me in the police van, and we continued to sing.

We sang our way to Clydebank and spoke freely with the police whom we encountered as one by one we were processed. Having established that the lentils in my pocket were neither a sinister plot nor a tasty snack, but in fact a broken shaker, I was taken to my cell.

It's surprisingly freeing, being locked inside a room for an act that you believe to be thoroughly correct. For innumerable logical, moral and legal reasons, it is obscenely wrong for us to be engaging weapons of mass destruction in our military defence, and not only allowing, but instructing members of our armed forces to prepare to commit war crimes. I say this particularly at a time when our departed Prime Minister, who is about to become a 'peace envoy', makes statements such as 'The problem with this country is that we put civil liberties before the fight against terrorism.' Thanks Tony, but sadly, and in fact quite terrifyingly, the opposite is true.

All evening we sang in the cells. We sang 'Peace Salaam Shalom', 'I shall be Released', 'Aye but I will sit here', some arias by Vivaldi and Purcell, 'Never give up', and literally countless others.

During a brief logistical oversight, we failed to notice that all of the choir leaders had decided to blockade the road, thus risking arrest, leaving our singers without waving arms to encourage them.

Upon our release, some of us were driven back to Faslane, and some departed sadly, but with a song in the street and warm hugs to send them on their way. With most sincere delight, we returned to find our friends still singing by the gates, and evidently having a wonderful time, so we joined them for a couple of hours, learning new songs, remembering old ones, and enjoying conversations with the police and eating mercifully dry sandwiches.

The sheer force of a group of people singing is quite something to be reckoned with not only by the physical power of many voices together, but also by the beauty and pain which is expressed so thoroughly through this medium. It is a resistance that causes the police to unwittingly tap their feet, or to feel a depth of sorrow that we all, by our common humanity, instinctively feel about death and destruction. It is quite something to be asked by your arresting officer to continue singing – to continue to express that which you have been arrested for. Music has the power to unite a group of people who are visually divided by uniform: yet all embody the same principle of trying to regain and retain a place of safety and justice, but employ different means to achieve this. I feel that this is largely understood by the people who protest at Faslane, and by the people who police at Faslane.

In recent weeks, many of my friends have been somewhat preoccupied with the fact that I've been arrested, and have unfortunately missed the point completely. I did not go to Faslane to be arrested, although I was fully aware that this would happen. If I had wanted to get arrested I could simply have committed a crime much nearer to home. I went to Faslane to remove my consent from our national defence strategy of the threat and use of genocide. I express myself through music, so I go to this place and I sing.

We sang in the rain, and we sang in the road. We sang in the police van, and we sang in the cells. They released us, and we sang our way back to Faslane.

As those wonderful singers slowly left Faslane to return to their ordinary lives, I was left with a great depth of sorrow. I was almost bereft at the loss of people who will willingly and ceaselessly sing with me, and who sing, as I do, with great strength of purpose. I was saddened by the unthinkable terror that we could release in one moment, and by the great length of the road ahead, but I was also galvanised by the knowledge that my action was not solitary, that it is part of a many stranded movement of people to create change for the better. Before I left Faslane, I wrote a song with only the words 'Be still my sorrow'.

As I drove home, exhausted from four days of singing, I let out a guttural roar until there was no breath left in me.

Notes for the Guidance of Accused Persons

RIVER WOLTON

Clydebank Police Station, 5 October 2006

The cell door shuts. Keys turn. Shock. Disinfectant. High-gloss off-white walls. A ventilation system churning. Four places where Dean C has left his mark. Can I write my way out of this? Out of the panic that lurches when I look up at the locked door with no handle, the smeared eyepiece, the toilet cemented to the floor, the flush button, the call button.

A young woman looks in through a hand-span flap. 'Tea? Milk? Sugar?' Her surgically gloved hand passes through a freshly-sharpened pencil and a sheaf of paper. There's a green and white nylon blanket with someone's hair embedded in it and a thin blue PVC mattress. I lay my wet socks on the floor. There is nothing on which to hang anything. A round light fitting, two square ventilation grills. A list of my rights and allowable requests is pasted to the door.

Opposite the door is a concrete 'bed' three inches high. This morning the air was soft, hills welling up through the mist on each side of Gare Loch. Through the rain the shops looked closed, but they aren't; they're hanging on. Eureka Pound Shop. Mehran Curry House. Golden Valley Chinese Takeaway. The Anchor Inn. Out on the rippling water a submarine sliced the surface, sleek black steel, like a bizarre latter-day Nessie. Forty-eight nuclear warheads on board. Each with the capacity of eight Hiroshimas. One of the quartet of submarines that rest and refuel at the base behind the barbed wire. Victorious. Vanguard. Vigilant. Vengeance.

As they lifted me from the road and carried me to the police van their hands were shaking. It's all right, I wanted to say, Don't be afraid. I noticed my own trembling and remembered the nonviolence training. Relax. Grow heavy. My head lolled. I looked up at the sky; rain pattered onto my face. You can't kill the spirit, she is like a mountain. Some of these cops were not yet born when we were Embracing the Base at Greenham. They were kind in the van, their faces shining out of their uniforms, warming up to our jokes, complaining that they worry more about council tax than Trident, and that their shift will not be over until 11pm. 'It's hopeless,' insists a young police-man, 'We're all going down sooner or later, there's no saving the world.'

After a few hours I'm almost acclimatised to this – four walls, a ceiling, a floor roughly six foot square. The comfort of Law, penned in, right. What subverts it is not just a competent grasp of the 1996 ruling in the International Court of Justice (that declared the use or threatened use of nuclear weapons illegal in international law). What cracks it open is absurdity. This after-noon we danced the hornpipe on the roundabout opposite HMNB Clyde Faslane's North Gate, directed by Ronin in a sailor suit and painted clown's face; while behind the fence lay weapons on which an absurd amount of money has been and will be spent. Weapons that did not stop 9/11 or 7/7, that cannot distinguish between a terrorist, the armed vanguard of a rogue state, or an infant. Weapons that would be absurdly lethal if they fell into the 'wrong' hands. 1,500 Hiroshimas aimed at ... where? Russia? North Korea? Iran? Bombs beyond any definition of bluntness. Skimming the loch's surface in their metal cradles, easing through the North Atlantic.

The cell door opens. Fingerprinting. A policewoman gently takes my arm and escorts me to the Forensics room where I am photographed above my misspelled name. 'You don't have to smile' she says, 'People don't usually look so happy'. Then she rolls each finger against a glass plate and the prints are magnified on the screen. There is a small white scar on my left thumb. 'I bet you get some palm-reading jokes.'

'Only from you lot.'

Newspapers are delivered, thanks to our support team. By the time they reach my cell, the choice is between *The Times* or *The Telegraph*. I have been allowed to keep the book that was in my bag – *Trident: The People's Case for Disarmament* by Angie Zelter. I read it into the night, sleeping patchily, my head under the blanket. Every few hours they open the flap, 'Shift change. Everything all right?'

6 October 2006

This is not unlike a long-haul flight: the light stays on when you're desperate to sleep, now and then you're offered water and a vegetarian option, there's a persistent drone and no view. My back and shoulder ache from the thinly padded concrete, but at least I can lie down – better than a flight on that score. I eat the 6am breakfast – baked beans, a soggy hash brown, sausages. Police station tea. Scalding. Sweet. The bloke who was brought in last night starts banging on his cell door and yelling.

The dusty glass squares in the ceiling lighten. I'm sweaty, teeth furred, trying not to wonder if they ever wash this blanket or mat. Friends seem far away, the legal supporters, people clearing up, keeping track of us, sending press releases, meeting. Those at home feeding the cat, wishing me well.

Can't forgive myself for failing to close the lock over Jill's ankle, thus fastening us together and making it harder to move us, causing more disruption in the base. When I boil it all down, worry and pettiness creep in. Each individual step becomes isolated, pointless. How can I render into specifics the certain knowledge that the whole is greater than the sum of its parts? How Colette's face-paint and furry feet, Lesley's Grim Reaper costume, Bob's saxophone, Rosa's fairy-wings, Maggie's smile, Meryn's young wisdom, Jill's drawing, Kiri's optimism, Hazel's efficiency, Heather's calm, Jane's steadfastness have given me the ground to step onto.

I am weary of this toilet. It faces me unapologetically, seatless, with its light ornament of folded toilet paper, as if it was the only other being in this cell. I cannot love you, toilet. You are marked with the piss, shit, blood and vomit of strangers. The past occupants of this cell and their digestive systems. Not me, not mine.

This Stabilo Opéra HB 2½ is now a fuzzy stub. Should I ring the bell and ask them to sharpen it? It seems an absurd request. Another in the string of absurdities. What time is it? Are the legal team trying to get us out? It's hard not to fight against the lockedness of the door. Grey. Graffitied. Blood spats. Kick marks. Panic proliferates at the thought of indefinite time in here. Not being able to turn on a tap, take a shower. Meanwhile people wait out decades in cells across the world, sentenced for crimes they did not commit, or did, through poverty, addiction, living in the wrong place at the wrong time. Tibetan monks and nuns remain equanimous through years of torture at the orders of the Chinese government, Palestinian women give birth in Israeli prisons and are separated from their infants, and men lie shackled at Guantanamo.

The modicum of filtered grubby daylight grows stronger. Will we be charged? Breach of the Peace: the reason given for our arrest. I'm acutely aware that this system is not as brutal as others, that the eight of us here are white, English-speaking, with friends who know where we are.

Tired now. Wanting a toothbrush. I read *The Times* again. 6,600 Iraqis died a violent death in July and August. The French team are poised to beat the Brits in the National Conker Championships.

I hear voices echoing as if in a cathedral. Has someone switched on Radio 3? You can't kill the spirit. Old and strong. I join in. It's impossible to sing and hear the others at the same time so we become disjointed, a ramshackle of song. The acoustics in the cell are wonderful. I try a few more numbers. I have dreamed on this mountain. Freedom coming.

Another cheery policewoman – I almost called her nurse – brings more water and tells me it's nearly 12 midday and lunch is on! I see Jill's blurred face through the eyepiece in the cell door. Kiri calls out that she's so bored, she's never been this bored in her entire life, can anyone think of anything more boring than this. That cheers me up.

Lunch is the same over-heated vegetable curry as last night. It comes with news that we'll be out in half an hour, an hour at most.

The duty officer does the rounds. 'Hi there! Everything all right?' I wave and give the thumbs-up. He smiles. What would it be like to trust in humanity? All of us wanting – in the end – happiness, freedom from pain. What if our politicians were far-sighted? Trident replaced with nurses, firefighters, schools, a cure for AIDS. How much peace could you build with a billion pounds?

Will there be people waiting outside? Will they have tea and cake? Will I be able to make a statement? I want to be articulate. I want to quote the ICJ ruling and the legal stuff from Angie's book. I feel blurry, longing to slump into creature comforts. I desperately want more stimulation than *The*

Times front page telling me again and again 'The future's bright, the future is Dave Cameron'. I want a wash.

I'm all geared up to go when she comes back: 'Another half hour, 20 minutes.' Incarceration sits on me like a stone. You can go. No you can't. I try to sink into 'not knowing' but I'm jerked forward by anticipation. Chocolate. Hot shower. Anything. And it's only been – what – 20 hours or so? In moments, there's nothing but sheer boredom, the footfall of the guard, metallic water. Would my senses become refined if I were here longer? Would I hear the rumble of the ventilation system as a distant waterfall, the thunder of a motorway, a lawnmower? Would my sour sweat become a comfort? The toilet bowl a beloved friend? Armitage Shanks, my companion? I'm grateful for the ability to write and read, for my sight, for the light – brightening again now, the way it does on Highland afternoons. Glad that I have made a stand. That I do not stand alone.

Footsteps. The flap opens. A cheerful woman with mascara, foundation and a strong Glaswegian accent: '10 minutes. Get your bit and pieces together. There's people waiting, a real party atmosphere!'

The doors open. We see each other for the first time.

'Cell Food', Jill Gibbon

'The Cell', Jill Gibbon

CHAPTER 7

Critique in Action: Academic Conference Blockades

JUSTIN KENRICK and STELLAN VINTHAGEN

The Story behind the Idea

THE IDEA OF AN 'academic seminar blockade' emerged during discussions between Stellan Vinthagen and Angie Zelter as they explored how bringing a great range of social groups to take part in the Faslane 365 blockades could, in their own distinct ways, have a really powerful impact on the public, by demonstrating that people from the whole of society are against politicians pursuing present policies. The strength of such a blockade was not seen as physical-technical-economic. Peace activism can't win by making the financial costs too big, nor through making the practical everyday business of the base impossible. The state is too strong in a non-revolutionary situation. Peace activism can win by making the political and moral costs too high: by draining legitimacy from the base and so making its continuation impossible.

The seminar blockades at the gates of Faslane in 2007 continued a history of similar successful protests. During the second half of the 1980s there was a nonviolent blockade campaign in West Germany at the US nuclear weapon base Mutlangen, a campaign in which Stellan participated. People gathered regularly at the base, singing, reciting poems, enjoying friendships, praying and celebrating community, while they blockaded the base, making the movement of the Pershing II mobile system difficult. Various social groups gathered. With time it became one of the most impressive social movements against nuclear weapons in Western Europe during the cold war. A blockade is quite a negative and one-dimensional action form, when you think about it. Sitting down, saying stop, and refusing to move... But in Mutlangen the nonviolent resistance creativity didn't know any limits.

Nurses blockaded in their uniforms, teachers gave lectures to their students, priests celebrated mass with their congregations, and many others did similar things, bringing forward their profession, their life, and placing it literally on the road. All that people valued, all they held sacred, all they wanted to defend from a nuclear war – everyday life, civil society, friendship, community and professional work – became their weapons in the nonviolent war with the Imperial armies of mass destruction. When people who had been prisoners in Nazi concentration camps during the Second World War, blockaded wearing their old camp uniforms it put the 'law-enforcement' of the West German police and the 'defence force' of the US soldiers in a problematic perspective. When the symphony orchestra Lebenslaute on 15 September 1986 played Bach, Beethoven, Schubert and Mozart in the first 'music in' or 'Konzert Blockade' of the campaign, the police let them play for a whole day. The soldiers got a day off. But when the symphony continued the next day, the whole ensemble got arrested. And, when a group of judges and lawyers blockaded the base, the mass-media of the whole country became crazy. The absurdity of the official nuclear policy of the cold war – correctly named MAD (Mutually Assured Destruction) was publicly enacted in the court room when a Judge (judging the case) was arguing with his peer, another Judge, who was in the dock as a defendant. In this live performance the doubtful legal status of nuclear weapons was on full display.

An 'Academic Seminar Blockade' can be seen as a special form of action within the Mutlangen tradition. It is possible to understand it, in a similar way to the other blockades at Faslane during F365, as a form of *constructive resistance*, a form of 'saying no by saying yes': a form of resistance in which you resist by using and doing that which you defend. If you want to defend community and celebration, you have a feast on the road, eat, dance and celebrate life – while blockading. If you want to defend academic inquiry and critical reflection, you have an academic seminar on the road. To our knowledge the first Trident Academic Seminar on 7 January 2007 was also the first such constructive resistance by academics in the form of an academic seminar as a blockade. Before this, 'academic blockades' had only been associated with academics boycotting academic cooperation with certain other academics in dictatorships or similar repressive contexts, for example in Hitler's Germany, in Iran or in Israel. Our hope is that this new form of academic exercise will become a part of the academic repertoire and help to create a university movement of 'creatively and politically engaged academics'.

People participating in the seminar blockade were inspired by being able to take such a positive and proactive action, one in which we did not simply protest against the existence of nuclear weapons but engaged in direct action to stop them from being used: a form of direct action where we simply engaged in the professional work we did as academics, by giving a scientific seminar. The special thing about it was that the seminar was simultaneously a blockade of a nuclear weapons base, since it was a seminar held directly on the road in front of the gate to Faslane base: it was a blockade in which scientific discussion blocked the work of the base! This is a beautiful form of action, one in which our words and deeds are aligned, one in which our theoretical discussion is our political practice, one in which we literally pit our bodies and our profession against the Weapons of Mass Destruction.

This was not just the usual sit-down-and-get-arrested blockade, it was an outdoor seminar of scholars concerned about nuclear weapons. The seminar blockade used the normal equipment of a university seminar – papers, tables, name-tags, conference folders with copies of papers and a white-board. The main difference was that the seminar happened at the gates of a nuclear base, not at a conference room inside a university building. As with other conferences there was an academic theme, for our first Academic Trident Seminar this was: 'Academia Vs. Weapons of Mass Destruction'. Academic papers, with appropriate references, were circulated through being placed on the F365 website and then, on the day, seminar participants presented their academic papers, and after each set of presentations there was the usual chance for questions and answers as well as time for small 'break out' groups to discuss the papers in smaller groups.

This creative and politically engaged form of academia only worked by being both a seminar and a blockade. The two extreme possibilities were that the police might have arrested everyone directly as they sat down on the road, or, that they would not arrest anyone. The way we managed this at Faslane was to have the morning session of the seminar at the side of the road, close to the entrance to the base, then have a nice lunch by the side of the road, and then at a given moment the whole seminar moved on to the road in front of the gate. We continued to present and discuss papers, as we had before. It would not have been enough to have had the seminar close to the gate, without blockading it. Nor would it have been enough to have simply sat down on the road straight away and risked being arrested immediately. It had to be given the best chance of being both a real seminar and an attempt to blockade. The academic seminar blockade was not just about 'making a statement' but about doing nonviolent direct action against the preparations for mass destruction: it was about transforming words into deeds without losing the capacity of words and discussion to open out the space for us to think deeper about the problem we are confronting and about a range of possible solutions and responses. As we found in the first of our two academic seminar blockades, as the police chose not to arrest anyone for a long time it then became possible to go on having post-seminar discussions and thus blockade for many hours.

Why Academics Should Blockade Nuclear War Bases

There are a lot of possible general and personal reasons why we, as academics and scholars, should participate in a blockade of a nuclear weapons base. From our perspective, here are a few key reasons:

1   It can stimulate dialogue in society. Our profession is about interrogating complicated issues, bringing different perspectives to bear, and through this informed dialogue developing a more reasonable understanding of the issues. Engaging in such an action does not involve ignoring the law or violating a democratic government's policy. Instead the status quo is openly challenged by our bodies and arguments, not through violence or through slogans, but through the presentation and discussion of perspectives in a context in which we are prepared to be arrested and to take the consequences of our actions, with a willingness to explain in court why we see this action as necessary and legitimate. We would be hoping, by our actions, to convince others to act and vote against nuclear weapons.

2   It is believed that nonviolent direct action against nuclear weapons is legal according to international law.[1]

3   For some of us such an action can be seen as part of our objectives as academics: to popularise and bring our knowledge to a broader society, to contribute with our knowledge to the public dialogue, which in Sweden is called the '3rd objective' and besides teaching and research is part of our job-description.

4   We can't be only academics. We are also citizens in our societies, like anyone else, and thus responsible for what our governments are doing in our name. As such, we have to recognise that our actions

---

[1] For more information on several important acquittals see www.tridentplough shares.org.

(and our non-actions) have an effect. There are times when we need to take sides and stand up and be counted.

5 When we act we show that we are taking our own analysis of the world and our society seriously. If we believe in what we say (e.g. that nuclear weapons are a threat to humankind and its survival, that the rule of law is undermined by a nuclear armed alliance waging a 'war against terror', etc.) then that has certain political implications, which we have to act upon.

6 In contrast to a lot of other professional groups in society we have relatively protected jobs where it is difficult for us to be sacked for voicing political opposition, at least those of us who are professors or have tenure. It would most likely be regarded as a violation of academic freedom to sack a professor who – whether in her or his free time, or as part of his or her participation in conferences – engages in civil resistance.

7 Universities and scientific knowledge are known to be heavily influenced by military and defence interests. A major share of research in the world is steered by military agendas. In order to be 'objective' or 'neutral' we then need to show that there are also academics who dare to show their clear opposition to nuclear 'defence'. We know, and others will understand, that by our actions we risk the loss of possible public funding for defence and security research and any job opportunities in the arms industry. But by the same token, we increase the tolerance and plurality of academia, opening up new areas of research and funding.

8 We become examples and role-models for our students, either as obedient critics or as disobedient critics, depending on how we act. It is our choice and regardless of what we choose to do we build an understanding of what it means to be an 'academic'.

9 The action is possible to understand as action-research and is thus already part of the academic tradition. We learn more about how a social system works by a controlled intervention (our action) and a study of its reactions (observation and interviews of concerned people). The action can thus be seen as in itself an opportunity for research for those interested in this field.

10 It is an old tradition that university people – students as well as

teachers – are engaged in radical politics and protest. Let's honour that tradition!

11 If not now, then when? If we are not nonviolently blockading the preparations for mass destruction when it can be legal to do so, then when would we academics say no or voice our firm opposition to something in society? Do we have to wait until mass destruction does occur?

12 If not we, then who? If we as academics cannot take part in the blockades, being a relatively privileged group, who is then supposed to do it? Who is then supposed to take responsibility for nuclear weapons? Our students who live with the insecurity of not yet being recognised as serious/real academics? A normal objection is the perception that: 'I will have more political influence (on nuclear politics) if I am seen by the public to be objective and neutral'. Well, if that is true, then there will not be any lack of academics who will have that greater influence... But, imagine what it means if that is not true, imagine if it is the other way around. What if those academics who voice their criticism of the government's policies in articles and papers – but who remain obedient to the implementation of those policies – are those who create the false and dangerous impression that nuclear policies are created by a deliberative democracy and an informed understanding of reality? Then obedient criticism becomes a vital (and indirect) support of nuclear mass destruction.

The 1st Academic Seminar Blockade: A Moment of Academic Activism

The first academic seminar blockade was held outside Faslane nuclear submarine base in January 2007. It was an interdisciplinary international conference titled 'Academia Vs. Weapons of Mass Destruction', but perhaps it should have been titled 'Our Coming Out of the Ivory Tower Party'. One of the things that was most striking was the way the passionate and humorous discussions with colleagues and students and police outside the base, contrasted so forcefully with the atmosphere in research ratings dominated institutions.

This first conference had been organised by Stellan Vinthagen and Angie Zelter, and it was extraordinarily successful on a range of levels from participants making connections and building support networks, to the sheer enjoyment of the process, to the seminar effectively closing down the base for several hours and achieving an extraordinary degree of media coverage, especially in Scotland where the following May elections saw the election of a Scottish government committed to getting rid of nuclear weapons.

The conference took place in a way which peacefully blockaded the entrance to the base for six hours, over a hundred colleagues participated, and in the end 16 students and 16 academics were arrested and spent the night in the police cells. There were strong connections made between academics and students across disciplines and institutions, and during the seminar blockade we moved easily between giving academic papers, breaking into small discussion groups and joining the students in performing an impromptu and hilarious rain-soaked version of Shakespeare's *Twelfth Night*, almost managing to get the police to join in with walk on parts. It was January, it was Scotland, and it was wet and freezing.

What we hadn't expected was that we would be so successful in blocking the base. We had assumed we would be arrested within minutes of sitting on the road (participants in the previous months of daily protests had all been arrested immediately) so those of us who chose to block the base by sitting on the road were not prepared for the hours we were allowed to sit and freeze there. At one point in the wet, cold, darkness, many colleagues decided that they were just too freezing to continue sitting there and were prepared to finally abandon the blockade. At that moment the pleasant police woman who was in charge of the policing made the announcement that if we didn't get up then we would be arrested within half an hour. We can only assume that she was a good friend of Angie Zelter's, because the consequence of this reassurance that arrest, police vans and warm cells were on their way imminently was that no one gave up on blockading at that point but continued for the next two hours until the welcome arresting moment finally arrived. It was warm in the cells, and the same spirited discussions continued in these 'break-out groups': in the cell in which Stellan, Justin and Richard Jolly found themselves, our discussions focused on many things, including on how academia can help us to actively envision and enable society to free itself from the nuclear state. While being managed by the police and their routine we also had an excellent opportunity to reflect on the role of prison in society.

Judging by the large number of academics and students who came to participate and observe, by the large numbers of police actively listening to the papers and informally asking questions, and by the unexpected amount of positive media coverage we received across a range of newspapers and television stations (coverage which actually focused on the choices we face concerning, for example, addressing climate change or perpetuating war), there is clearly a desire for academia to be relevant. Not relevant in the narrow ways defined by our university audit culture which sees relevance in terms of student 'employability', league table positioning and business measurements; but relevance in the far broader sense of refusing to turn relationships into numbers, and instead making the space with students and colleagues to reflect on the world and to work to reclaim the global and intellectual commons of democratic debate and accountability from those who insist that 'there is no alternative' to current practice.

That there are real alternatives to current practice was evident in the range and quality of papers given in the seminar. These papers were in response to a call which welcomed papers connected to the theme 'Academia vs. Weapons of Mass Destruction'. The call suggested papers on the following themes:

- Why I am here today.
- What arguments are there for academics to engage in civil disobedience and nonviolent direct action against nuclear weapons?
- In what sense is academia militarised or part of the nuclear mass destruction system, and what can we do about it?
- Why and how academia can be a social force for peace, social change or nuclear disarmament?

In addition, the call suggested that papers could deal with issues such as:

- How the dominant world-view and social structure undermines our knowledge base.
- How the military is involved in research funding.
- How corporations buy up research findings.
- How research results that are 'controversial' or are seen to be in opposition to corporate/established positions are withheld.
- How human intelligence and knowledge is not used for the good of all or for the continuance of life on this planet but for short-sighted 'profit' for the few.
- What is happening to academia today?! Within my own discipline? Is it becoming less radical, and more directed by funders to be policy

relevant and usable for governments? Has it become an industry for producing academic certificates? If so, what can we do about that?'

At both our January *Academic Trident Seminar Blockade* and the June *Faslane International Academic Blockade and Conference* (the FAB-conference) we got a wonderful response. The range and quality of papers being presented demonstrates this. A few examples include: 'Trident and the Law' by the lawyer Anabel Dwyer; 'Faslane Statement' by Sir Prof Richard Jolly; 'Ethical Analysis of Trident: The Application of Different Ethical Theories' by Senior Lecturer Dr Marion Hersh; 'The Future of the UK's Nuclear Deterrent: an Ethical Critique of the Government White Paper' by Prof John M. Hull; 'Nuclear Deterrence as a Red Herring' by Prof David Dwyer; 'Why Am I Here? Personal Reflections on Four Decades of Global Change'; by Ass Prof Bertil Egerö; 'Curbing Militarism in Japan and the Role of Academics' by Prof Toyoshima Kouichi; 'Gender and the Nuclear Weapons State' by PhD student Claire Duncanson and Dr Catherine Eschle; 'Weapons of Mass Destruction, Terror, and Human Security' by Prof Mary Kaldor; 'Sociology, Science and Nuclear Weapons' by Prof Bridget Fowler; and 'Trident and Public Opinion – Evidence from the 2007 Scottish Election Study' by Dr Rob Johns. In all 29 papers were presented and participants came from the UK, Sweden, Japan, the US, the Netherlands and Spain. Scholars came from departments such as biology, education, theology, government, sociology, politics, international relations, engineering, Arab & Islamic studies, anthropology, physics and astronomy, English, peace studies and East European studies, among others.

We had panels on, for example: Nuclear Ethics and Democracy; The Responsibility of Academics and Scholars; the Consequences of Nuclear Weapons – Trident and Nuclear Weapons of Mass Destruction.

The Global Context of the Academic Blockade

The academic blockades – as part of the Faslane 365 year long blockades of the Trident nuclear submarine base on the Clyde – have been an important struggle in a network of struggles that are spreading like wildfire. That may sound over optimistic but in fact it is in many ways an indication of the extent to which humans in general now feel that their very survival is at stake – whether they are the dispossessed in the Global South or students and academics in the Global North.

Donald Nonini[2] paints a frightening picture of current global conditions when he writes that:

> during the last three decades, corporations allied with Northern scientists and universities, national and regional governments, and international financial institutions (IFIS) have, through a variety of mechanisms associated with neo-liberal globalization... acted to dispossess large proportions of the world's population of their common resources and enclose them for profit making. Those belonging to the corporate alliance... have acted as if the people who have long depended on these resources for survival are no longer entitled to use them – or even to exist, since they have become increasingly superfluous to capitalist production.

Nonini points out that people are resisting this process, and that the context for this resistance has changed dramatically. Capitalism has always undergone periodic crises of over accumulation, but Nonini points out that there is a qualitatively different crisis unfolding in 'the form of multi-dimensional and increasingly ubiquitous degradations in the conditions of material life crucial to the existence of capitalism'. In the past the destruction of local livelihoods and ecosystems has been localised and corporations have simply moved on to plunder elsewhere, but now the 'weardown of local commons has been transformed into weardown of commons everywhere'. Nonini goes on to argue that 'the catalyst for the current crisis has been the massive devaluation of labour globally since the 1980s, brought about by the rise of post-Mao China. The new financing and credit mechanisms that lubricate ongoing global demand by increasing the debt-bearing capacities of middle and working classes in the North have only deferred the current crisis, and there are signs that the huge debt burden is reaching its structural limits'.

In this context, Nonini argues that corporations seek to reinvest capital surpluses by making massive incursions into the life supporting commons, drawing on market forces and state violence in order to overcome resistance to this 'universal commoditisation of the use-values central to the survival of human beings' such as forests, fresh water, public goods, intellectual property, etc.

---

[2] All the Nonini quotes are from Donald Nonini, 'The Global Idea of the Commons', in *Social Analysis* 50(3), 2006, pp. 164–177 (14)

Nonini points out that 'These oligarchic-corporate state hybrids appear structurally incapable of engaging in successful strategies for remediating the productive conditions that heretofore have been sustained by the various kinds of commons', but more optimistically he argues that 'social movements organised around the concerns of women, farmers, indigenous peoples, and transnational labour migrants, and those committed to environmental justice, workplace safety, resource conservation, health care, disability rights, and many related interests, are now posing and will continue to pose major threats to corporations' savage 'business as usual' and to the oligarchic-corporate states that support them'. Nonini argues that these struggles against the corporate alliance are 'multi-fronted, occur at more than one level of engagement, and are worldwide in scope. Appearing much of the time as uncoordinated, decentralised, and spontaneous, these movements are increasingly taking form self-consciously as connected to, and even part of, a broader global counter-movement'.

In a similar vein, Brian Barry[3] argues that the end of the corporate status quo is an ecological certainty given the ecological collapse which he argues is imminent as a result of the unrestricted pursuit of profit made possible by the corporate 'machinery of injustice'. Barry asks whether this will drag human society with it into ecological collapse, or whether the prospect of this will galvanise radical action built on social justice? The latter possibility may seem far-fetched but on the final page of his book, Barry argues that over the last hundred years Europe alone has moved from decade to decade from optimistic moves towards peace and justice to pessimistic moves towards war and injustice, and back again. Thus the future is far more uncertain than we can imagine and that is probably a reason for hope. A related point is that made in relation to state socialism in Russia where people in the West and East assumed it would last for centuries, whereas now in the post-socialist world it seems self-evident that historical changes meant that it could not have lasted. Our question is: why does fundamental change appear impossible before it happens, and why does it appear inevitable after the event? One key to the dynamic involved in relation to dramatic changes such as the shift to post-socialist Russia and to the dramatic changes Nonini and Barry anticipate, can perhaps be found in Bent Flyvbjerg's interpretation of Foucault which sees 'the privilege to engage in conflict and power struggle

---

3 Brian Barry, *Why Social Justice Matters*, Polity Press, London, 2005.

is part of freedom'[4]. Flyvbjerg argues that social conflicts produce the valuable ties that hold democratic societies together, and that a 'basic reason for the deterioration and loss of vitality of the Communist-dominated societies may be in their success in suppressing overt social conflict'.

However, a very similar point could be made in relation to the virtual hegemony of some key central assumptions in mainstream political and media represented thinking in the Capitalist-dominated current world order. Key economistic assumptions concerning material scarcity as only improvable through a future obsessed technologically developing society, and concerning a human nature which is assumed to be dominated by a materially self-interested competitiveness, are hardly questioned in the mainstream media, educational and political establishments. This very totalising account is one which everyone is supposed to subscribe to. Paradoxically, the fall of 'Communist-dominated societies' is used as further 'proof' of the 'naturalness' of our 'Capitalist-dominated' social order, whereas the lesson from that fall may be quite the opposite. The lesson may be that a totalising belief system has no resilience to integrate experiences and realities beyond itself, and so although from within its fall looks impossible (since there is nothing outside its reality, its account is taken to be reality), once it is so bloated with self-belief that is exactly when it is likely to fall, and fall fast.

So, where does academia come in to this? In seeking to examine how the world works we need to examine how we – as individuals and as academic disciplines – have been and are complicit or resistant to the actual historical processes of power which enable, or which crush, more just and peaceful forms of social relations. Perhaps the key is to recognise that our involvement in politics is unavoidable, and that therefore our positions need to be explicit and contestable rather than unspoken and uncontested. Politics is the struggle to establish what is of value, to decide (collectively or individually) what it is that makes life worth living and it involves seeking to construct theories about the world and strategies to change the world to enable such values to be realised[5]. Academics can and should be central to this process of envisioning and realising the kind of society we want, and

---

4   Bent Flyvbjerg, *Making Social Science Matter: Why Social Inquiry Fails and How it Can Succeed Again*, Cambridge University Press, Cambridge, 2001, p.108.

5   David Graeber, *Toward an Anthropological Theory of Justice: the False Coin of our own Dreams*, Palgrave, New York, 2001, pp.88 and 21.

'the real choice is between thinking about such questions explicitly or leaving them implicit – in which case one will inevitably end up drawing on one's own culture's unstated folk beliefs' and simply repeat the mistakes of the past, rather than learn from them.

The University Context of the Academic Blockade

The report *Study War No More*[6] highlighted the fact that 'Global military spending has been increasing steadily over the past five years, reaching a massive $1.2 trillion (£0.6 trillion) for 2006, a figure likely to be an under-estimate'. The report points out that in this context the UK 'spends significant amounts of tax payers' money on military Research and Development, currently around £3 billion from the Ministry of Defence alone' adding that the Ministry of Defence's Defence Industrial Strategy (DIS) and the Defence Technology Strategy (DTS) mark 'an expanded effort to involve universities more deeply in military R&D, by seeking, through the government's Defence Science and Technology Laboratory and the recently privatised QinetiQ, closer relationships with university scientists and technologists in the UK and abroad. Thus universities as centres of such expertise increasingly augment the R&D effort undertaken in UK and US military corporations.'

The *Study War No More* report highlights that research which aims to help tackle poverty, climate change and ill-health – and thus help to provide basic security for human populations – is under-funded ($50 billion in 2004) compared with a military R&D of around $85 billion in 2004. The researchers found that between 2001 and 2006, more than 1,900 military projects were conducted in the 26 UK universities covered by their report. They 'estimated the total value of these projects to be a minimum of £725 million', that over half were conducted in university engineering departments, and that through 'sub-contracting research to universities, which have world-class, publicly-funded staff and facilities, the military sector can keep overheads down and, in the case of military companies, profits up. The ease with which military organisations can influence university departments, through purchasing research and services and providing sponsorship, is indicative of the general trend towards commercialisation in higher education'.

---

[6] FOR and CAAT, *Study War No More: Military Involvement in* UK *Universities*, Fellowship of Reconciliation and Campaign against the Arms Trade, London 2007.

The report goes on to point out that public money from Research Council's collaborative research grants schemes heavily subsidise many of these military projects, and that this public financing of military research makes these projects more attractive to universities. Academics actively seek out military money because they are under pressure to attract research funding, especially since government policies have severely narrowed the possibilities of departments securing research money for disinterested research.

This needs to be understood as being part of broader and deeper changes being imposed on the rest of society. One way of understanding the forces at work here is in terms of the imposition of the Neoliberal agenda. Shore and Wright[7] describe the way in which this 'neo-liberal governmentality' has become endemic in universities. They define 'neo-liberal governmentality' as the use of 'the norms of the free market as the organising principles not only of economic life, but of the activities of the state itself and, even more profoundly, of the conduct of individuals'. They go on to describe how this involves not only the imposition of coercive discipline on the individual, but also new ways of ensuring the individual will themselves ensure that they comply with such a programme: a process which involves a combination of 'external subjection' and 'internal subjectification'.

In universities this has involved the rise of audit culture through which narrow measurements of achievements are used, normally related to publications and the securing of grants from government research boards which themselves narrow the field of research deemed appropriate. Individual success according to such criteria are measured by management, and Shore and Wright argue that this involves 'The substitution of trust by measurement, the replacement of academic autonomy by management control, the deliberate attempt to engineer competition and a climate of insecurity... The logic of the modern audit system is to produce not 'docile bodies' but 'self-actualised' auditable individuals.' This 'audit culture relies upon hierarchical relationships and coercive practices' whose 'key aim is to engender insecurity in the workplace'. For this reason 'the so-called 'quality revolution' with its rhetoric of 'empowerment' and 'accountability' is geared less to

---

7 Cris Shore and Susan Wright 'Coercive Accountability: The Rise of Audit Culture in Higher Education' in *Audit Cultures: Anthropological Studies in Accountability, Ethics and the Academy,* ed. Marilyn Strathern, Routledge, London and New York, 2000, p.61.

enhancing quality itself than to strengthening managerial control over the workforce'.[8]

Shore and Wright, citing Bleiklie, usefully identify three different layers of the university that have built up over time: firstly, the autonomous cultural institution in which the individual can pursue research for its own sake; secondly, the public body in which research is geared to the public good, and thirdly the market-oriented Neoliberal corporate enterprise driven by a logic of profitability in which individuals, departments and universities are pitted against each other in a win or lose competition for students, grants and prestige. These models overlay each other, and are associated with different and contradictory layers of expectations to which the academic is supposed to respond: expectations of independence and quality; expectations of loyalty and relevance; and expectations of maximising economic efficiency and one's individual position. Clearly the currently dominant third layer is not only the context in which funding is directed to some areas of research such as the development of weapons, but the logic as a whole also mirrors the mentality of the War economy itself.

The *Study War No More* report highlights the way in which universities have changed from being basically centres of learning and disinterested investigation to becoming what the report calls 'R&D contractors' in science and technology. This has profound implications for openness and democracy as corporate interests tend to favour secrecy, a monopoly of intellectual property rights and the silencing of dissidence. Alongside this, the commercialisation of universities can have a negative impact on those subjects which are not supported by big business. The report concludes with wonderful understatement 'that these trends are not good news for those in universities'.

Although the report focuses on disciplines such as engineering, subjects such as social anthropology – which might be thought of as being about as far from being useful to the military as any university subject could get – are not immune to this process. The military and defence-related funding currently being directed at anthropology demonstrates just how entangled universities are becoming in the military, and in an approach which sees war as a part of the solution rather than as a fundamental part of the problem.

---

[8]   Cris Shore and Susan Wright 'Whose Accountability? Governmentality and the Auditing of Universities'. *Parallax 10* (2), 2004, pp.100–116.

However, the response of most anthropologists to this process gives us hope that an effective resistance to this process can be mobilised.

For example, in America the Pentagon has implemented a new $40 million program called the Human Terrain System (HTS) which has begun recruiting graduates with degrees in anthropology to serve as cultural advisers in the military in Iraq and Afghanistan. Steve Fondacaro is a retired special operations colonel recruiting anthropologists to the HTS. In his justification for the HTS programme, his use of the term 'target population' is instructive: 'Cultural anthropologists are focused on understanding how societies make decisions and how attitudes are formed. They give us the best vision to see the problems through the eyes of the target population'.[9]

In response in September 2007, a group of scholars formed the Network of Concerned Anthropologists and drafted a 'Pledge of Non-Participation in Counter-Insurgency'.[10] By late October, the executive board of the American Anthropological Association issued a preliminary statement calling the Human Terrain System project 'an unacceptable application of anthropological expertise.' At the very least, as David Price notes, the Human Terrain System violates fundamental research ethics which: 'require that research subjects have voluntary meaningful informed consent, that they're told, you know, what's going to be done with the research, and that no harm come to those who are studied.'

In the UK the Economic and Social Research Council proposed funding research into the diverse causes of 'radicalisation' and transnational political violence. The ASA, the professional body of Anthropologists in the UK, were joined by the sociologists' professional body in opposing a research initiative which is clearly linked to 'UK Counter Terrorism policy overseas [and is therefore] prejudicial to the position of all researchers working abroad, including those who have nothing to do with this Programme.'[11] *The Times Higher Education* supplement reported the matter as follows: '*The Times Higher* learnt that the Foreign and Commonwealth Office had been inviting selected

---

9   Kambiz Fattahi, US army enlists anthropologists 2007 http://news.bbc.co.uk/1/low/world/americas/7042090.stm.

10   Roberto J. Gonzalez, 'Standing Up Against Torture and War: Why Anthropologists Should Vote on the Resolutions', in *Anthropology News*, March 2007, http://www.wm.edu/anthropology/Gonzalez-AnthNewsMarch2007.pdf.

11   April 2007 resolution of the ASA, http://www.theasa.org/news.htm.

academics to bid for funding under a £1.3 million project called 'Combating Terrorism by Countering Radicalisation'. The project is focused on countries identified by MI5's Joint Terrorism Analysis Centre. The FCO project, run in partnership with the Economic and Social Research Council and the Arts and Humanities Research Council, provoked a furious response from academics who claimed it was tantamount to asking researchers to act as spies for British intelligence.[12]

Although the 'furious response' led to the cancellation of the initial research project, it was then basically recreated in a very similar form and is now up and running. The militarization of all aspects of the university continues, and resistance to that militarization continues at all levels from seminar blockades outside Faslane nuclear submarine base to resolutions passed by overwhelming majorities at the meetings of professional bodies.

Relinquishing Coercive Power: Remembering Relational Power

Universities should provide a space from which people can critique and challenge the dominant assumptions driving the global insecurity wrecked by insatiable economic growth, and by reaching for military 'solutions' and threats where working to rebuild relationships of trust would instead restore and reweave the fabric of peaceful human relations.

The fact that universities so often provide ideological support for the power of the status quo should come as no surprise, however, since, as David Graeber points out, even critical social science thinkers end up repeating the dominant 'economism' in which 'the assumption is that 'objective' or 'scientific' analysis means trying to cut through to the level on which you can say people are being selfish.'[13] Graeber points out that the assumption that people's motives for acting come down to maximising self-interest permeates our thinking, yet is based on a cynical assumption concerning human nature: that no one ever does anything primarily out of concern for others. It is an assumption which legitimises a military and economic system which reduces social relationships (which involve a whole range of moral obligations grounded in reciprocity and mutuality) to objects. Graeber points out that:

---

[12] 26 October 2006

[13] David Graeber, *Toward an Anthropological Theory of Justice: the False Coin of our own Dreams*, Palgrave, New York, 2001, p.29.

'There is no area of human life, anywhere, where one cannot find self-interested calculation. But neither is there anywhere one cannot find kindness or adherence to idealistic principles: the point is why one, and not the other, is posed as 'objective' reality'.

Perhaps one of the key ways in which we are persuaded of this cynical view of human reality, is through the dominant understanding of power. Bertrand Russell wrote that just as physics is fundamentally concerned with understanding energy, so the social sciences are fundamentally concerned with understanding power. Perhaps what is needed, then, is for us to refuse to reduce our understanding of power to the dominant definition which sees it as the ability to make the other (whether human beings, other living things or objects) do things which they would not otherwise have done. This understanding of power as coercion dominates our understanding of international relations, relations between humans and other aspects of the environment, and also of course our experience of hierarchical contexts such as universities. It is not surprising, therefore, that it permeates the analysis of how social change happens that is dominant in universities.

The academic seminar blockades relied, for their success, on people choosing to engage in peaceful creative action despite the insistence of mainstream society that this isn't a way to change anything. That so many people participated, so effectively, and with such good humour and creativity, demonstrates the existence of a very different sort of power. To grasp the nature of such creative power one has only to reflect on the fact that, although looking towards the future radical progressive social change so often looks impossible, looking to the past radical progressive social change often looks as if it was inevitable. The question is: what makes the difference in the present? And the answer may well be that it is the very different experience and practice of power that is engaged in by those seeking to enable progressive social change.

The power at play here is a completely different power to that of coercion. It is one of creative and collective action, in which there is often an experience of an alignment between the little actions one is taking part in and the larger picture of global politics and global change. This alignment is sometimes experienced as a clash between the truth of what needs to happen and the truth of what is actually happening in the world, and sometimes it is experienced as truth unfolding, as the world changing unexpectedly in line with one's understanding of what has to change. Distinguishing between these experiences can be tricky. For example, when we sent out the call for the second academic blockade, one academic who had taken part in the first blockade wrote to us all to say that there was no point having a second academic blockade since the vote in the London parliament after the first blockade had confirmed that the UK government was going to push ahead with upgrading Trident anyway.

From his perspective there was a clash between our actions and the broader political reality, and we had been defeated. From up here in Scotland, however, the situation looked quite different. Here we were moving towards a Scottish parliamentary election in which a party which opposed nuclear weapons had a chance of winning, and in fact it did win. In the analysis presented by one of the academics at the second academic blockade in the month after the election, an analysis referred to by the new Scottish government ministers as well, this electoral success was partly because campaigns such as Faslane 365 had worked so hard to keep the issue of nuclear weapons uppermost in the public's mind. The new Scottish government immediately established official dialogue with those who had been protesting, and set out to establish ways of stopping the upgrading of Trident.

Perhaps all great social change emerges out of the accumulated impact of thousands upon thousands of small acts of compassion and defiance which collectively act to enable people to realise that ideals are not unattainable. Perhaps these acts demonstrate that, on the contrary, such ideals are the realistic expression of fundamental and realisable human needs for peace, justice and dialogue. Perhaps, in seeking to stop the work of the Trident nuclear submarine base, academics and all the other creative protesting groups sought to add their small acts of compassion and defiance to a world wide movement calling on those in politics, in the media and in wider society, to realise that the future is entirely up to us, and we can make it.

This notion of creative power as arising out of the relationship between our deepest hopes and the willingness to engage in – often seemingly hopeless – action to bring these hopes to fruition, echoes Cree indigenous notions of power. For the Cree of Northern Quebec: '...power is an emerging coincidence between the anticipation (social thought) and the configuration of the world (event), a congruence that this anticipation helps to actualise through action...' Power is a social process, a relationship in thoughts and actions among many beings, whereby potentiality becomes actuality... Power in the Cree sense may have analogies to a concept of truth, i.e. thoughts that come to be. We might say that in this view the power that is worth seeking is truth unfolding in social relationships, rather than power as a control of one person over another.'[14]

This brings power and coincidence together in a way that is counter-intuitive from within the orthodoxy that permeates the social sciences and permeates our dominant world order. It does, however, suggest quite a startling potential resolution to the question of whether progress can only be made by seizing state power, or whether we can change the world without taking power. The implication being that rather than seeking to seize power or refusing to take power, we can act in a way which reconfigures, redistributes and reorientates power through remaining open to those who appear to still be holding all the power in terms of the 'control of one person over another'.

A small example comes to mind from just after being arrested during one of the blockades at Faslane, when we were being held in one of the hired vans the police were using. When one policeman was left on his own with us for a brief spell, one of us handed him a badge which said 'Question Authority' on it. He looked at it and smiled, saying 'my boss wouldn't like this'. On hearing that he was welcome to keep it, he hesitated before smiling again and putting it in his pocket. His willingness to receive this gift was perhaps made possible because the words on the badge and his action were perfectly aligned: he was questioning authority as he pocketed the badge; he was identifying with the spirit of our action out of choice, as we were being arrested and taken to the cells, we were also building relationships of trust and asserting that the desire to ensure a peaceful society both clearly motivates many to join the profession of the police force, and clearly motivates many of us to object to the state of nuclear terror.

Engaging in actions such as this, not only reminds participants of our wider responsibilities, and builds our networks of support that enable us to challenge complicity in the ongoing structures of violence, it also encourages others to do likewise. The question to ask, perhaps, is not why did some academics engage in this form of nonviolent collective action, but what stops academics in general from acting in this way, given that – in the

---

[14] Harvey Feit, 'James Bay Crees' Life Projects and Politics: Histories of Place, Animal Partners and Enduring Relationships', in *In the Way of Development: Indigenous Peoples, Life Projects and Globalisation,* eds. Mario Blaser, Harvey A. Feit and Glenn McRae, Zed Books, London, 2004.

global context – they are in a privileged position from which to insist on sane solutions?

Perhaps a large part of why it is hard for academics to do this is because of the way the academy is held and dominated by the same core assumptions that permeate wider society concerning who we are. To release this hold is not simply a theoretical exercise. Releasing this hold requires recognising that ninety per cent of the institutional practices of universities is embedded in hierarchical disciplining structures which themselves forever reinforce in our experience the sense that reality comes down to the individual in isolation competing with others and judged by some higher order: reinforces our sense that reality comes down to isolation, insecurity and competition.

Academics like Cris Shore, Sue Wright and Marilyn Strathern[15] have shed bright light on the audit culture of universities, and on the way in which this shapes the core understandings in academia. Telling the story of the way in which the social sciences have been part of a process of governmentality which has served the dispossession of indigenous and colonised peoples overseas, and helped shape policies which have maintained structures of inequality at home, is part of the process of reclaiming the social and natural sciences as egalitarian fields of cooperative and creative learning which have the potential to recognise the complex nature of reality and help reshape society for good. Telling the story of how the academic disciplines are practised within a hierarchical setting which is framed to make us act as if we were economistic beings self-calculating our way through the academy, is part of the process of reclaiming and replenishing rather than denying and exploiting the emotional and intellectual commons we share with our students and colleagues.

The academic blockades were a powerful part of this process of strengthening our resolve and our connectedness, and educating ourselves as much as others. Such engaged activity in which words are actions and conferences are blockades, can restore our sense of humanity and our ability to return to the universities and turn our academic practice into the practice of

---

[15] Cris Shore and Susan Wright 'Coercive Accountability: The Rise of Audit Culture in Higher Education' in *Audit Cultures: Anthropological Studies in Accountability, Ethics and the Academy* ed. Marilyn Strathern, Routledge, London and New York, 2000.

active engagement with colleagues, with students and with the creative making of a world where we each know that the surest route to experiencing our own well-being is through enabling the well-being of others.

How Do We Do it the Other Way Round? Taking Activism into the Academy

How Do We Make Academia Relevant for Activism?

Clearly, academics need to stop being tools for contemporary hegemonic power in the way that has become normal: providing 'analysis for hire', new power techniques and tactical tool-kits, and ideological legitimacy to the status quo. By perpetuating the assumed non-ideological 'impartiality' or 'objectivity' of science we just become useful tools for those who have the coercive power to implement our findings, innovations, knowledge schemes or theoretical models. In Europe academics have, in turn, been willing instruments of the Church, the state, and now, the market. We need to base our work on a critical understanding of how power permeates academia: in the formulation of research questions, the funding of projects, the application of methodology, the acceptance of findings and publication, as well as the promotion of careers. It is only by starting off from a critical standpoint that we can make 'real impartial objective' science and, more importantly, make a 'human needs relevant' science.

Alongside the dominant forms of coercive compliance, academia also has a strong history of critical work and a refusal to simply comply with power. Universities, especially university students, have a long-standing tradition of rebellions against various injustices. The classic rebellion of 1968 was not confined to Paris and Berkeley, it was international. But we also have the 1988 resistance in Burma, the 1989 student occupation of Tiananmen Square in Beijing, as well as those in many universities in Africa throughout the 1990s.

Academic history has always contained undercurrents of counter-hegemonic or marginal discourses. It is partly possible to understand the universities of the Enlightenment period as a form of resistance to the hegemony of medieval Christianity. The numerous earlier critical traditions, such as Marxism, liberalism, feminism, environmentalism, post-colonialism and peace research, are major sources of contemporary critical projects. In many ways they have today become established and integrated within academic hierarchies. Sometimes this can simply mean that they provide theoretical frameworks and understandings within which coercion-compliant research can be conducted; but often this can mean that they can provide the basis for radical interventions aimed at questioning and challenging dominant power relations. In this latter form, they can protect disciplines, resources and academic status, and serve as learning-experiences and protective environments for new critical actors.

So, What Is the Role of Engaged Academics, the Role of Intellectuals, in Social Change?

One way in which 'organic intellectuals' (Gramsci) or 'movement intellectuals' (Eyerman & Jamison) combine theory and practical action (praxis or integrated theory) is by being analytical within their engaged work on movements.[16] They don't ask academic research questions emanating from the interests of academia, university disciplines or funding agencies. They do academic work emanating from the interests of movements. They question prevalent knowledge, established structures and hegemonic discourses, and they look for the possibilities of social change and the role of social movements within that change work. In doing this, they don't serve the propaganda interests of these movements, they are not trying to be the spin doctors or ideology designers of movements. They serve the interests of movements by critically identifying and analysing that which hinders radical social change, and by expanding the avenues of critical action deemed possible. Sometimes this can involve being disloyal to both academic hierarchies and movement leaderships.

The analytical work of these intellectuals involves both the deconstruction of hegemonic discourses and the reconstruction of critical theory. The practical actions of these intellectuals serve an essential purpose, to fuse theory and action. It is impossible to understand and analyse the political strategies and tactical roads towards real social change without also engaging in practical political work yourself. That is because radical and political action, the praxis of critical theory, is a matter of practical knowledge: about *how* to do things. Any *practical knowledge* – be that typing, reading a book or

---

[16] Ron Eyerman and Andrew Jamison, *Social Movements – A Cognitive Approach*, The Pennsylvania State University Press, USA, 1991.

organising a civil disobedience campaign – can only be learnt by doing it.[17] In the same way that a dancer, football player, car driver or child learning to bicycle, only learn from trying, making mistakes, adjusting and readjusting – all practical knowledge is a matter of combining the mind and the body. Thus, intellectuals who strive to be relevant to a radical politics need to do radical politics and reflect on that practice.

The only real privilege that comes with being an academic is the availability of resources to aid thorough reflection; resources such as time, interested colleagues, an office, access to the literature, equipment such as computers, and so forth. However, with that privilege comes responsibility, a responsibility to use those resources in the interest of – and to the benefit of – the wider community and humanity from which those resources are drawn, and to whom they really belong. The responsibility of engaged academics is to serve the interests of all, which means serving the interests of those who are not being heard: to serve the interests of the poor, the hunted, the tortured and all others who suffer the consequences of a militarised, genocidal, repressive, racialised, sexist, class-dominant, homophobic modernity.

We need to be problem oriented in order to prioritise those kinds of problems that plague humanity – dictatorship, repression, poverty, injustice, unsustainability, and so forth. In line with this, we need to take an approach like that taken in medicine: we need to be explicitly normative, we need to take the side of those who suffer and we need to try to expand the possibilities for solutions. As such science needs to be a matter of applicable knowledge, serving the needs of those whose needs are not being recognised or addressed, of those who are suffering. But, unlike medicine, we need to not simply work alongside the dominant inequalities and discipline people according to dominant discourses and techniques, we need to reconstruct science, not just social science, so that we stop serving war, repression and private profit. We need a science that take the side of peace, justice, liberation and community.

How Do We Make Academic Work Relevant?

How do we build an actively engaged academy from the inside? Clearly there is a need for the systematic, collaborative and innovative change of

---

[17] Pierre Bourdieu, *Practical Reason: On the Theory of Action*, Polity Press, Oxford, 1998.

'normalised' academic work so that critical and engaged academic work becomes more possible, more normal and more effective. In Sweden a network[18] of social movement scholars, 'laymen researchers' from social movements and movement activists was formed in 2005. Since then this collaboration has created a number of conferences in which recent studies of movements and the movements' own evaluations and analyses are discussed together. What unites participants is their common interest in the way critical reflection can inform social change, and can be changed by social change. In 2007 a broad range of scholars created the global Resistance Studies Network[19] based at the School of Global Studies at Gothenburg University in Sweden, in which seminars, blog discussions, journals, and books on 'resistance' are produced. In Scotland similar networks of engaged academic activists are emerging such as the Public Interest Network based at the University of Strathclyde[20] and the academic activist network NASPIR[21]. As well as academic activist research networks focused on research there is also – in Sweden, Scotland and elsewhere – a growing interest on the part of postgraduate students in taking postgraduate courses which enable them to critically reflect on social change through being actors in progressive social change movements. The recent Masters course at the University of Glasgow on 'Global Movements, Social Justice and Sustainability' is a good example of this growing interest and of the space for critical reflection which Universities can make available.

In order to forge an integration of academic work and social movements, research work by scholars and students need to become relevant to those social movements. Issues, research questions and research processes need to be guided by how far they are relevant for the type of problems social movements struggle with. But this needs to be done through a critical approach which is also directed towards social movements themselves, thereby ensuring that researchers don't end up simply making propaganda for organisations, and instead building on the (potential) value-alliance between engaged academics and social movements, alliances built on core-values such as democracy, equality, emancipation, and truth.

---

[18] The Network of Critical Movement Studies and Social Change.

[19] www.resistancestudies.org.

[20] www.publicinterest.ac.uk.

[21] www.naspir.net.

The Importance of Academic Activist Networks

It is virtually impossible to make a difference as a critical academic if you act alone and isolated from your peers. To be successful, resistance and social change work needs to be developed and sustained from within a supportive and challenging community. Such a context can provide the necessary nurture, contacts, support and advice that enable you to survive hardship, crisis and everyday difficulties. It is important not to underestimate the difficulties than can arise from choosing an unconventional academic career.

Other related networks which can be helpful in creating the necessary academic community might be the Northern Network of Critical Global Scholars (North-Net)[22], the Anarchist Studies Network[23] or the WebRing for Communication and Militant Research on Precarity.[24]

Postscript: Visioning the Future: Academics at the Final 365 Blockade

On the last day of the year-long Faslane 365 blockades, four of us drove from Glasgow early in the morning and Becka parked a mile or so from the base. We got out and were greeted by a beautiful view out over the mountains and the misty glens. A couple of policemen and two workmen were standing there – one of the workmen said he hoped we'd carry on blockading so that he wouldn't have to go in to work in the base that day! We walked down through the hills and through the morning mist, to be greeted by a chaos of colour and sound and lines of bright reflective policemen being swirled around by multicoloured protectors blocking all the roads.

One of the most powerful images from that final 1 October blockade was of a smiling determined woman in a wheelchair locked on to another woman who together kept one road closed for what seemed like hours. One of the most touching moments was a mother being escorted by police to where her partner was being arrested, so that their young child could give him a kiss before he was taken away. There was fantastic humour by the clown army and people on stilts spreading crime scene tape everywhere, powerful

---

[22] http://www.northernnetwork.blogspot.com/.

[23] http://www.anarchist-studies-network.org.uk/.

[24] http://www.geocities.com/immateriallabour/precarity-webring.html.

singing and drumming from the band 'Seize the day' and from the choirs. There was a handful of politicians from the anti-nuclear Scottish parties, including the government. There was an extraordinary Iona Community Church service that ended in the middle of the road with a young church minister arrested despite promising his wife he'd be home that day.

The four of us, who had participated in the academic seminar blockades, managed to hang our 'Universities against Trident' banner on the perimeter fence, alongside many others. The blockade that final day was uplifting, but as Catherine pointed out later, it was strange to be there without holding a seminar in the road in our own inimitable way.

1 October was the last day of the Faslane 365 blockades, but it was another day in the gathering storm for peace. In the following weeks some of us were able to accompany other blockaders to meetings with members of the Scottish government, and attended the extraordinary summit in Glasgow on disarming Trident called by the new Scottish government. In extraordinary times extraordinary things happen.

When we got back to the car the mist had cleared. The beautiful glen that had been hidden beneath the mist when we arrived was in fact the Loch with the huge nuclear base in it. It will be a peaceful Glen and Loch again one day... and this is part of the story of how it happened.

Students and the Strident Tent State

JO TYABJI

From 28 June to 3 July 2007, some hundred students from across Britain converged on Peaton Wood for the week-long national student blockade of Faslane and Coulport – the Strident Tent State. My involvement began a year and a quarter before when I first heard of Faslane 365, and started talking to friends and family about how and when to go, and with who. At that time a group of students at my university organised a day-long event in a nearby park called the Noughties Festival. It was somewhere between a festival, a fun-fair (there was one!) and a rally, sending out the 'Noughty Message': 'Hiroshima and Nagasaki – never again', and setting it to music. Inspired by this, I started thinking about an 'event' that would run alongside a national student blockade, gathering people together to envisage a nuclear free world, and the practical steps needed to get there.

Talking was spurred into more immediate action by a friend who pointed out that while it was all very well to aim to gather students from across

Britain and beyond for a large summer blockade, unless we took part in Faslane 365 earlier on by mobilising within our own universities and communities there may not be a 'rolling blockade' to take part in. He was part of the early Nottingham students' blockade, one of many really successful blockades throughout the year which were mobilised by students. On his urging I went back to uni in September and started mobilising for a smaller blockade in January, to coincide with the academics' blockade.

The January blockade was a really good experience, and a steep learning curve. The months before were a crash course in the kind of awareness raising needed to both get the message out about Trident around our town and colleges, and gather enough people for an effective blockade. After debates, talks, die-ins and film showings we ended up with 25 students from Oxford, Sussex, Cambridge and Edinburgh. We spent the first day of our slot, Saturday, 6 January, protesting at the gates, and performing a scratch *Twelfth Night* in nearby Helensburgh. We handed out mince pies to passers-by and told them who we were and why we were there. On the Sunday we were joined by 70 academics, who held an open air seminar in front of the gates – and then of course in the road. We were locked on for six hours, a satisfyingly long time, though as it was a Sunday there was less traffic than there would otherwise have been. We had chosen to go ahead and blockade on the Sunday rather than a week-day in order to join up with the academics, and the trade-off was definitely worth it: the presentations in the 'seminar' approached the concept of 'deterrence' from a wide range of disciplines – international relations, politics, human psychology, even maths. It was really good, after the final flurried weeks of entirely logistical preparation, to sit back in the rain in the road and remember why we were there. Dr Rebecca Johnson spoke about her work as founder of the Acronym Institute for Disarmament Diplomacy, and the pennies started to drop. With the examples of Climate Camp, the Noughties Festival and our own shared experience to feed off we evolved our plan for a national students' block into a week-long event that would unite action with critical interrogation of everything that lies behind a policy of nuclear deterrence.

Personally, my vision for what such a week could achieve, and what I thought it needed to achieve, was informed by an Oxford Research Group workshop that I attended in the June before Faslane 365 started. It was arranged by a group of Oxford Quakers, who were to take part in the blockade, to look at some other means and approaches to opposing nuclear weapons. I was surprised to learn that to some dialogue and direct action were viewed as antithetical, as I saw Faslane 365 as part of my ongoing opposition to Trident, and as only one way in which I would make my convictions clear. I was intrigued and attracted to the idea of long-term contact between citizens and decision makers, painstakingly keeping the channels of communication open in order to patiently work towards persuasion, while continually recognising that there is always some common ground somewhere. I had no idea whether I could hold a position like that for a sustained period of time – I'd had some experience campaigning against the arms trade, for example, and wasn't sure I could keep in view whatever slim common ground I shared with an arms trader. It was emphasised that the more person-to-person approach of opening and sustaining dialogue, and the atmosphere-shaping, pressure-raising tools of nonviolent direct action are both extremely useful and necessary. Some participants weren't at all sure a single person could do both at once, I wanted to try – I still do. In January, listening to Rebecca in the rain, it seemed possible: Rebecca comes from a background of direct action, taking a firm principled position in a very visible and challenging manner, but she has also become expert in the intricacies of disarmament diplomacy, without ever leaving behind her roots.

We (eventually!) called the event the Strident Tent State after the example of the Sussex Tent State, inspired by a practical protest which began at Rutgers University in the US in 2003, to demonstrate against the unprecedented cuts to state education funding in the wake of the wars in Afghanistan and Iraq. Rutgers Tent State University (TSU) creates an alternative, democratic university in the midst of the campus, protesting at the status quo and creating an alternative in the same act. A coalition of organisations bring workshops, seminars, speaker sessions, art, music and creativity, involving and uniting students, staff, community members and grass roots organisations. The central focus of the Rutgers TSU was 'education not war' – to restore the funding cuts and draw attention to opposition to the war. There are obvious links, though not all of these became clear to me until I was actually at the Strident Tent State, sitting in a workshop run by one of the organisers of the Rutgers TSU, who had amazingly heard about Strident while on a visit to the UK. Initially we just wanted to adopt the spirit of inquiry and interrogation we thought the idea of a 'tent state' held – a space created to explore how things are done, and how they should be done differently. It would help us see our blockade as part of other forms of opposition, not a one-off flash in the pan, but a stepping stone to other things. In the spirit of academic involvement in 'real' issues I even wrote my linguistics coursework on Tony

Blair's introduction to the White Paper on Trident – its amazing how nuclear weapons are a 'deterrent' when they're ours, and 'blackmail' when they're Iran's.

After the January blockade there was a small but feisty group of people up for organising the as-yet unnamed event, but we were really conscious that we wanted to be gathering people from across the country to organise and envision with us how it was going to be. We decided to set up a 'national planning meeting' for the same day as the anti-Trident and Stop the War march in London on 24 February 2007. Westminster Quaker Meeting kindly gave us the use of a room in the Friends Meeting House on St Martin's Lane, which allowed us to flier what felt like the entire march and invite them to a meeting that evening in the centre of London. We advertised to university mailing lists, People & Planet, Youth and Student CND, any student groups we could find on the Faslane 365 website, and mustered a pretty good turn out. We came away from this with three working groups – Logistics, Events and Promotion – and a sense that it was really going to happen. We had our site, thanks to Jane Tallents and Sam Lloyd Jones telling us about Peaton Wood, and now we had some sort of structure for organising food, travel, mobilisation and booking all the speakers and workshop leaders we wanted to get hold of in the four and half months left to us.

We decided to do the 'scratch *Twelfth Night*' at the January blockade in order to give a time and place for interaction to take place with the local residents of Helensburgh. Many local people were very supportive of the blockade, as we found from the car-horns, waves and thumbs up from people driving past. However, some time after our January blockade, residents of Helensburgh, Garelochhead and the Rosneath Peninsula formed a group called Peninsula24seven, to protest against what they felt to be an unremitting and unacceptable disruption to the lives of local residents, particularly in the case of school children trying to get to exams and care workers needing to access the Peninsula urgently.

Our contact with Peninsula24seven came about because some of their members read our website, and the forum where we were trying to encourage participation and discussion of plans for the week. A post I wrote hastily and in the spirit of opening discussion was taken as a firm plan of action. Blockading groups had been using the grass verge opposite Faslane and next to the turning to Faslane Cemetery to camp on since October 2006 – we camped there in January 2007. My suggestion was to use the verge as a camping place for blockading groups who wanted to move closer to the base during Strident, rather than travelling from Peaton Wood on the day of their blockade. A member of Peninsula24seven posted on our forum explaining that the close proximity to the cemetery, and the use of the small cemetery car park for minibuses (and police vans!) was creating a lot of tension amongst residents. In January a man had reacted very angrily to us hanging a banner which read 'diplomacy = talks = peace / deterrence = threats = war' from the road sign which directs the turning to Faslane Cemetery. To people who knew nothing about us, particularly the elderly wishing to visit the graves of loved ones, I can see that a series of unknown groups of people could be a dismaying prospect. I immediately replied saying that we had no intention of behaving disrespectfully, and that we wouldn't camp or use the area anywhere near the cemetery if it was the cause of so much upset.

I asked the writer if he would be willing to talk to me, to increase our mutual understanding and also to give me advice on how to avoid unintentionally antagonising the residents of the surrounding villages. It was the start of a series of extremely interesting and difficult conversations. Difficult because we both had to start by stripping away our assumptions about each other, but wholly beneficial as I learnt an enormous amount about the way blockading groups were perceived by some parts of the surrounding communities. For example, I learnt that a lot of people had been very upset when a blockading group hung a skull and crossbones flag from the road sign by Faslane Cemetery. The extreme anger of the man who had got out of his car to shout at one of us in January made emotional sense when taken in the context of a series of events, and the sense of invasion of a sacred space obviously felt by some people. The sporadic and often very brief contact between each new set of blockaders and local residents meant that blockaders often came across as patronising. For example, the member of Peninsula24seven I spoke to first had grown up in the area and was very much opposed to the existence of Trident, to the expansion of the base he had seen in his lifetime, and to the annexation of land in the surrounding area by the MOD. He described how the local economy had been swallowed up by forced purchase orders.

Unfortunately, rumours that we intended to use the cemetery during the Strident Tent State grew into rumours that we were going to hold a disco and barbecue in the cemetery. Appalled at this misinformation, we contacted Peninsula24seven, and began a dialogue that ranged from attempting to reassure the group of Garelochhead residents who had been distributing fliers claiming this, local press and even the MSP Jackie Baillie who had extraordinarily raised this in the Scottish parliament without checking its veracity, to a wider dialogue about the Strident blockading groups. Hannah (another of the organisers) and I arrived in Scotland, two days before the Tent State officially began and we released a joint press release with Peninsula24seven. Sadly 'peace protesters and local residents agree to work together' doesn't make a great headline, but the local paper still published a small piece reporting that we weren't 'at loggerheads', as had previously been claimed. The whole process was a steep learning curve, and there was probably no way we were going to end up agreeing on every point, but I was very glad to talk to the three members of Peninsula24seven, and learn more about their different view points – even this limited contact brought us a long way.

On 27 June, after a day and a half of intensive work setting up tents and transporting kitchen equipment, people began to arrive. Nick, one of the organisers, travelled from his home in Wales all the way to London in order to drive my parents' car up to Scotland full of equipment. Others did equally heroic feats of transportation, from samba drums to just themselves – not easy through all the flooding! I have a photo of the first complete strangers to turn up – suddenly Strident wasn't a figment of our imaginations any more, but a living breathing space being created by these new amazing people. Needless to say they weren't strangers by the end of the week. By the weekend I had given up on knowing the names of everyone who arrived, as between 100 and 150 people passed through. Most stayed the whole week, bar the time they spent in custody, and others came and went as life dictated. There were even people arriving on the last day, who had determinedly slogged it the length of Britain to take part.

The first blockading group headed off very early on the morning of the 28th, and the workshops started up. People who had just arrived pitched straight in to gathering wood, cooking, planning actions and joining discussions. Hannah had spoken to me about the importance of the Tent State being a shared space, a community we would build together to demonstrate how inclusiveness, equity and consensus can work, and now I saw it working. My previous experience of consensus decision making had all been through young Quaker events, but at Strident I learnt some of the processes needed to ensure people listen and are listened to in any group. There were late night discussions around the fire, early morning blockades, workshops on political process, clowning and protest. We bathed in the Trident-trawled Loch Long and swam out to the MOD police boats that were invariably positioned opposite the camp. The week was a strange, awe-filling mix of beauty and determination, work and song and dance. One of my favourite memories is of the people who'd been cooking one particular lunchtime singing 'I'm gonna lay down my sword and shield' as we queued up for the (always delicious!) food they were doling out in generous portions.

As a community I think our greatest achievement was the way we responded to the terrorist attack at Glasgow Airport on Saturday 30th. It wasn't immediately clear what had happened, and what this would mean for the Strathclyde Police. Memories of the way news filtered out over the days after the 7/7 bombings made it hard to assess whether we would be pulling police resources away from a real need to be in Glasgow. Sam and I were police liaison over the course of the week (another incredible learning curve!), and were asked by our point of contact in the Strathclyde police not to blockade for 24 hours. We took this to the camp, and a meeting was held to decide what to do. I think everyone felt that the terrorist attack was reason to be even more firm in our belief that, far from protecting anyone, nuclear weapons exacerbate the state the world is in. The question was how to get this across without being glib about the real security risk surrounding the attack – both Faslane and Coulport were on high alert, and Strathclyde were on tenterhooks at the prospect of further attacks in Glasgow. Almost 20 years on from Lockerbie, it had shaken people a lot. At the start of the meeting there were some radically divergent points of view, but the process of the meeting meant we emerged with absolute consensus: we would assure the police, MOD and civilian, that we wouldn't engage in any disruptive protests, such as blockading, until midnight on Sunday 31 July. This was over the 24 hours we'd been asked for, and reflected the fact that we felt as soon as Strathclyde police had had time to redeploy their resources we wanted to show in the strongest possible terms that our opposition to Trident had not wavered, but was strengthened by what had happened. On the Saturday night some of us went and held a candlelit vigil at the gates of Coulport, where the warheads are kept, in memory of all victims of terrorism and war, including the state-committed atrocities of Hiroshima and Nagasaki. On Sunday, we protested in a non-disruptive fashion at Faslane and Coulport, and of course peacefully as ever. On Monday, bearing in mind that Strathclyde were not so stretched that they couldn't police a motorcross event nearby, 37 people were arrested as we blockaded both gates of Faslane and all three roads leading to Coulport.

There is far more to tell, of course. There were two sets of documentary makers at Strident, one aiming to take their film around festivals, and the other aiming to take it into secondary schools. Over the course of the week we heard about organisations and networks we could get involved with from Nuke Watch to the Clandestine Insurgent Rebel Clown Army, via the new EU-wide 'Ban All Nukes Generation'. On the last day we had a 'what next?' meeting, where lots of people said very firmly that the Tent State needed to happen again, and that they could see a future for Strident as a network for people to organise actions, direct or indirect, against nuclear weapons. There is lots more to be done, Faslane 365 has put us in a really good position to go on and do it!

Faslane 365

LEON ROSSELSON[25]

Autumn trees are red and gold in the light of the breaking dawn
The wind rakes the waters of the Loch and the rain drives down
And we gather at the gate of the submarine base where a thousand
    Hiroshimas are deployed
Behind that grey iron fence topped with razor wire.
And the police are there to uphold the law and they clear the way so the
    early shift
Can service the machine whose end is nuclear war.

And we stand at the gate with our placards and our banners and we sing
Our voices are scattered and battered by the wind yet still we sing –
WE SHALL NOT GIVE UP THE FIGHT WE HAVE ONLY STARTED...

I'm wet and I'm cold and I'm losing the will to live
And I'm wondering, as are the police, what we hope to achieve.
But there's a gang of dangerous armed extremists up there making plans
They've got to be stopped and we haven't got much time.
Conspiracy to murder and to cause explosions, that's what they've got in
    mind
And to be silent is to be complicit in a crime.

---

[25] Leon is a well-known songwriter and singer and sang this at the Power of the Word Block, 5 June 2007.

So we stand at the gate with our placards and our banners and we sing
Our voices are scattered and battered by the wind yet still we sing –
NO MORE KEEPING QUIET FOR ME, NO MORE, NO MORE...

At 11am from the base a hooter is heard
And we stand in silence to remember the glorious dead.
And down at the Cenotaph they'll be there, wearing solemn faces, our
     mind-locked leaders
Who believe you can settle disputes with a nuclear bomb.
Hard power war junkies intent on making sure
There'll be millions more dead to remember for generations to come.

So we stand at the gate with our placards and our banners and we sing
Our voices are scattered and battered by the wind yet still we sing –
TRIDENT, TRIDENT MONEY DOWN THE DRAIN
IT CAN KILL ALL LIVING CREATURES AND THEN KILL THEM ALL AGAIN...

From the hills to the north of the Loch through the misty rain
I can see the heavy grey shape of a nuclear submarine.
Any enterprising terrorist with a rocket launcher could easily take it out
In which case Trident, as a deterrent, wouldn't be much good.
And, I wonder, would they really use it? They've got to mean and to say
     that they would
But if they use it, it wasn't a deterrent and we're all screwed.
So we stand at the gate with our placards and our banners and we sing
Though our voices are scattered and battered by the wind yet still we sing –
TRIDENT OUT CLOSE THE BASE TRIDENT IS MASS MURDER...

A gust of wind sweeps the clouds away and the sky is clear
How beautiful the Loch would be were the base not there.
So it's 76 billion pounds for a weapon that can't be used.
Are they mad? Or are we with our hopeful chants and our naïve faith
In our peaceful power to challenge the state and our belief that people are
     good
And wouldn't want to turn children to ash and poison the earth.
So we stand at the gate with our placards and our banners and we sing
Our voices are scattered and battered by the wind yet still we sing –
WE SHALL NOT GIVE UP THE FIGHT WE HAVE ONLY STARTED
WE HAVE ONLY STARTED WE HAVE ONLY STARTED...

CHAPTER 8

Local Impact around the Rosneath Peninsula

JANE TALLENTS

2 APRIL 2007 – six months into Faslane 365 and once again we were at the North Gate of Faslane at 7am, putting our banners up. But this morning was different. We were expecting a group of protesters, not one more group of anti-Trident protesters from far and wide, but local people coming to protest against us. I felt sick, I was nervous and I really didn't want to be there. But as a member of the Faslane 365 steering group and as a local resident of 23 years standing I knew that I had to be there, to take responsibility and to listen to what people had to say.

An impressive hundred or so of the newly formed anti-protest group (later called Peninsula24seven[1]) arrived on foot from the nearby village of Garelochhead. Although it was the first day of the Easter holidays a good number of young people had risen from their beds before 7am to join in. The banners and placards were very creative saying things like 'Protesters Peace Off'. Encouragingly, they had, like us, made a commitment to conduct their protest in a nonviolent way.

The media, having not given us the regular kind of coverage we would have liked to have seen, given the newsworthiness of every one of our blockading groups, predictably turned up that morning in search of conflict. With a sinking feeling in my stomach I agreed to do a live interview on BBC Radio Scotland alongside Ian Todd, who had taken the role of spokesperson for the locals. I don't feel myself to be a natural at media work, but again I felt that as the local member of the steering group I could at least try and put our side of the argument in a clear but non confrontational way. I must admit that I was also worried that some of the people who were there with us for the first time did not begin to understand the complicated local scene and would unwittingly make things worse by saying things that locals felt

---

[1] www.peninsula24seven.co.uk.

to be patronising or dismissive. The BBC interviewer was fairly predictable, as was Ian Todd. We both had our say but were polite to each other.

I crossed back to 'our' side of the road, saying hello as I passed the other group to Maxine, a local taxi driver who lives near to Faslane, and whom I've known for many years. We were a much smaller group. We had resisted the urge to summon everyone we could get hold of. This wasn't about whose gang was the biggest! We had also asked the Clowns, members of CIRCA, the Clandestine Insurgent Rebel Clown Army, not to come clowning at the North Gate that morning as they had intended. We had not made this request lightly. Many of them had travelled a long way to come together to protest in their unique way and they had picked the dates – 1 and 2 April – to coincide with All Fools Day months before. But we felt that it might be misunderstood and even the presence of clowns might look like we were making fun of locals or dismissing their concerns. The clowns had had a long meeting the previous evening which some members of the steering group had attended while they reached consensus about not clowning as they has planned. In the end a few of them came up to the gate in their non-clowning attire and made a really helpful contribution. Katy was also there with her tea stall so that we could offer locals a cup of tea. But few of them ventured to 'our' side of the road.

So what had led to this situation? Here were two groups of people standing on opposite sides of the road, both wanting peace but apparently having radically different ideas about what that meant.

Ever since nuclear weapons arrived on the Clyde there have been protests. There were sit-ins against the US Polaris presence in the Holy Loch in the 60s. At Faslane most of the early opposition was expressed through marches and rallies. When Faslane Peace Camp was set up in 1982 it caused quite a stir in the Helensburgh area. While many Faslane workers, both navy and civilian, live in Helensburgh (population: 15,000) it doesn't look like a garrison town. Faslane is six miles away, out of sight up the Gare Loch and the married quarters for navy personnel are situated on the outskirts of the town. The influence of the navy is definitely felt if you live there but it is not so obvious to the visitor. In fact the base sometimes feels like quite a well kept secret as the tourist information plays down the existence of nuclear bombs in amongst the magnificent scenery. The only times the navy are evident are when there is a NATO exercise and the sailors descend on the numerous pubs provoking patrols by van loads of both military and civilian police and during the annual navy public relations event, the Faslane Fair.

However, the geography of the area is quite complicated. Although Helensburgh is the nearest town to Faslane most of the people who live there do not go past Faslane on a daily basis unless they work there or at RNAD Coulport[2]. The Rosneath Peninsula (known locally as 'The Peninsula') with the villages of Cove, Kilcreggan, Rosneath and Clynder along with Garelochhead have a population of around 7,000. Peninsula residents travelling into Helensburgh for work or shopping usually pass by Faslane. The Hermitage Academy in the town is the secondary school for the area and buses (which have often dropped off base workers on their way through) pick up the school children from these outlying villages. There is another route to Helensburgh avoiding the North Gate of Faslane but it involves a seven mile detour and during winter weather is not the best of roads. Obviously a number of people travelled into the area to work too, notably teachers at the primary schools and doctors and nurses to the surgeries at Garelochhead and Kilcreggan. It was the people who lived and worked in Garelochhead and the Rosneath Peninsula who were most upset and started the anti-protest protest.

I had always thought that these people, who just pass by Faslane every day, no longer actually see it or think about it but in the course of the year of blockades I found out that this is not true. I was also surprised at just how many residents said that they didn't want nuclear weapons.

Although the Peace Camp was initially rather a culture shock for local people, with its up-front approach to protest and resistance and the alternative lifestyle of its residents, after 25 years it is now part of the scenery, whether disapproved of or secretly admired. Even the increase in activities when Trident Ploughshares got started in 1998 only produced sporadic complaints. Just as the base had become an accepted way of life the anti-nuclear protests were also part of the scene. This accepting or resigned attitude changed when the Faslane 365 plan became public. We had hoped to announce it with a carefully worded statement in advance of the blockades beginning but this approach was pre-empted by an alert local journalist who picked up news about the plan from a journal in the US.

When the idea of a year-long blockade was first mooted there was a good deal of discussion in the anti-Trident campaign about whether it was

---

[2] The Armaments store where warheads are kept below ground when they are not deployed on submarines. The UK made warheads are fitted to the missiles leased from the US in the huge Explosives Handling Jetty at Coulport.

the right tactic at this point in time, whether we could actually pull it off and whether the negatives outweighed the positives. There was an early meeting in October 2005 where all the feedback from Trident Ploughshares and beyond was collected together. I myself had mixed feelings. The potentially problematic impact of our actions on local people was a big issue for me. Although it was pointed out that factors other than protests could and did cause traffic disruption in the area I did not want us to underestimate the scale of the difficulties. Regular detours of seven miles were going to be costly and time consuming. As a result we spent a lot of time discussing how to liaise with local people.

We had the idea of running a series of public meetings in the area just before the start of the blockades to explain what we were doing and hear local concerns and we began exploring who could help us run these. Angie and I had a meeting with Liz Kingsnorth, who runs Nonviolent Communication[3] courses and she agreed to facilitate our public meetings but recommended that we should first attend one of her courses. I found the two-day course both intense and rewarding, particularly the insight that a key to communicating with anyone is empathising with them. I had previously tried to put my feelings aside when talking locally about nuclear weapons but this approach taps into your own feelings to listen and communicate in a very human way. I booked up halls on three consecutive nights for July 2006 in Cove, Garelochhead and Helensburgh. However, as time went on Liz began to have major reservations about facilitating our meetings. She felt uncomfortable about a negotiation and dialogue process in which one of the parties makes it clear in advance that there is a central issue on which it won't negotiate (in our case whether or not we would blockade[4]). There was also the concern

---

3 See www.nvc-resolutions.co.uk.

4 Angie tried to explain our position: 'my own viewpoint is that the 'conflict' if one wants to look at it like that is between the protesters and the military/political decision-makers that have forced nuclear weapons upon us, which affect the whole planetary community, not just those in Scotland or the UK. I do not see the conflict as between the workers at the base, or locals or anyone else we are likely to meet at or around Faslane. This is why the stopping of the blockades is not on the agenda, in the same way as the stopping of the nukes at Faslane are not on the agenda. What was on the agenda was how to enable local people's concerns about any effects that the protests and how they were policed might have on their lives and which might jointly be addressed by the protesters, the police and locals'.

that having open meetings at which the press would likely be present was to set ourselves up for failure. It might be better to do the liaison work away from the fanfare of publicity.

Accepting that they might well not be constructive we cancelled the meetings. This meant that the only structured communication with locals before the blockades started was various articles and letters in the *Helensburgh Advertiser*[5] following the 'Shocking New Plans' story in February 2006. Once Faslane 365 was under way there were regular reports of actions alongside stories of local disruption. In March 2007 the editor gave us the opportunity to answer critical readers' questions in our own words.[6]

However, our first face-to-face meeting with local people as a group turned out to be with the Peninsula24seven protesters on the verges of the A814 outside Faslane North Gate on 2 April 2007. We had thought quite carefully about how to respond to their presence. We decided to really listen to what they had to say and to show them respect. We made a couple of new banners especially for the occasion. One of them contained my personal response to the often stated local plea 'we just want things to get back to normal.' Our banner read – 'We all want to return to normal, NUCLEAR WEAPONS ARE NOT NORMAL...'

Some of those present were quite angry and wanted us to know about problems we caused. We went over to 'their' side of the road to engage with them. A week previously a Faslane 365 group had blocked the main road (A814) and the three hours it took to remove them and clear the road for through traffic seemed to be the final straw for some people. The problems highlighted were:

- School children being late for school or not getting there at all.
- School children missing exams.
- Primary school teachers being delayed from getting to school.
- Carers being delayed from getting to old or disabled people.
- People not being able to get to doctors and hospital appointments.
- People being late for work and losing pay.

On that morning at the North Gate it was difficult for us to hear some of these things. I did get quite upset at one point in response to an accusation

---

[5] The *Helensburgh Advertiser* is a weekly paper: www.helensburghadvertiser.co.uk.

[6] See Appendix 9.

that we were just messing around having fun and didn't care that we were making people really upset and angry. I said that although we try to have fun in the way that we protest they should be in no doubt about how angry and upset we were underneath it, angry that our government for so long has promised to disarm and meanwhile were just planning to continue to have a new generation of nuclear weapons, angry at the waste of resources, upset at the effect that nuclear weapons have had on human beings so far, from the uranium miners, to the Pacific Islanders, not to mention the legacy of Hiroshima.

There was a group of young people there who were very articulate. Some of them knew my son so they recognised I was as local as them. They explained how hard they were working for their exams and that some of them had already been late for prelims because of us. They wanted us to stop blockading so that they could get to their Standard Grade and Higher exams in May. They said that they found the exams stressful enough without worrying about getting there on time. We promised that we were listening and that we would go back and think very hard about all we had heard and pass it on. The Northants No Nukes group who were also there that day took some very careful notes of what was said and included them in their blockading report on our website.

The steering group shared all that we had heard. We decided once again to approach the police because a change in the way that they dealt with the tailbacks would have a profound effect on the local traffic. However without any sign that the police were going to cooperate with this we had to address how high feelings were running. We decided to contact the blockading groups who were due to come during May when the exams were on and ask them to consider not blockading until after 9am. We had always been clear that we were just facilitating a process and the actual tactics including timing was for the individual groups to decide. However we felt that people needed to know what was happening on the ground to inform their planning and that we were right to make a request about what we wanted. As a result all the groups who came in May left their blockading until after 9am. This was certainly appreciated especially by some of the young people who thanked us for listening to them.

On 16 April 2007 there was a public meeting called in Rosneath to discuss further response to F365. As most of us in the steering group were away Angie and Adam went to this along with some members of the local CND group. This was a fairly awful meeting mostly because the chairing was incompetent and people were allowed to become abusive. Angie and Adam had decided they were going along primarily to listen but as soon as they went in Ian Todd told them to come and sit in the front row which meant they became the focus for a lot of the anger. The two police officers, one MOD and one Strathclyde, were also sitting at the front table and this gave the impression that they were aligned with one side of the debate.

The following week Helensburgh CND had a public meeting in Helensburgh to discuss 'Trident and Jobs'. John Foster was there to explain the results of the study jointly commissioned by Scottish CND and the Scottish Trade Union Council (STUC)[7]. It had found that if the money earmarked for replacing Trident in 2024 was used differently then jobs would be created rather than lost. Jackie Baillie MSP was also speaking and as usual she said that if Faslane stopped having nuclear weapons then the government would shut it down altogether leading to a loss of 11,000 jobs. People from Peninsula24seven were sitting in the front row and although talking among themselves to start with they did listen and ask some good questions. Inevitably the effect of F365 on the locals came up and the third member of the panel Rebecca Johnson was able to explain why she was a member of the steering group. Discussion continued over cups of tea and one of the Peninsula24seven women apologised to Angie for how she had been treated at their meeting.

Unfortunately local politicians had also quickly seized this opportunity to make political capital out of the situation. They failed to make any constructive approach to us. Local MSP Jackie Baillie supported the Labour position on Trident, assimilated the Peninsula24seven position uncritically and in the Scottish parliament gave a completely distorted and dishonest account of the situation. We turned this around by using it as an opportunity to write to all the MSPs (some of them just newly elected) to both correct Jackie Baillie's misinformation and explain what we really were doing and more importantly why.

Peninsula24seven held their next demo at the North Gate of Faslane on 7 May. As it happened there was no blockading group that day and steering group members decided that we were not going to go to Faslane just because Peninsula24seven were going to be there. In the event we had a call to say that after an hour at the North Gate on their own Peninsula24seven had

---

7 'Cancelling Trident – The Economic and Employment Consequences for Scotland', www.banthebomb.org.

decided to go and stand on the other side of the road from the Peace Camp. Brian and I from the steering group went out to see what was happening. There were about 40 people including quite a lot of children. It was pretty quiet and there were no police to be seen. When some of them came over to the camp to pose for a photograph we went to talk to them and it was nowhere near so hostile as previously. People were invited to come for a cup of tea and a couple of teenagers did. There was a fairly calm exchange and there was acceptance that we had made some changes in response to local concerns.

The Church of Scotland has been opposed to Trident for many years. When Dumbarton Presbytery called a meeting to discuss the forthcoming General Assembly and the proposed resolution called a 'deliverance' about Trident Replacement I was invited. Before making a local deliverance of their own I suggested they should speak to some of the church members around Faslane. There was a real need for someone to get even a few folk together to look at the issues raised by our blockading but also the wider debate around having nuclear weapons in the middle of our community. The local politicians were not interested in dialogue and I hoped the church could play a role.

John Harris of Bearsden Church accepted this challenge and set up meetings in Garelochhead Church and St Columba's in Helensburgh. The local ministers were asked to find a few of their congregation who 'had an interest in Trident'. At the first meeting on 17 May, Brian Larkin and I went along from the steering group, and Julia Mercer, who had taken a six month sabbatical from her work to stay at the Peace camp and support Faslane 365, especially the religious groups, was there too. The meeting was very intense and brought up some interesting points. The Garelochhead Parish Church minister, Rev. Alastair Duncan explained how local people felt hurt by the way they were portrayed by the peace movement. It was politicians that made the decisions about our defence policy and they didn't feel they deserved to be called war criminals etc. They also felt that they were made into scapegoats by being caught up in our direct action. When we discussed alternative employment including the study which had just been released by the STUC they said that they had no faith in any of that and that the people who undertake such studies are not realistic about the alternative jobs that they could do. The second meeting in Helensburgh was much more of a theological debate.

At the end of June the students came for a week setting up the Strident

Tent State near to Coulport. They had liaised with Peninsula24seven and issued a joint statement. Shortly after this some of the main organisers of Peninsula24seven began acknowledging on their web forum that campaigning was hard work and took a lot of time. As the schools had finished for the summer and our blockading groups were not coming quite so thick and fast the momentum went out of local opposition.

Could we have handled things better? On reflection I think it was a mistake not to stage some form of meeting with local people long before the blockades started. By failing to be proactive we found ourselves always responding to negative events and the resultant exploitation of the situation by politicians and the media was predictable.

There are a lot of local people who do not want nuclear weapons on their doorstep and who have no love of the Royal Navy including some of the people who joined Peninsula24seven. Once the difficulties that our tactics were causing were expressed so forcefully it made it harder for anyone locally to show their support for us. On the other hand tension caused by our actions put us into a rough and ready kind of dialogue which no other part of the anti-Trident movement seems near to even contemplating at the moment.

Another factor was the organisational relationship between the steering group and the individual blockading groups. While both sides of that equation fully understood the steering group role as a facilitator of the actions of wholly autonomous groups, it was not an easy concept to convey to outsiders, to the local people, the police, or the public at large. This inevitably put more pressure on the steering group, wrongly perceived as the leaders of a conventional organisation. In the event, the liaison between the steering group and blockading groups was overall very effective, helping the individual groups to respond to local concerns.

Ultimately, we can only assess our interactions with local people by the principles of nonviolence. I do feel that sometimes we anti-Trident campaigners are less than fully nonviolent in the way we refer to people who are involved in the nuclear weapon system. Phrases like 'Devil's pay for devil's work' or 'Straight on for hell central' do not help to build bridges, nor are they based on real knowledge of the workers, their motivations and experiences. Living as I do within a community which is implicated in Trident you become aware that the reality is a lot more complex than can be conveyed in a few black and white slogans.

The issue of nonviolence also applies to how much inconvenience and distress we are willing to cause (directly or indirectly) as part of our protest or disarmament actions. There is no easy answer to that. Since every action has an impact this concern could be quoted in defence of no action at all. Ultimately the biggest effect we could have in this area is if Trident is disarmed. The Faslane workers are our potential allies; and if we can find a way to work together to call for a nuclear free Clyde with real funding for an alternative employment programme and proper restoration of the environment that will be a call which is hard to ignore by any government

F365 and Faith Groups

DAVID MCLACHLAN

The centrality of churches in the anti-nuclear movement was well illustrated by the (now) First Minister of Scotland, Alex Salmond. The occasion was the Bin the Bomb Rally held on Saturday, 24 February 2007 at George Square, Glasgow. A march had taken place around the city centre and the marchers assembled in the square to hear what would be said from the platform of the stage. Following on from Rev. Alan McDonald (then Moderator of the Church of Scotland), Cardinal Keith O'Brien, and Bruce Kent – Salmond shared his realisation with the assembled crowd – he was the first person to speak at the rally who wasn't a clergyman!

My own denomination, the Church of Scotland, has for many years argued against the possession and threatened use of nuclear weapons. The changing political landscape, with the emergence of New Labour and an end to the unilateralism of previous Labour Party Conferences did nothing to deflect the church from its position of sustained opposition, and I think that on this issue at least the church has a proud record of principled opposition. Now, if anything, the situation is even better, with all mainstream churches basically saying the same thing, and the Christian Church in the UK united on this issue as never before.

Why should churches and other faith groups get involved in this issue? One answer is that people of faith live in the same world as everyone else, and the political arguments currently advanced for the need to maintain the UK nuclear deterrent sound as weak to them as to anyone else. A report passed by the Church of Scotland's General Assembly in 2006 said: 'We will continue to ask the basic question of Trident or any replacement: what is it for?'

For the Christian church there are specific issues that arise from the teachings of Jesus. There are Christ's commands that his followers should be peacemakers, and that we should love our enemies. Over the years this has created a division among Christians between those who are pacifists and those who believe that war may be justified as a last resort – in defence when all other options have failed, and where the responsive force is kept to the minimum necessary. But this is still a far cry from first-strike nuclear weapons which destroy indiscriminately – not simply enemy combatants, but innocent civilians and the environment in which they live. There is also the fact that Jesus seemed to be angered more by hypocrisy than anything else. There is today a breathtaking hypocrisy surrounding the UK government's stated need to continue with a nuclear deterrent while denying that right to other countries.

All faiths concern themselves with moral questions and the most fundamental objection of all to the existence of nuclear weapons is that they fail the moral test. The indiscriminate nature of these killers make them incapable of use in a proportionate way, and the idea of threatening to destroy the planet (or vast areas of it) is seen by most people of faith as deeply immoral.

Ultimately, what we spend vast sums of money on, (and what we don't spend vast sums of money on), comes down to values, and thus to morals. The billions to be spent on a Trident replacement could instead be spent on hospitals and schools or to tackle poverty in many places around the world. What we decide are our priorities in spending is a deeply moral question. These issues matter greatly to people of faith.

In Scotland, Christian leaders like Cardinal Keith O'Brien and Moderator Alan McDonald have worked hard to keep the issue in the public eye and have provided a united front with Catholic and Protestant churches sounding the same message. They spoke together in Glasgow on 27 June 2006 at a packed public meeting organised by Clergy Action. This meeting took place only days after Gordon Brown first made the statement that he wanted to see Trident renewed and so was met with a lot of publicity. Since then they have joined forces for the Long Walk for Peace, spoken out at the Bin the Bomb rally and issued letters about the NPT, and signed a joint letter to the Scottish people at New Year 2007 where their prayer for the non-renewal of Trident was stressed.

These sentiments are echoed in other church statements north and south of the border. For example, the Rt Revd Peter Selby, Bishop of Worcester said:

'Nuclear weapons could never be justified; the reasons that were given in support of our having them have become less and less plausible. To renew Trident is to allow an opportunity for a real gesture towards disarmament and peace to pass us by.'

Revd R. Graham Carter, President of the Methodist Conference, concurs: 'The Methodist Conference of 2006 overwhelmingly expressed its opposition to the renewal of the Trident nuclear weapons system... Britain has the opportunity of giving a lead to other nations in nuclear reduction and peace-making. If the opportunity is not taken, it seriously weakens any argument against other countries' development of nuclear weapons. We need to develop more imaginative ways of making peace rather than retreat into the old 'cold war' ways of thinking.'

Last November, the Roman Catholic Bishops' Conference of England and Wales expressed similar sentiments when it stated: 'We urge the government to take a long-term view and act with courageous leadership by seeking to make this breakthrough toward total nuclear disarmament.'

Christian groups were the largest faith groupings at Faslane 365. That is perhaps not surprising. Despite the decline in religious affiliation, over 70 per cent of people within the UK still claim to be Christian, so Christians make up the biggest faith communities in the country. Another reason for the church's involvement is that the church has been here for so many years as part of society and has built up links and relationships with government. Over the years there has been a great history of Christians being involved in the political process and lobbying governments on issues of concern.

Though church groups, Quakers and Buddhists were most represented during the blockades, Muslims signed a statement of support for the aims of F365. And, of course, other groups taking part in the campaign will have included people of different faiths among their numbers.

Faith groups are often able to mobilise another section of society. Many of the people coming to the faith groups blockades have not been the 'usual suspects' of the past. Christian groups offer a chance to sing, to worship and pray and usually to share communion in a really unique setting.

Faith groups were also vital in providing behind the scenes support for the campaign as a whole. It was worship centres and church halls that provided accommodation for many of the groups over the year – especially those who had travelled long distances. They also worked at keeping the issue in the news both locally, nationally and internationally.

Three of the Christian groups most involved in the joint Christian blockades were Clergy Action, the Iona Community and CANA.[8] The way in which faith groups worked together was well illustrated by the blockade on 1 November 2006. On that day Clergy Action, the Iona Community and CANA overlapped with the departing Quakers from Cumbria who invited us to share in their final act of worship. In our block there were representatives of the three organisations along with priests from the Church of Scotland, Church of England, Baptist and Catholic churches, as well as individual lay people who came out to join us. In all, our numbers were around 45–50 that day. During the course of that afternoon we took part in another three services – one led by the Anglicans of CANA, one by the *Iona Community*, and a Communion led by *Clergy Action*. This was followed immediately afterwards by a march down to the front of the main gate to coincide with the 4pm shift change, where the actual blockade took place and some arrests were made.

---

[8] Clergy Action (my own organisation, which has now changed its name to SCANA (Scottish Clergy Against Nuclear Arms). This may seem confusing, but the hope is that this name will link us with the work that is being done south of the border.), are a small group of people with a history of mobilising the churches in Scotland on this issue. They have organised services of Communion at the Gates of Faslane during blockades of previous years, as well as actively supporting action for F365. Many have been arrested during protests. Clergy Action set up the public meeting with church leaders Rev Alan McDonald and Cardinal Keith O'Brien which generated good publicity. They ran a postcard campaign during the run up to parliament's vote called **MAKETRIDENTHISTORY**. Over the years they have organised vigils and written letters and articles to keep the issue of nuclear weapons before the churches.

The Iona Community is an ecumenical Christian Community founded by Rev George McLeod, with members and associates around the world. Part of their aims include action for justice and peace and the integrity of creation. Members are committed to opposing nuclear weapons, campaigning against the arms trade and for ecological justice. Rev Kathy Galloway, the present leader of the Community, led worship during the day of the Big Blockade marking the end of the year of activity on October 1st 2007.

CANA (Clergy Action Against Nuclear Arms), based in England, are another small group of committed clergy, ministers and laity concerned about war and peace issues, and in particular those with a nuclear dimension. It was set up in the 1980s and encourages supporters to preach and teach about issues of peace and justice and to lobby the government and witness at demonstrations. They produce papers for consideration on peace related topics as well as a regular newsletter.

The following statements were made to the press after our release:

> The Rev. Ainslie Walton (Church of Scotland) Glasgow, said, 'It is sheer hypocrisy for the UK to tell other countries they cannot develop nuclear weapons while we are designing and intending to deploy a whole new generation for ourselves. Blair and Brown told the world they wanted to Make Poverty History. £76 billion would go a long way to making that true. If this kind of money can be found for war purposes let's use it instead for peace.

Rev. David McLachlan (Church of Scotland) of Langside Church, Glasgow said:

> I want to claim my faith back from those 'Christian' world leaders who lie to their public, start wars to destroy other countries, do little to help the world's poorest, while finding £76 billion to threaten death on an unimaginable scale. I don't know what Bible they read. It's not the one I've got. Giving aid to the needy instead of creating more nuclear weapons would go much further in making this world a safer and better place.

Rev. David Paterson (Church of England) of Oxford said:

> Our 'independent' nuclear deterrent is a myth. The nuclear weapons Britain holds can only be used with US permission. We should have our own defence system. Do our neighbours in Europe, all of whom (except France) have no nuclear weapons, go to bed each night in fear of attack? If they can defend themselves without resort to nuclear bombs then so can we.

Rev. Colin Anderson (Church of Scotland) Glasgow said:

> Jesus is the Prince of Peace and calls his followers to work for peace across the world, the possession of nuclear weapons does nothing to promote peace but only adds to the aggression and posturing of division.

Rev. Kay Stiven (Church of Scotland) Edinburgh, said:

> The government wants to spend £76 billion and has not agreed that parliament should even get to vote about it. How is that for good housekeeping! The fact is that there is no situation whatever that could morally justify using nuclear weapons. Therefore we shouldn't have them.

At another action on 9 March 2007 members of CANA led by Canon David Partridge, with students from Wescott House Theological College, travelled north to meet with members of Clergy Action and the Iona Community. They were joined by Rt Rev. Stephen Cottrell, the Bishop of Reading, who presided over a Eucharist in the rain across the road from the main gate of the nuclear base. The service ended with a procession down to the gates and there were some arrests.

In his sermon, Cottrell referred to the beatitudes of Christ and his call that we should be peacemakers. 'A peacemaker looks very much like a trouble-maker! Indeed most of the people who have done the most good for peace in the world have caused a lot of trouble for those in authority. And I am not just thinking of Nelson Mandela and Lech Walensa, Desmond Tutu and Trevor Huddleston, Dietrich Bonhoeffer, troublemakers every one of them, but of ordinary men and women; ordinary men and women like those of you who have born witness at these gates... It is a vision that looks crazy to the world. But it is our only hope. While the eyes of the world eye each other with suspicion, build the barricades higher, post sentries along its borders, secure vast arsenals of weapons, and makes pre-emptive strikes against each other calling it defence, we look to Christ, who teaches that all are made in God's image and that all are worthy of God's love.'

Some very effective blockades were staged with a minimum of activists. The Saturday before Advent Sunday seemed like an appropriate day to stage a Nativity Play and that was what the radical Prayer 158 group decided to do. Mary, Joseph and a (lock-on) donkey arrived at the base gates only to be told there was no room for them at this inn. The police however did find room for them in the cells that night.

Ten Quakers were arrested on 4 March 2007 after 40 invaded the road outside the main gate for a 15 minute Peace Witness. Participants ranged in age from 16 to 75, and included civil servants, probation officers, students, architects, teachers, poets, tax consultants, and even brush-makers! Helen Leach, from Leeds, said, 'I feel compelled to be here because I'm a Quaker; and if you want to live in peace, you must do something about it – however small it may be'. Ruth Corry explained, 'As a grandmother I want to make a small contribution to the security of my grandchildren.' Jenny Biggs, from York, said, 'We believe that we should respect the laws of the state, but we believe too that our first loyalty must be to God's purpose'. Quaker groups appeared throughout the year from such places as Mosedale, the South of England, and York.

On Pentecost Sunday a group of marchers from an Interfaith Walk arrived at Faslane as part of their 86 day trek from Dublin to London. Only six people took part in the entire walk – though they were joined by hundreds of supporters along the way. One of the walkers was a Japanese Buddhist monk.

The Glasgow Buddhist Centre organised a day of meditation at the gates after having held several meditative vigils at other times.

A group of trainee priests and ministers, supported by their theological colleges, arrived at Faslane in June to witness for peace. The group of 28 included Anglican and Roman Catholic ordinands, Methodist ministerial candidates and staff from four theological colleges. The participating colleges were The Queen's Foundation in Birmingham (ecumenical), and the Durham colleges Cranmer Hall (Anglican), Ushaw College (Roman Catholic) and the Wesley Study Centre (Methodist). The spokesperson for the group was Professor John Hull, 'Our faith demands that we condemn the planned renewal of the Trident nuclear weapons programme, not simply because these weapons are immoral, illegal, a dreadful waste of money and cannot be justified politically in today's post-cold war era. But because their use would cause destruction on such a scale that the very ability of creation to create would be destroyed. And that is an offence against God that cannot go unchallenged.'

One thing is certain – people of faith will continue to be part of the opposition to nuclear weapons as long as they threaten life and peace.

Feminism and Nonviolence: The Challenge of Women's Actions

REBECCA JOHNSON, LIZ KHAN, RAUDA MORCOS, SUE FINCH and LIEVE SNELLINGS

Women kicked off Faslane 365 on 1 October 2006, 25 years after marchers from Cardiff set up the Greenham Common Women's Peace Camp in 1981. With workshops and blockades on the first two days, Greenham women merged on the third with Women in Black, a feminist, anti-militarism network that started in Jerusalem in 1988. The penultimate blockading group on 27–28 September 2007 was also women only, organised by London Women in Black. In addition, 'Grannies for Peace' and the 'Older Lesbians

Network' also organised women-only blockades during the year. It was fascinating to see how so many former Greenham activists turned out to be the driving force behind many of the 'mixed' blockades.

Women have been at the heart of peace and anti-nuclear movements worldwide. Faslane 365 was unusually welcoming of women-only groups, but in the wider peace movement there still seems to be a lot of resistance when women want to organise autonomously *as women*, or when we bring a feminist analysis of patriarchy and violence into campaigning against weapons and war. Women in Black started with a vigil in Jerusalem on Hagar Rublev's birthday, 8 January 1988. As an Israeli woman of Moroccan origin, she wanted to bring Jewish and Palestinian women together to oppose the occupation of Palestine. Women in Belgrade picked up the idea when their government went to war on its neighbours, as Yugoslavia disintegrated with appalling carnage, including 'rape camps'. By 2006, Women in Black had become a worldwide movement – a network of autonomous groups committed to making visible our feminist, anti-militarist, anti-nationalist resistance to war and male violence.

Our analysis is not based on biological determinism or some simplistic idea that women are naturally more peaceful. Nor does it stem solely from the fact that most violence is perpetrated by men, whether they use machetes, guns, rape or weapons of mass destruction. Our feminist analysis goes beyond male and female bodies to question masculine and feminine roles. At the core, however, is the recognition that women experience a continuum of gendered violence and that from domestic life to war, male violence is generated, sustained and related in patriarchal cultures.

All national militaries are dominated by patriarchal structures and concepts of masculine honour that include male bonding around notions such as honour, loyalty, obedience to authority and contempt for 'weakness', portrayed as 'womanish'. Our language is embedded with these images that equate masculinity with strength and reason, and femininity with weakness and emotion. It is no accident that the Microsoft Thesaurus gives the following alternatives for the word 'emasculate': weaken, enfeeble, render impotent, reduce, render powerless, make ineffective.

Weapons in patriarchal cultures are fetishised and sexualised. Until the early 1990s, one US army training rhyme involved pointing first to the rifle and then to the penis: 'This is my weapon, this is my gun; this is for killing and this is for fun.' Not surprisingly, sexual violation of women and girls continues to be a feature of war. Raping women serves both as the ultimate tool of occupation and a reward for military success, quite literally ramming home the humiliation of the vanquished. Individually men may be the victims of these cultures of violence, but collectively they keep building and sustaining the institutions, including heavy reliance on the manufacture, trade and control of weapons and the political and economic reliance on military-related industrial infrastructures.

Such connections are not new, and few if any men in the peace movement would try to deny or justify such abusive practices. The linkage between Trident and gender may be less familiar. Nuclear weapons, with their capability to destroy life on a massive scale and threaten the very survival of Mother Earth, are the 'ultimate weapon' and thus the apex of coercive killing power. As a political instrument of power projection and status they also carry a peculiarly masculine symbolism, that does not derive solely from their penile shape. The Hiroshima and Nagasaki bombs were nicknamed 'Little Boy' and 'Fat Man' respectively. India's nuclear tests and subsequent declaration that it had become 'a nuclear weapon state' in May 1998 was justified by Hindu nationalist leader Balasaheb Thackeray, who said, 'we had to prove that we are not eunuchs'. Even more crudely, in the 1980s a vigilante group opposed to the Greenham Women's peace camp published a grotesque cartoon in the local *Newbury Weekly News* that depicted a 'peace camper' atop (or skewered by) a sexually enhanced cruise missile in a cross between a rape and a ride.

But the importance of women's perceptions and engagement in peace-building goes much further. Without glossing over the differences and developments within feminism and among different campaigns and women's experiences, women-only organisation and practice is rather different from traditionally male ways of working. Even where men have taken on board feminist analysis and critiques of power, there is a tendency to assume that their heroes and ways of working are the norm. While some may theorise about whether violence is justifiable in liberation struggles, there is still the assumption that for peace and anti-nuclear movements, 'passive resistance' is desirable and that nonviolence is nonviolence, the same for everyone.

Women's experience is different. In most societies, men learn to act violently when they feel fear or anger. So male-based nonviolence, like the teachings of Gandhi, tended to require that such emotions be suppressed and overcome so that 'the other cheek' and a peaceful demeanour are turned towards an oppressor. Many women who come into the peace movement have already faced domestic and sexual violence at the hands of male relatives or others. While some would lose control like men in situations of fear or anger, many had learned that this was a quick route to being beaten up or raped. Some would freeze, perhaps hoping the aggressor would get bored or move on to more exciting prey; others learned to placate and soothe the aggressor. In this way the power of the aggressor was rewarded and the women would be left feeling even more powerless. Most men – including police forces – still expect women to be inert and ineffectual in the face of violence. They view women's passive behaviour either as normal or as an expression of fear and weakness. So female passivity does not challenge them, but may actually excite them and reinforce their sense of masculine power.

Feminist nonviolence as developed at Greenham and taken up in different ways around the world probably owes more to the suffragette example of politically challenging actions than to the Gandhi heritage, with the added strand of women's own experiences of deterring violence from physically stronger males. If nonviolence is to work as a philosophy or technique to challenge and change violence globally, it must not disempower its practitioners or reinforce the expectations of the aggressors. Feminist nonviolence therefore does not place emphasis on suppressing anger and fear; we recognise that such emotions are not 'wrong' or 'bad', but that they will undermine us and create further dangers and violence unless we channel them into actions that will transform oppressive power, symbols and behaviour.

So women would paint humorous messages or lob handfuls of bright pink porridge at the sinister dark mottled camouflage onto nuclear weapon convoys that we stopped or slowed, simultaneously ridiculing and marking them. Not only is dried porridge horrible to clean off, but a few photos make it impossible for the military authorities to keep up the lie that no one can get near enough the nuclear weapons to pose a threat. The aggressors cannot then believe that they avoided a more serious attack on their nuclear weapons or bases because we weren't clever enough or close enough, but only because we *chose* not to emulate their forms of violence. Fighting fire with water and earth, for example, rather than with fire.

The strongest acts of nonviolence come when undertaken from a sense of personal responsibility, not obedience or loyalty. One of the central axioms in 20th century feminism was that the personal is political, with the corollary that the political is also personal. To take this a step further, feminism taught that the person is most powerful in all her aspects. We challenged the weak/strong dichotomies of constructed masculinity and femininity, and in our nonviolent thinking and actions we evoked both reason and emotion, rationality and passion, organisation and anarchy, means and ends, sense and sensibility. Greenham's mixture of feminism and anti-nuclear, anti-war activism challenged patriarchy, traditional pacifism and some of the self-styled arbiters of 1970s feminism. We stretched and changed all those boxes, and inspired other women to develop nonviolent feminist challenges to male violence and militaries around the world.

At Faslane, the women's actions made links and crossed boundaries. Rauda Morcos, coordinator of ASWAT, a new organisation for gay women in Palestine, came to the first blockade and ran a workshop that linked her personal struggle for acceptance and survival as a visible lesbian in a deeply homophobic and misogynistic religious culture with the political struggle of Palestinians against Israeli occupation and control. The connections and contradictions of her experiences gave powerful reminders of the cross-cutting layers of different kinds of patriarchal violence and exclusion. As an early Women in Black booklet noted, the movement includes women on many ethnic and national backgrounds, cooperating across their differences in the interests of justice and peace. Women in Black is about building bridges across differences and borders, working for a world where difference is celebrated, and does not lead to inequality, oppression or exclusion.

We had a group of Belgian lesbians who piled into a local bed and breakfast and taught us to cackle like weird, wonderful witches. Greenham songs were revived and sung loudly – 'we are the witches who will never be burned; we are the witches who have learned what it is to be free...' Grannies sat and knitted, concealing bolt-cutters under their coats. Women wove colourful webs across the fence and barriers or put up pictures of their grandchildren or lovers. One got arrested carrying a cup of cocoa. Others for dancing across the road – or on top of a lorry heading into the base. Three locked arms inside two Hackney recycling boxes filled with foam and concrete, with assorted biscuits and crackers on concealing gingham tea towels across the top. As it turned out, this did not halt the traffic for long, but that wasn't what mattered – what really mattered was that three friends overcame our anxieties about being locked-on and 'trapped' and we're now thinking of how to do it better next time. And that sharing, learning, laughing and loving is really what feminist nonviolence is all about.

'In the Police Van', Jill Gibbon

CHAPTER 9

Policing the Blockades

ANGIE ZELTER

'ONE HUNDRED AND NINETY-TWO days of protest, 131 different protest groups, in excess of 1,200 arrests, and more than 600 lock-ons. Altogether this represented the most determined protest that the MOD Police (MDP) have encountered for many years.' Thus began an article on the Ministry of Defence News Website on 9 January 2008.[1]

The earlier MOD Annual Report[2] also makes an interesting read for those who want to get a policing perspective. Under the Agency Outputs section[3] it states that 'disruption and disorder caused by protesters' is one of five main crime and security risks faced by the Ministry of Defence and Armed Forces[4]. Then Assistant Chief Constable Gerry McAuley[5] states that, 'The MOD Estate has seen a marked increase in protest activity, particularly in Scotland with almost daily protest at HMNB Clyde, and a determined sea-

---

[1] This quote was from the Defence News, Home and Environment that you can find on http://www.mod.uk/DefenceInternet/DefenceNews/Estate And Environment/ModPoliceRespondToFaslane 365AYearOfProtest.htm. The December 2007 Issue, No 133, of *Talk Through*, the Magazine of the Ministry of Defence Police, is also worth looking at on http://www.mod.uk/NR/rdonlyres/B1415470-BC8B-47E1-90C0-E206AF6748A0/0/tt133.pdf.

[2] Annual Report and Accounts 2006–2007 of the Ministry of Defence Police and Guarding Agency http://www.official-documents.gov.uk/document/hc0607/hc06/0624/0624.pdf.

[3] Page 10 of 'Ministry of Defence Police and Guarding Agency – Annual Report and Accounts 2006–2007'.

[4] The others are terrorist attack and the threat of it; theft of key assets; major financial fraud; unauthorised intrusion onto the defence estate).

[5] Director of Divisional Operations – his whole piece can be found on page 24 of the 'Ministry of Defence Police and Guarding Agency – Annual Report and Accounts 2006–2007'.

borne action on the Clyde which led to the boarding by MDP of a Greenpeace vessel and its temporary seizure.' Later on in the Report[6], Chief Supt. Steve Walker states that it has been 'a particularly demanding year for officers in Scotland Division' with the two overarching challenges being 'the enduring terrorist threat and the threat to public order presented by various protest groups'. He goes on to say, 'the emergence of a newly formed anti-Trident pressure group known as 'Faslane 365' began to test MDP resourcefulness in October 2006. The group exists as an umbrella organisation for assorted groups of protesters who are given to civil disobedience in pursuit of their aims. The stated objective of Faslane 365, which comprises foreign as well as UK nationals, is to maximise disruption to site operations through protest stunts and persistent attendance at the entry gates of HM Naval Base, Clyde. Their aim was, and remains, to capture media coverage which it is hoped will further influence debate on the subject of next generation UK nuclear deterrence policy.'

Walker continues under a sub-heading 'Protest on the Clyde', saying 'Over the six months up to 1 April 2007, Strathclyde Police and MDP jointly policed the protests with some 700 arrests made in total. Many unusual and demanding policing situations presented themselves over this period. For example, some 350 incidents involving 'lock-on' tactics by protesters had to be dealt with. MDP has special expertise in dealing with lock-ons, but the process of safely removing locks and dealing with the subsequent arrests is a long one. Through the collective efforts of the DSG, the permanent MDP complement at Clyde, officers from RNAD Coulport and on occasion support from the MDP Operational Support Unit (OSU) based at York, disruption to Faslane has overwhelmingly been kept to a minimum. This was largely a result of swift deployment of specialist officers, working in very close support of Strathclyde Police public order operations.'

As these extracts from Ministry of Defence show the Police have been present in large numbers over the year and for this reason alone deserve a chapter to themselves. Ostensibly being the upholders of law and order, they have been caught in the middle of a long and intense battle for hearts and minds. The many ironies of arresting protesters for breach of the peace when those protesters see Trident as a massive breach of the peace has not been

---

[6] Page 26 of the 'Ministry of Defence Police and Guarding Agency – Annual Report and Accounts 2006–2007'.

lost on anyone. It has also been apparent that many of the more considerate and thoughtful police have felt high levels of discomfort when asked why they are protecting, rather than preventing, preparations for war crimes.

In any nonviolent struggle it is important to always distinguish between the person and the role they may be playing at any particular time and to attempt to find the inner human being behind the clothes, uniforms, outward appearances, even actions. We are trying to change our society so that it dismantles nuclear weapons and changes its foreign and defence policies to be in line with real, sustainable and ethical security that is appropriate for the 21st century. We need to encourage every sector in society, including the police, to make sure that their duties and responsibilities are in accordance with their humanity. The police, especially, need to be encouraged to stand up for their role as impartial and professional law upholders, to see the global context for our actions and not be corrupted to only look at little individual crimes and ignore big state crimes, for that way lies the continuing corruption and disintegration of the values of our society.

We (the steering group of Faslane 365) have therefore encouraged a friendly and courteous approach to the police in all our dealings with them. This includes all the police we meet at the gates of Faslane where we continually invite them to join with us in our disruption of the nuclear base, at the police cells while we are being 'processed' after arrest, and at our more formal meetings with them. As a steering group, we never liaised on behalf of the blockading groups but we did have regular meetings to enable a freeflow of information and concerns that we could then share with both sides – police and blockading groups. We usually arranged for two or three of the steering group to go to the meetings and we always tried to start and finish with a reminder to the police that the activities going on inside Faslane are criminal and are, in our opinion, preparations for war crimes. We explained that allowing this 'business as usual' to continue undermined the rule of law and that we expected them to uphold the law by instituting a proper investigation into the nuclear war preparations and helping us to prevent these crimes from continuing.

Mostly, the police tried to duck out from this responsibility by saying they could not get into 'political' discussions but we quietly responded it was not merely 'political', it was about the law. Preparations to kill hundreds of thousands of non-combatants by using bombs so powerful that they will destroy not only the military target but also the surrounding cities and people, and that will poison the environment for decades to come, are unlawful. We were not usually able to continue the discussion for long but we firmly planted this, our major concern, at the beginning and end of all our discussions.

We started with a letter to the local Helensburgh Police in June 2006, a few months before the start of the year of blockades due to begin on 1 October 2006. We decided that it would be signed by Jane as she lived locally and knew Kenny Boyter (the local police inspector) very well from her many years of protesting at Faslane. A copy of this letter[7] was sent to all of the groups who had already signed up to the blockading rota so they could see what the steering group was up to. In the letter we introduced the Faslane 365 blockades, its commitment to nonviolence, the autonomous nature of the organisation and how each blockading group would be responsible for its own police liaison. However, we said that we were in touch with all the groups and could pass on any information and concerns that the police might have if they would find that useful. We also wrote that we assumed they would police the blockades in a manner similar to previous blockades with health and safety as a priority.

There then followed various informal talks with Kenny Boyter and other local policemen involved in the policing of the usual protests, including those around Hiroshima Day and the annual Trident Ploughshares Camp at Peaton Wood. Nothing much was communicated except a reassurance of the nonviolence of the Faslane 365 blockades to come.

It was not until the end of September 2006 that we received a letter from the Divisional Commander, Chief Superintendent Mitch Roger, which clearly stated the police position and set the context for the year.[8] From our point of view it was quietly professional and considerate of our rights as protesters even though it did not take on board our arguments about the crimes going on inside the base. The police position was that 'On no account can prolonged disruption of the community be considered acceptable or the safe workings of the Naval Base be compromised as a result of your protest activity.' The police position was clear – Faslane 365 was a 'protest', not citizens trying to prevent preparations for mass murder.

We understood it would be hard to win over the police to such an extent that they would support us and try their utmost to get the nuclear weapons out of Faslane. After all, approximately 11,000 people were employed in Faslane, it was an 'official' military base, it appeared to be a 'normal' and

---

[7] See letter at Appendix 3.

[8] See letter at Appendix 4.

'legitimate' part of society. Whatever we might think or say and whatever the reality of international law there were unlikely to be any policemen or women willing to confront such an 'established' base, however sympathetic they might personally be.

Nevertheless, things were changing – the continual anti-nuclear protesting over more than 50 years had worn away the veneer of legitimacy, morality and usefulness of nuclear weapons, the unpopular wars in Iraq and Afghanistan had raised serious questions of international humanitarian law, and the threat to the whole international nuclear non-proliferation regime was providing a political context where our arguments might open up deep cracks and provide one of the catalysts for real change. Our work and our dialogue continued.

Already, in this first letter, the Chief Superintendant mentions that he has 'received representations from the local community via their elected representatives' as there was 'no doubt whatever that blockading the gates at Faslane to prevent the entry of vehicles will cause significant disruption to other traffic in the vicinity of the Base, preventing the local community going about its lawful business unhindered'.

We replied on 30 September[9] carefully trying to distinguish between lawful local traffic and base traffic which we considered to be unlawful. We also started the long discussion, that continued throughout the year, about how the policing of the blockades, especially how the base traffic was dealt with, would impact upon the lawful local traffic.

The blockades began on 1 October 2006 with women camping and demonstrating at the North Gate in the official demonstration area behind the police barriers and with blockading of the bell mouth and of the road around the roundabout. By the end of the first two weeks there had been eight different blockading groups and 74 arrests had been made by the police. Some of the groups had not been able to get into the area in front of the gates to blockade and so had started blockading the road leading to the main gate. Both Jane and I were telephoned by Inspector Kenny Boyter and were asked if we would meet with Chief Superintendent Mitch Roger as there were 'concerns that the Faslane 365 protests were being conducted on the A814'.

On 16 October 2006, Adam, Jane and I went to the Divisional Police HQ at Dumbarton. There had been a very successful blockade by the Nordic group that morning when 42 people were arrested. There had been a tripod

_____

9 See letter at Appendix 5.

erected on the A814 just North of the Peace Camp alongside a lock-on, another lock-on at the turn off to the South Gate and a lock-on and sit-down protest at the North Gate. The variety of groups and tactics used by the preceding groups ranging from mainly demonstrations/vigils/visual presence with perhaps two or three blockaders to more sustained blockading pressure with 10 to 15 blockaders and then to a sudden jump of 42 blockaders meant that the police could never be sure what would happen. Neither could we! Pressure was also beginning to mount on the police from locals who felt their lives were being disrupted by the blockades, reports in the local papers talked of school teachers failing to get to school on time and children being looked after by janitors until the teachers arrived, of locals failing to get to work. We also had concerns about some of the police, especially Ministry of Defence police, being rough with blockaders and the positioning of barriers that reduced the space for 'legitimate' protest i.e. the demonstrations around the gates. So we all had a great deal to discuss.

The three of us were introduced to the four officers present. Apart from Inspector Boyter we met Superintendent Willie Thornton, Superintendent Joe Cattrell, and Chief Superintendent Mitch Roger. After the introductions I started the 'conversation' by stating our concern at the major war crimes preparations taking place at Faslane and asking for their support in dealing with this and explaining the blockades in terms of prevention of crime. They listened politely but soon steered the conversation around to matters of more concern to them. During our hour of discussions we all said what was on our minds and at the end of the meeting I felt we had come to a clear understanding of our different positions.

Both 'sides' were committed to 'fluffy' nonviolent protesting and policing and while there was an inevitable 'clash' between Faslane 365 wanting to shut down the base and the police being committed to keeping it open, nevertheless there was a right to protest that the police would respect.

We made it clear that members of the Faslane 365 steering group did not 'represent' any groups but were merely a channel of communication. Both sides agreed that it was important to keep open this communication channel and that another meeting might be scheduled to review issues in a few weeks time as it was useful to have a chance to feed back issues arising from the police side and from the protesters' side. We said that the issues raised would be communicated to the blockading groups, and would be posted on our website too, including an encouragement to all blockading groups to liaise with the police through Inspector Kenny Boyter.

The police told us they had made a policy decision not to use (at this present time) their forward intelligence team (a video unit) or riot gear or other 'hard' policing tactics and that they were briefing all police units, on our nonviolence and 'fluffiness', who were told to respond in kind. They were working to protect our right to protest and be safe. We, in our turn, passed on feedback from the blockading groups that had taken part so far of their appreciation of the mainly professional and safe policing. However, we both had concerns that we raised from our own observations and discussions with participants.

We all agreed that road conditions would be getting worse with winter approaching – mist, fog, icy roads, less daylight etc. could all make safety issues even more important. And both sides raised examples they had seen in the last two weeks of protesters lying down in front of a car driving quite fast around the roundabout at the North Gate when the driver may have been caught unawares; of a protester diving under a car and hooking onto a rear axle; of a tripod that was erected in the A814; of a driver who bumped his car into a woman protester with a dog; of a policeman roughly shoving protesters off the road rather than just interposing their bodies and/or arresting.

We suggested that speed limits should be reduced for the year to encourage slower approaches to the gates of Faslane and especially to the roundabout outside the North Gate. The police said they already had this in hand.[10] We said we would stress to groups the importance of wearing high visibility vests and giving vehicles plenty of time to slow down.

There was some concern raised by ourselves about free access for emergency vehicles. We reminded the police of our safety and nonviolence guidelines and explained that if police communicated the approach of an ambulance or fire engine to the blockaders we were sure they would immediately clear their blockade, in line with our nonviolence guidelines. Trust was essential from both sides and this trust should not be abused as it was essential that no lives would be lost in our nonviolent struggle against weapons of mass destruction.[11]

We also took the opportunity to tell the police that the barriers around the bell-mouth of the North Gate had been lengthened twice since the

---

[10] This in fact never happened due (we were later told) to the length of time needed to liaise with the Highways Department.

[11] No emergency fire or ambulance vehicles, to our knowledge, were delayed or stopped by our year of blockading.

beginning of Faslane 365 and now prevented protesters and locals from crossing the road safely off the roundabout area and off the A814. The barriers plus the heavy police presence at the gates might give an impression to protesters that they could not establish a blockade at the North Gate and thus possibly encouraged groups to blockade the A814 – as being the closest they could get to the gate. We also said that the fencing that had been put up around the central roundabout area had taken another large area away from protesters' use. The police said at this meeting that the positioning of the barriers at the gates would be reviewed again. However, despite this and other reviews, the barriers stayed more or less in the same position as they were two weeks into the year, throughout the whole year.

The police raised the problem of locals not connected with the base being affected and that the disruption to the local community was a problem. The steering group acknowledged that some locals would inevitably and sadly be affected. But this would be considerably reduced if the police allowed protesters into the area right in front of the gates where they had the resources to arrest them if this is what they felt was needed. Meanwhile, the base traffic could be redirected until the blockade had been cleared. This would keep the roundabout clear and local traffic moving. I think that the main reason this was never done was because it would have involved a loss of face – an admittance that we were having an impact on base traffic. It would also, of course, have required more police resources who would have been needed on stand-by as it was never certain which groups would be blockading and when or for how long. The uncertainties were very great and made planning difficult.

During the whole discussion there were quite a few occasions when the different perceptions of legality, crime prevention, disruption to the population, breaches of the peace and effects on people's lives came up and of course we made it quite clear that feelings ran high amongst the protesters too and that they felt their values and way of life were being seriously disturbed by the presence of Trident and the illegal preparations to commit war crimes going on inside Faslane. These differences of perception were acknowledged by everyone present. We left the meeting after a final challenge to the police to put pressure on their political masters to deal with the gross illegality of Trident by disarming and to organise a Police Block!

This first meeting set the tone of all the meetings we had throughout the year – quiet, courteous, professional, sometimes amusing, and useful for both sides. Having dealt with the Metropolitan and Thames Valley Police and various other police forces around the UK I can fairly say that the Strathclyde Police have proved much superior in their dealings with nonviolent protesters. The police have much power and it is difficult to ensure it is not abused. Strathclyde have done a good job of controlling their use of power.

Two weeks later Adam, Anna-Linnea, Rebecca and I had another meeting but this time in Helensburgh with Inspector Kenny Boyter. He wanted to discuss Christmas Day and New Year's Eve as he had noticed we had blocks booked in the rota for these days and they are the busiest time of the year for the police. He said the police would value not having to police our blockades over that time so that more of their staff could be with their families. Would we cancel these blocks?

Rebecca was organising the Christmas Block and was therefore able to liaise directly with the police about this block. She offered to have a presence only at the North Gate over Christmas Day and Boxing Day and that if the MOD closed the North Gate over this time and only used the South Gate the Christmas Block would not blockade the South Gate. After negotiations between MOD, Strathclyde and the Christmas Block the police were able to have a minimal police presence over these days, the main gate remained closed and the vigil and blockade of Faslane occurred at the main gate only.

That was the first issue dealt with. But we also raised some safety issues about the hauling and dragging of protesters either before or as they were sitting down or locking on. It was agreed that it was better not to violently drag activists away but to lift them carefully and if this took longer it was nevertheless better in the long run. When we raised our concern that the MOD Police were using pressure points on protesters at the South Gate and that this was a major provocation that was unnecessary and also possibly dangerous, we were told the Strathclyde Police had talked to the MOD about this and they suggested that we also talk to Chief Inspector Brian Johnstone, MOD Head at Faslane, and were given his telephone number. Jane and I met with Brian Johnstone later and had a satisfactory exchange of views and information. On 5 November, I also met, outside the base, Sergeant Jimmy Carr of a Yorkshire based MOD Police Unit that had used the pressure points and he said Strathclyde had talked to them and they were not going to use pressure points any more. Quite a few of the complaints we had about police behaviour were connected with this particular MOD Police Unit.

It is worth mentioning at this point that the civil police, Strathclyde Police, had a very different attitude to the MOD Police. They welcomed dialogue and were keen to keep everything as low-key and nonviolent as possible.

They are responsible for policing outside the base and whenever a block was advertised on the rota they always had police stationed around the base. The MOD police, who have responsibility for the inside of the base, also do regular patrols around the outside of the base and often had to deal with blockades that were not advertised on the website rota and when there were no Strathclyde police present. It was never easy to communicate at the higher level with the MOD police and there was a certain tension and rivalry between the two police forces. The MOD appeared much happier to push and shove, do rugby tackles and in these rather confrontational and rough ways try to prevent blockades setting up in the first place. The Strathclyde Police, also vigilant in trying to prevent blockades setting up, gave precedence to keeping the atmosphere light and nonviolent. If the MOD police had been in charge of the operations planning I think that protesters would have been hurt and emotions would have run high. It would have been harder to keep everything nonviolent. That said, I have to praise the local MOD 'cutting team' who released people from the lock-ons in a considerate and professional manner, taking the time needed to do it without hurting anyone. As the year progressed the behaviour of the MOD police came more in line with the Strathclyde police.

Another problem that had arisen and that we raised with the police was the incident of two Strathclyde police detaining a protesters' coach at the bus stop opposite the Faslane Peace Camp on 27 October 2006 where it had stopped to drop off a few people. The two police officers ordered the drivers to stop and were in the process of delaying the coach when I had come along and questioned them about why they were unlawfully detaining these people and whether they were arresting everyone on the coach and if so what for? The police officers did then let the coach go on. Kenny Boyter said that he would look into this as stopping coaches was not a tactic they intended to use, although this was a right they had. We had no other incidents of the stopping of protesters' coaches the rest of the year.

We asked why some police were not allowing banners to be hung on the fence. Kenny said this, like camping outside the gates, was a matter for the MOD. We said that in fact camping is not covered by the by-laws at Faslane and was therefore something that the Strathclyde would have to deal with. Kenny agreed to have a word about the banners. On 5 November 2006 I spoke to MOD police and to Jimmy Carr again about the banners and they said they would not stop us putting them up, though in fact MOD police had come around that very morning to try to prevent the banners being put up as it interfered with the fence alarm system. Throughout the year the issue of whether banners can be put up and where they can go up has varied. Sometimes, we were allowed to put them up everywhere including on the base signs, around the roundabout fencing and on the base fences either side of the gate. At other times we were not allowed to put them up anywhere on the fences. Protesters have continually insisted that they be allowed to hang their banners, some even saying that if the police really want to arrest them just for hanging banners then they should do so. But in the vast majority of cases banners have been allowed on all the fences and police barriers except for those around the roundabout, which were judged to be a safety issue as they blocked off views of approaching traffic.

At the same time as these meetings were going on in November 2006, I wrote to the Strathclyde Police complaining about preparations for war crimes being carried out at the Faslane Naval Base and asking for a police enquiry into these crimes.[12] Several other people resident in the Helensburgh area, including members of the steering group, signed this letter. The Assistant Chief Constable of Strathclyde Police wrote back on 1 February 2007, saying that the Area Procurator Fiscal advised him that 'the circumstances ... do not justify the instigation of criminal enquiries or proceedings'. This was a most unsatisfactory reply that we are continuing to deal with at a higher level.[13]

To some, what is official is legal and there needs to be no investigation. And there has been the hurdle, that the courts will not address, of the Crown Prerogative and the problem that here in Scotland, defence issues are 'reserved to Westminster'. However, neither the Crown nor Westminster have the right to breach international humanitarian law, neither can gross illegalities be 'reserved'. And defence is not really defence when it is in contravention of international law, when in fact it includes deployments of weapons of mass destruction that can never be used in conformity with the law. The 'legalised' killing by a member of the armed forces protects them from the charge of 'illegal' killing or, in ordinary language, 'murder'. It is international law that sets the boundaries of whether the killing is lawful or unlawful. If it is not, then it is murder in times of peace and in times of war it is a war crime. Hence, Scotland has every right to intervene to stop

---

[12] See letter at Appendix 6.

[13] An approach was made to the Lord Advocate and the legal submissions made can be seen at Appendix 7.

weapons of mass destruction being stored or deployed on its land or in its seas. The police force, as the institution formed to protect the innocent, investigate crimes, and prevent crime is failing in its duty to the public if it does nothing about state crimes. It is of course a difficult thing for them to do – they have an institutional process to follow, they are obedient and obey the orders and guidelines of the Procurator Fiscal and ultimately the Lord Advocate. We can all use the argument that it is our bosses or someone else's responsibility, that we personally cannot do anything to stop various wrongs, it is not in our power. But of course, this is not true. We all do have the power to object and to ask questions, to refuse to obey unfair or wrong orders. The police could carry out investigations, could arrest the base commanders, could at the very least pass on messages of concern to their institutional and political masters. There would be consequences of course – they might lose their jobs! – but there always are these choices.

By March 2007, our local police liaison, Inspector Kenny Boyter, had moved out of the area to become a Chief Inspector at Campbeltown. He had always been a kindly and fair police officer with whom we had been able to liaise in a responsible and helpful manner over many years. We wished him well in his new posting and I gave him a copy of my book *Trident on Trial* as a farewell gift! The officer replacing him was Inspector Gavin Bone. Kenny introduced us to him in March and he seemed willing to keep on the constructive dialogue to enable us all to keep the policing and acts of civil resistance against weapons of mass murder as nonviolent and peaceful as we all wanted it to be.

At the March meeting we dealt with complaints from the MOD cutting teams about concrete lock-ons that had old saw blades embedded in them and that these fractured when being cut through and that a policeman had been slightly hurt from the flying pieces. The cutting teams quite understood our desire to build and experiment with lock-ons that were difficult to get through but wanted us to pass this information on to blockading groups in the hopes that they would only use materials that would not cause damage to the people cutting through them to release the protesters. Kenny Boyter and Gavin Bone also indicated that they would consider more serious charges if saw blades were used in lock-ons in that way again. Regardless of the threat of more serious charges, we felt that this was a reasonable request and in accordance with our guidelines, and that we should try and use other materials. We passed this information on to our Groups and put it on the website.

In April we felt the need for another meeting with the police and we also decided that we needed to put it in writing for their later consideration.[14] We dealt at length with the issue of liaising with other groups as we thought there might be the beginning of a divide and rule policy. It appeared that the police were concerned about the rising number of un-announced actions that did not appear on the rota. There was also the continuing problem of disruptions to local traffic. The meeting ironed out misunderstandings but also made it clear that the police would not be able to re-direct traffic and thus help ease disruptions to locals.

As 2007 continued the police became more accustomed to the blockades and a little more relaxed. They could tell from their own experience and from reading our website that our nonviolence was a real and deep commitment on our part. The number of groups and the days of presence had also declined. The first three months (October to December) had been very intense with 42 Blocks covering 60 days. The next three months (January to March) there were 30 Blocks covering 42 days and the following three months (April to June) 34 Blocks covering 50 days. The last three months (July to September) there were only 25 Blocks covering 36 days. But more importantly from the policing perspective, many of the blockading groups were much smaller with fewer people. However, they could never tell exactly who would turn up or when, or even if, they would blockade, and whether the blockades would consist of sitters or lock-ons. Blockaders arrested throughout the year varied between no arrests and 43 during any one blockade day.

The policing costs, greatly exaggerated at the beginning of the year of blockades as being in the region of £1.75 million a month, turned out in reality to be roughly £6 million over the whole year. This was reported in the *Sunday Herald* on 16 September 2007 which featured an in-depth article on Faslane 365, entitled 'Touched by Trident'. The journalist, Karin Goodwin, had interviewed Chief Inspector Andy MacDonald, one of the regular officers at Faslane with whom we had sat down at meetings on a number of occasions. According to the article he had found it a tough year, co-coordinating hundreds of officers shipped in from divisions across the region. He admitted, 'I'll breathe a sigh of relief after 1 October'.

I was glad to find that my analysis of Faslane 365's relationship with the Strathclyde Police was also shared by him. Karin Goodwin reports him as saying 'The organisers were very open with us about the intentions of the

---

[14] It contains a good summary of our position and is reproduced in full at Appendix VIII.

protest... All the information was available on the website. I'd say we had a good working relationship with them'. The article finishes with the Chief Inspector saying, 'A 365-day blockade was a tall order... And in the main they have managed to keep the protest going for the full year. I could understand if they thought it had been a success.'

The issue of policing costs has been one brought up by those in opposition to our actions, along with the more serious one of taking police away from their important responsibilities of preventing crime. Our perspective on this is fairly predictable. We agree – the police should be preventing crime and surely one of the greatest crimes they should be preventing is the crime of threatening and preparing for mass murder! We argue that the police should be joining us, not trying to prevent us, from disrupting plans for nuclear annihilation, that we are peaceful and do not need policing, that the crimes are taking place inside the base not outside it. However, we also argue that protest is a legitimate part of any democratic system and has to be paid for like any other service and that any policing costs that do accrue should be paid out of the Ministry of Defence budget not the civil police budget.

One of the components of the policing costs that was completely unnecessary, and we would argue, an abuse of judicial process, was the decision by the Procurator Fiscal (PF) to keep the vast majority of those arrested (well over 1,000 people in all) in police cells overnight. Normally the police do not keep people overnight unless they need to question them or take them to court the next day. It soon became clear that the PF did not want to prosecute so many people and had no intention of taking them to court the next day. Our suspicion is that it was a way of keeping people away from the base until their Block was over and that it was used as a 'punishment', that a night in police cells would 'deter' people from taking part and would also be a way of sentencing them without due process through the courts. Whatever the reasons, the police and PF went through a lengthy charade, that lasted the whole year, of pretending that the PF needed time to consider whether to take people to court and then to type up letters to give to prisoners when eventually released. It became clear that the majority of the police were just as unhappy with this waste of time and resources as we were. We heard mutterings of discontent about why they were arresting protesters and keeping them in police cells when they were not going to be prosecuted.[15]

---

[15] More details on these issues are explored in Chapter 6 – Legal Support.

Inspector Gavin Bone phoned us on 20 August 2007 to say the Divisional Commander Mitch Roger wanted a meeting with the steering group about 1 October. They had thought the year was going to end on 30 September but they understood why we wanted to end on a working day with a Big Blockade. But Faslane 365 would then end would it not? We reassured them that Faslane 365 would end then. But of course, we pointed out, protests would go on until nuclear weapons were removed from Faslane. Protests had been going on for over 25 years and were here before Faslane 365 and would continue afterwards. Faslane 365 would end but anti-nuclear protests would continue in a different form for however long it took to reach nuclear disarmament.

Our discussions about policing the Big Blockade on 1 October were similar to ones we had held when discussing the Trident Ploughshares (TP) Big Blockades of previous years.[16] The last TP Big Blockade had been over two years previously during the G8 at Gleneagles and we were keen to know whether the Faslane base would be closed for the day as it was then. We were told this was not their intention this time, that the policing would be similar to the Big Blockades before that. Chief Superintendent Mitch Roger said he read our website assiduously and even had it on his home computer and had noted that we were aiming to start the blockade at 7am. We confirmed this and asked him to confirm that he would not be stopping coaches and transport from getting to the base to drop people off. He undertook not to stop coaches and said we could offload people opposite the cemetery car park turn-off. He made it clear that no one would be arrested if they stayed behind the police barriers but if they stepped into the road and refused to move when warned then they would be. At this point we mentioned that the police barriers could trap people on the road even if they wanted to move off it and asked that it be shortened and a break put in it to allow people to come off the road when warned. He said he would do this. We

---

[16] Trident Ploughshares had organised Blockades at Faslane on the following dates:- 15 February 1999 **Blockade** (41 arrests); 14 February 2000 **Crimebusters Blockade** (185 arrests); 12 February 2001 **The Big Blockade** (385 arrests); 22 October 2001 **OKBLOK** (170 arrested); 11, 12, 13 Feb 2002 **Block 'n Roll** (190 arrests over three days); 22 April 2003 **The Really Big Blockade** (171 arrests); 23 August 2004 **Carry On Up the Clyde** (70 arrests); 4 July 2005 **G8 Faslane** (four arrests – the base was closed for the day).

also raised the problem of a policeman recently forbidding a protester to take pictures of her friend being arrested and taken away by police and asked why this had happened. We were assured that it was not illegal to take pictures of police and we could continue doing so.

I knew of a group coming from Leicester that would include Muslim women some of whom might be veiled and I asked that, if arrested, they be treated with respect and that only women police officers deal with them. I was told quite shortly, 'We are diversity proofed'! I reminded him of the fact that the blind professor had not been allowed his dicta-phone, a blind person's equivalent of paper and pencil, in the police cell and that I just wanted to be reassured that the Moslem women would be treated with respect as it was much harder for them to protest in the current political climate.

While we were discussing the variety of people who would be coming to the Big Blockade it became apparent that the police had found it very hard to keep their cool when the Clowns were 'feather-dusting' them. This information was passed onto the clowns whose amusing antics are designed to keep confrontation and frustrations down through humour and who had not perhaps taken on board the fact that police cannot move away if feeling discomfort like we can.

We asked what the release procedure would be as throughout the year blockaders had mostly been held overnight at police cells but on Big Blockades mostly blockaders were released later that day. Mitch said that from the police point of view they would like to release people as soon as possible but that this would depend on the Procurator Fiscal. In the event people were being released at the very same time as the blockade was finishing and I was talking to Chief Inspector Andy MacDonald who was telling me that people were probably going to be held overnight! I asked him to check and he finally confirmed that people were going to be released straight away. As far as we know very few are being taken through the courts even though 189 people were arrested that day.

I wrote a final letter of thanks for the year-long process of liaison and the manner in which the protests had been policed. It was sent along with our celebratory poster of many of the pictures of blockades and banners from the year, which I hope will remind them of why we were there. Of course, it contained a final appeal to them to do all that they could to get international and national law upheld and to rid Scotland of Trident once and for all.

'Protester with Police', Jill Gibbon

PC 365

THEO SIMON[17]

When first I enlisted, I did it with honour
Unfairness to fight and the peace to maintain.
Now I'm standing here like some glorified bollard,
Once more at the gates on the road to Faslane.

Each morning we come here to block the blockaders
Defending the terror deployed in our name;
Folk who joined the Polis to make the world safer
Now paid to stop other folk doing the same.

---

[17] Theo Simon of the folk group 'Seize the Day' sang this at the Power of the Word Block on 5 June 2007 to the traditional tune of 'The Deserter'.

But if there can be WMD here in Scotland,
Why not in Korea? Why not in Iran?
The world's greatest war-crime's preparing to happen,
And we're standing here to make sure that it can.

With hospitals failing and street stabbings daily
And climate-change stayin' at the top o' the news
Westminster still wants a wedge out of my wages
To spend on a weapon they never can use.

And if they should use them, what is there to say?
And how to square that with where I stand today?
I'm just 25 and I want to have children…
I'll not keep the peace for them policing this way.

I whip out my cuffs and lock onto a lorry,
My colleagues all staring like I am insane.
Then one by one slowly they break ranks to join me
On the PC 365 blockade of Faslane

Protesters ecstatically reach for their mobiles
Broadcasting the news to the planet at large
Where the statement I issued is widely reported:
'For health and for safety, we had to take charge.'

Now doors open for me, and medals adorn me
And children applaud me for letting them live…
When the daydream is broken by words harshly spoken
Sayin' 'Look alive, 365 – time to change shift!'

Bradford and Leeds Organise

LAVINIA CROSSLEY

A group formed in Bradford in September 2006 with the aim of organising a blockade at Britain's Nuclear Weapons base, Faslane. The make-up of the group varied widely, from 17-year-old students, who had recently become informed on nuclear issues, to people in their 60s, who had a life time of experience campaigning and a broad range of people in between.

In the lead up to our first blockade we met regularly in order to build up firm relationships of trust and support which would enable us to take action effectively together.

After the training session carried out by the dedicated team of Anna-Linnea and Adam the group began to work together and energise each other. As the group developed, affinity groups formed action plans and legal support was organised, along with a media team and drivers.

By mid-November 2006 we were making our way up to Glasgow. On the day of the blockade on an early winter's morning we arrived at Faslane, armed with chains, a CND lock-on and lollipop ladies with 'STOP Trident' lollipop sticks. The legal support were wearing their high-vis 'peace police' jackets and armed with pens to observe and document the action.

As we approached the base, we encountered 30 to 40 police. We had expected a police presence but the sight of so many was very daunting for some members of the group, myself being one of them. Tensions were high. The plan we had arranged now seemed difficult to implement with such great numbers of police. However, the anticipated signal was given, and we all ran towards the North Gate, at the same time as the police ran towards us to prevent us from getting into the road. After a little 'nonviolent' pushing and shoving, many of us were in the road and locked on to the CND sign or to each other, and were now blocking the main road in front of the base. A little while later, the lollipop ladies slipped away and effectively blocked the South Gate. A little messier than planned, we had achieved our blockade.

Our legal and media support efficiently recorded our 28 arrests as we were carried away. The men and women were separated and taken to different police stations. The men were put in cells of three, but the women were in solitary confinement. A number of the group, myself included, found this a difficult experience. Being locked in a bare room with no control over when you will leave and no contact with others definitely had an impact on many of us, particularly those who were experiencing it for the first time.

Reminding myself of why I was there did give me strength, we were objecting to weapons capable of indiscriminate killing that can never be used, threatened or even possessed legally. Knowing that we were expressing our objection to such horrific killing devices made the experience seem more bearable. Thirty six hours later, we were released and chaos set in as we hugged each other and shared experiences of the time in the road and in the cells.

The block didn't go to plan, but it happened and for many, including myself, it strengthened my conviction to campaign against Trident and gave me an experience which was both challenging and empowering.

As we returned to Bradford with renewed enthusiasm the decision on Trident replacement was growing ever nearer. We believed as a group the pressure must continue. We campaigned harder than ever, writing to our MPs, marching on protests both locally and nationally, talking to local press on the issue of Trident replacement and planning our next blockade of the base.

A week after the decision to research replacing the trident submarines was made, we returned to Faslane once more, determined to block the base more successfully and armed with a much lighter and stronger device than our CND lock-on: superglue.

In mid-March we drove towards Faslane once more, this time the sky was bright blue and as we approached the North Gate from the beautiful surrounding hills the number of police we were met by was significantly lower than the 40 who had met us the first time... in fact there were none!

We piled out of the van and ran towards the North Gate, lay down in the circular formation we had practised, interlocked our arms and super-glued our hands together. It worked a treat! The first police to arrive, rather arrogantly announced how easily they would move us once more police had arrived to carry us away, until we replied that we were in fact glued together! The banner we had made (but unfortunately forgotten to bring with us) summed up our action nicely, it read: 'Sticking Together For Peace'. And we were stuck there for three hours, as the Strathclyde police gently prized our flesh apart.

This was the second of four blockades the Bradford and Leeds group organised, as well as different members taking part in Strident, Women's Actions and the SOCRAP action too. Our last blockade took place on 2 October 2007 to emphasise that the pressure and campaigning will continue as long as the weapons remain.

The group has supported each other through blockades, campaigns and now the resulting court cases. As a result of a year focusing on blockading Faslane and campaigning against Trident replacement, the group has now begun to focus on local issues relating to Nuclear Disarmament and in Yorkshire, Menwith Hill and Fylingdales provide us with an equally big challenge! However the challenge will be met with our objections, as in the last year a true sense of empowerment has come through working to implement change together.

The Bradford and Leeds group has been mobilised, as I think many other groups and individuals have through the Faslane 365 campaign, and the results of this mobilisation will be seen in many years to come. Watch out!

Conclusion

ANGIE ZELTER

IT IS NOW NINE MONTHS after the Big Blockade that ended the Faslane 365 year of blockades on 1 October 2007. I am sitting back at home in North Norfolk pondering the results of our efforts and where we go next.

On a purely practical support level we are not quite finished as there are still some cases to be resolved through the courts. The 1150 arrests resulted in only 75 prosecutions, but as of 6 June 2008, 14 still have to be resolved. However, the majority of cases have been heard and have resulted in 33 convictions and 28 acquittals. The high rate of acquittals is due to the fact that it is hard for the police to prove that such peaceful good-humoured peace protesters actually alarmed anyone with their blockades. The total amount of fines imposed to date has been £2,303 and of compensation imposed has been £3,000. Eighty five days of prison have been doled out along with 90 hours of compulsory work.

On a political level the Working Group on Scotland without Nuclear Weapons that the Scottish Government set up after the Summit last October has only met once and seems not to have got very far. The people of Scotland are ready for a major change and would like to get rid of Trident but cannot wait forever. There is just not time with so many other issues needing urgent attention.

The Faslane 365 blockaders and their supporters (to whom this book has been a testament) know that nuclear weapons are indicative of a mindset that is now completely outdated and even more dangerous than ever before. With climate chaos now descending on our fragile planet at an increasing rate we recognise the need to re-commit ourselves to a genuine and deep respect for universal human rights and to global co-operation on poverty reduction and sustainable living. We can no longer spare any of our limited global resources for nuclear weapons, or fighting wars, for national, religious or cultural rivalries. We need to respect all human beings equally and share out all our resources equally. Together, as a world community, we can struggle through a process of genuine reconciliation and act in the understanding of ourselves as global citizens. Nuclear weapons are the antithesis of all that is needed as we confront the current situation. They are a potent symbol of violent terrorism and abuse of power. Until Scotland finds its strength to stand up in dignity and refuse to have them based at Faslane then we will shamefully know we have still not removed the canker at the heart of our society. We cannot move on to fulfilling our potential as full human beings whilst still supporting a military machine and a foreign policy that seeks to threaten nuclear devastation, supports repressive regimes around the world and earns money from selling weapons and torture equipment.

Faslane 365 attempted to bring many different and important civil society groups together to speak of our values and hopes for a better and more humane world, to undermine the distorted power and mind-set of the US/UK alliance to control the world's resources for their own selfish ends, to disrupt the 'business as usual' mentality that is killing our natural world. But the struggle is not yet won and we must not give up before the end. If the present Scottish Parliament cannot find the strength and moral integrity to confront Westminster and insist that Trident leave Scotland then our protests must start again and we will have to be even more creative and stubborn and determined than before. And because we cannot afford to ignore the climate chaos that is urging us to reform so many of our hypocritical and outmoded ways of running our societies we will have to find ways of integrating our campaigning around many different issues at the same time. It is a challenge to which we can all rise. Our experiences at Faslane have taught us that we can integrate these different challenges at one and the same time and need to do so. A year after the end of Faslane 365, in October 2008, we will start a sustained vigil outside the Scottish Parliament, to remind our politicians that they are there to carry out the people's needs for a nuclear weapon-free world. We hope that many of the readers of this book will join it. But most importantly I urge you all not to lose hope. Let us allow our compassion and love to flower into nonviolent resistance against all abuses of power and into sustainable and inclusive life styles. Let us reach out to all global citizens and live the changes we want to create.

Big Blockade of 1 October 2007

BRIAN LARKIN

The year-long Faslane 365 campaign finished on 1 October with a fabulous celebratory Big Blockade in which many of the autonomous groups and individuals who had already come to Faslane earlier in the year returned and together disrupted the operation of the Trident base for most of the day. It was a fitting conclusion to an extraordinary year of resistance. An estimated 600 people converged on the base and quickly established the blockade at the North Gate which remained completely shut from just after 7am until after 10am and then at frequent intervals after that for the rest of the day. Eventually blockades were established at all three Faslane gates and for the first time both roads in to Coulport were simultaneously closed. Together we had succeeded in shutting down access to the entire nuclear weapons establishment in Scotland. By the end of the day 187 people were arrested bringing the Faslane 365 total to around 1,150.

At the North Gate the police were unable to control the crowd which soon poured into the roundabout and a festival atmosphere erupted. A People and Planet group were initially thwarted in the attempt to block the Oil Depot Gate, and for some time there was no blockade of the South Gate.

But the fearless Irene, and company, soon filled that gap and word arrived that the South Gate was blocked. A cheer went up from the crowd when the announcement was made. Shortly after that Ben returned with the message that both roads into Coulport were blocked simultaneously. People and Planet from a consortium of Scottish universities had at last succeeded in accomplishing what they had tried more than once before and shut down Coulport.

It's impossible to piece together an accurate account of such an organic-anarchic eventful day. This can only be a sketch.

Coaches from Glasgow and Edinburgh met up at the Helensburgh Pier at 6.30am. The training venues had been packed the day before. Additional vans came overnight from Wales, Oxford, Assynt, and Leicester with lock-ons ready, and joined with the assembled forces at Helensburgh. A coach of Finns and Swedes had come in to the Peace Camp a few days earlier. In the early morning darkness the Peace Camp was jammed with people at the outside fire. A police van, motor running, blocked in the Peacedrobe, a transit van which they feared was going to be used to blockade the A814 because it was precariously parked just inside the fence facing the road and looked as if it would roll onto the road any minute. Police were everywhere. They had set up a check point blocking the turn into the South Gate access road. And at the North Gate as dawn was breaking through thick fog the bell-mouth was lined with police while van loads sat opposite. Three women sang 'O my soul let it bring peace' in exquisite harmonies. Base traffic crawled through the roundabout as shift change was under way.

Then it happened. Activists emerged from the coaches south of the roundabout and crowded into the official protest area. With only one lane open traffic came to a standstill in the roundabout and groups of activists jumped out of vans and ran toward the gate, many with lock-ons already on one arm. The Bradford-Leeds lot were among the first. They got well in near the gate and super-glued themselves to the road. Police snatched some lock-ons but a core group of the well-practised activists from Leicester managed to get locked-on in a jumbled and twisted bunch right under the feet of the over-whelmed police. Other members of this group darted in to join on separately as they saw openings. When the crowd in the legal protest area had swollen to bursting point a section of the barrier was lifted up and passed back over the heads of the unruly crowd. The Swedes dove through the gap and got locked on in the bellmouth. A group of clowns surged forward adding to the melee. A giant squirrel carrying a 'Nuts to Trident' sign got down on the ground with nutty friends from Manchester. More Leicester folk poured into the gap. Bicycologists impeded traffic in the roundabout and before long the police had lost the upper hand. The people poured into the roundabout along with a cadre of photo-journalists. The frenetic and triumphant drum-beat of Seize the Day sounded 'We shall not give up the fight we have only started.' Anarchy ruled. The North Gate to the Trident nuclear base was shut.

Soon several Muriel Leicesters were wheeling and ambling about. A 12 foot tall grey wolf strolled through on stilts while Green MSP Robin Harper, in rainbow scarf, gave interviews to bewildered journalists. All the while the cutting team was hard at work as so-called sterile areas were established by the police around the locked-on groups. Blockaders who had not locked on were being carried off one at a time. This was labour intensive work. The cops obviously intended to try to clear the blockade as quickly as possible but they had a job to do it with so many bodies to be carted off. The uplifted voices of some of the Protest in Harmony choir joined from behind the barrier with their blockading cohorts. Hands were soon seen to raise and, just as the morning mist had cleared the glorious chaos magically subsided. All went quiet. Gate Support announced that the attempt by People and Planet students to shut the Oil Gate had been foiled. Neither was the South Gate road blockaded. People who were still arrestable were asked to go there. Despite shutting down the North Gate we had not totally shut down the base. A group of students poured pink paint over their own heads and sat in the roundabout. Police formed a ring round them but no move was made to arrest them. After a while it became evident that they were being left out to dry. Protesters had learned something from the Spaniards who had so successfully used red paint earlier in the year. But so had the police. A French copper was there, observing. Over on the South side of the gate voices were raised as Camilla Cancantata's Oratorio – 'Trident: A British War Crime' – was performed.

Soon word arrived that the South Gate Road was blocked. Irene who had already been arrested eleven times during Faslane 365, and two friends had got the job done. We had done it. Word came too that the Finns had partly blocked the A814 with a tripod in front of the Peace Camp. The resistance was full on. And to top it off word came that People and Planet had blocked both roads in to Coulport simultaneously. Thus the Big Blockade had succeeded in shutting down all road access in to the UK nuclear weapons establishments.

Meanwhile, Clergy Action were quietly celebrating Communion across from the North Gate. Messages of support were read out from Sheilagh Kesting, Moderator of the Church of Scotland, Idris Jones, Primate of the Scottish Episcopal Church, and from Cardinal Keith O'Brien, head of the Catholic Church in Scotland. Just when it seemed the police might regain control of the road a bunch of elderly ministers, veterans of Faslane blockades, sat down peacefully in the gateway. Amongst them were the wife of the founder of the Iona Community, a number of grandmothers and a 78 year old priest. Michal, our cook, roamed through the crowd handing out vegan power balls. Renate's CIA (Cows in Action) puppets were, like their colleagues from the police FIT team[1] with cameras, gathering intelligence, while an effigy of a policeman looked down from the fence on the roundabout, blissfully unaware of the chaos below. The stubborn old GOATs (Golden Oldies Against Trident) formed another wave of arrests and cheers went up as these elders of our communities were led off. I wonder how many times some of them had been arrested resisting the nuclear madness. Amongst them was the 89-year-old Betty Tebbs.

As the dancing in the street subsided, Jeely Peace café was open for business. A group of SNP MSPs arrived, bearing greetings from Alex Salmond. Two Green MSPs were there as well. And Jill Evans Welsh MEP (Plaid Cymru) returned to the scene of her crime accompanied by the magnificent scarlet Welsh dragon. Buddhists for Peace sat quietly in meditation, bringing an

---

[1] FIT stands for Forward Intelligence Team.

element of calm. The sun was shining now and people were shedding layers. One old crone with a staff was weaving amid the crowd topless. Again it seemed the polis were gaining the upper hand when a group from the Edinburgh Peace and Justice Centre, joined by Roz in a wheelchair, blocked off the North side of the roundabout. The police asserted control forming a cordon along the road edge. People continued to challenge this by crossing here and there without permission. Assynt Peace Group initiated a Ceilidh. Someone from the Irish Make Trident History group was breathing fire.

By early afternoon the Bicycology sound system was set up and those of us who had not been arrested enjoyed listening to music performed by David Ferrard, Leon Rosselson, Roy Bailey, and Seize the Day as well as a number of poems. Paula Bolton read a section of her *Trident Monologues*. Seize the Day performed again and just when it seemed all was winding down Theo and Richard breached the line of cops and dove into the road. The police dragged them out of the road while Theo characteristically laughed. He must be ticklish.

This last blockade came just after Helen Stephen had negotiated with the Commanding Officer for the group to be allowed to have a closing circle in the bellmouth. There was a wish to mark the end of this extraordinary year of resistance. The Commander withdrew permission for the circle in the road, but Helen spoke to him again and he agreed. The yellow sea of police parted and we entered the bellmouth. The circle widened out, filling the bellmouth and all of the near side of the roundabout, surrounded on all sides by police. An image of a monk was placed in the middle – a reminder of the severe repression often imposed when people speak out against injustice, a reminder that we here face such minor consequences for our acts of resistance. If the Burmese monks can risk imprisonment, torture, even death, we can and must stand against the violence of state sponsored terror here where at most we face two or three days in jail.

Many people had spoken of this moment as the end of the campaign. But Faslane 365 had come out of the hard work of people who had been actively opposing nuclear weapons for many years. It had brought people back to the struggle who had been away from it for years. And it had intro-duced people who had never before taken part in nonviolent direct action. Autonomous affinity groups had been formed. Skills had been shared and developed. The spirit of resistance had been nurtured. It was obvious that this was only the beginning, the renewal. So, it was fitting that in that moment we sang 'You Can't Kill the Spirit, Old and strong, She goes on and on...' We had been given five minutes but the weaving of the spiral seemed to last forever. No one wanted it to be over. You could feel the love, strength, determination. But at last it did finish. Coaches carried those remaining away.

But back in Helensburgh, at Legal Support Central, the work went on well into the night as phones rang off the hook. Those arrested had been taken to stations all over Glasgow. Some 21 were still unaccounted for. Then the calls started coming. Groups were being released early. Transport was dispatched and by 11pm everyone was out except Irene who was held on a warrant for another action down South.

The Big Blockade was covered that night and the next day in all the major media. There were photos on the front page of *The Herald* and *The Scotsman*, with full pages of coverage in the Scottish papers and full stories in all the English papers. The Big Blockade had definitely made an impact.

Early the next morning the other half of the Leeds-Bradford lot pulled off a Faslane 366 rainbow paint action. And the following day the Faslane Peace Camp and Finnish friends blockaded the South Gate and the next night after that a group of Swedes got inside Coulport, some by swimming.

They were undetected for several hours before presenting themselves to the MOD police[2]. This phase of the campaign had reached its conclusion, but these post-365 actions indicate that nonviolent resistance will continue until Trident is disarmed.

---

[2] The BBC carried a factually inaccurate report on this breach of Coulport security which repeated MOD claims that Andreas had been rescued from the water. In fact he had waved down the searching helicopter from the land and he needed no medical attention.

1 October

BRIAN QUAIL

We're here at the gates of hell
in the hills of Scotland
and we're singing;
we cannot forget the victims that died
children playing, mothers singing,
burning burning
crying for water, lost in hell on earth[3]
and the cars drive past
driving to work to visit
to do important things to go past
to do anything but stop and think
but we cannot forget, we cannot forget.

We're here at the gates of hell
in the hills of Scotland
and we're dancing
on the road strip the willow
drum and violin, hands clapping
feet dancing men and women together
celebrating life and joy
here at the gates of hell.
This is why we are here
to say yes to life and all it offers
and no to death and mass murder.

---

3 Brian has echoed and alluded to several of the memorable phrases that he and
others sang from the Oratorio written and composed by Camilla Cancantata
called 'Trident – a British War Crime'. The Oratorio was performed several times
during the year of blockades and the words can be found on the TP website at
www.tridentploughshares.org/IMG/pdf/CD_ Booklet_Feb05.pdf and a pdf of the
sheet music at www.Faslane 365.org/oratorio.

We're here at the gates of hell
in the hills of Scotland
and we're praying
if the Lord's disciples were silent
these stones would shout aloud
and the hills around echo
with a silent cry of anguish.
the Iona Community
and our friends encircled together
praying with words and silence
hearts and minds joined as one
we cannot forget we cannot forget.

We're here at the gates of hell
in the hills of Scotland
and we're lying
on the road linked together
we're staying here
because we cannot forget we cannot forget
shadows on the wall searing pain
the baby drawing breath, the children at play
vanished vanished burning burning
and we are here lying on the road.

365 days one year a few hundred folk
focused on the one truth that dwarfs all others.
the ultimate evil. Trident.

Oh you who pass by,
have you no ears to hear, no eyes to see?
Will you not open your hearts
to the cries of our victims?
Hiroshima, Nagasaki
Rongelap Kwajelien
Chernobyl and Enewetek
Castle Bravo and Tsar Bomba
Moruroa and Maralinga
Fangataufa and Semipalatinsk
we cannot forget we cannot forget.

We're here at the gates of hell
in the hills of Scotland.
We are the common folk
young and old
Scots and friends from distant lands
children of hope
singing hope into life.

Miles of weld mesh and razor wire
police guards vans security
sad slaves of our Moloch
our nuclear idol
whose appetite knows no quenching
to this god they are prepared to sacrifice
our children and all the children of the world.
The earth in all its mystery and loveliness
trees and birds
fishes and flowers
all living creatures
bright and dark.

But to this madness
we say no today
and every day and we will
go on and on
on till we prevail
on till Trident is a bad memory
on till we can raise a golden glass
to our freedom
and yours.

Names of Blockading Groups

Full list of participating blockading groups in date order from 1 October 2006 to 1 October 2007.

1	Greenham Women & Aldermaston Women	32	Tyneside
2	Women in Black	33	Sussex
3	Sheffield	34	Prayer-158
4	Assynt and Gareloch Horticulturalists	35	Power of the Word
5	Seize the Day	36	Irish Make Trident History
6	South West	37	TP
7	Cyclists	38	Luciatåget
8	Edinburgh	39	Leicester
9	Green Party (Scotland, England and Wales)	40	Staffordshire and Stoke
10	Scandinavia Group	41	Scottish Students
11	Galloway One	42	Christmas Crackers
12	SNP	43	Benelux
13	Glasgow	44	Oxford Students
14	White Van	45	Academics
15	Eastern	46	Elected Representatives
16	Quakers	47	Lawyers
17	White Van Again	48	Dundee
18	Cumbria & North Lancs	49	Kathleen's Birthday Party
19	Clergy/Iona	50	Kirkland Run
20	CND	51	Health Professionals
21	Stop the War	52	Cambridge
22	Manchester	53	TP
23	Palestinian Solidarity	54	Coventry
24	Solidarity	55	Pensioners for Peace – Valentines Day
25	London	56	Christian Block
26	Armistice Day Surprise	57	Greenpeace
27	White Poppies (Northern Friends)	58	Di and Nick
28	Y Ddraig Goch	59	Quakers
29	Gogledd Cymru	60	CANA
30	Leeds & Bradford	61	Leeds Uni
31	Bucks & Buddhists	62	Trident Replacement Vote
		63	Alternativa Antimilitarista
		64	York
		65	Bradford

66	Merry Folk	108	Faslane Peace Camp
67	Tea Party	109	SCND Groups
68	Oxford	110	Magnificent Seven and Ffriends
69	French	111	Japanese
70	Bananas	112	Next Generation
71	German	113	Peace Boat
72	Nottingham	114	Assynt
73	Clowns	115	Teachers
74	Northants	116	TP
75	Older Lesbian Network	117	Scottish Councillors
76	Vanunu Freedom Ride	118	Hereford
77	CIA and friends	119	Grannies for Peace
78	Glasgow	120	Quakers
79	Trident Ploughshares	121	SOCRAP
80	Picnic for Peace (Aberdeen)	122	Cyclists from Everywhere
81	Irene	123	Star Wars
82	Portobello and Lothian	124	Scottish Lawyers
83	Environmentalists	125	Palestinian Solidarity Group
84	Kingston Peace Council/CND	126	Scottish Teachers
85	Calderdale Against Trident	127	Bomspotting
86	Unity	128	Dundee People and Planet
87	Family Block	129	Women Only
88	Newcastle	130	Rutherglen and Cambuslang CND
89	Y Draig Goch	131	Aberdeen CND
90	Quakers	132	Big Blockade
91	Anglican Pacifist Fellowship		
92	Peace Pentecost		
93	Dance and Movement		
94	Footprints for Peace		
95	Choirs		
96	Power of the Word		
97	Silent Disco Faslane		
98	Theological Colleges and Courses		
99	Birmingham		
100	Manchester		
101	Scottish Socialist Youth		
102	Candlenight 10pm–7am		
103	Quakers from Mosedale		
104	Shambolic Warriors		
105	Academics		
106	National Students Block		
107	Somerset Peace Groups		

Brainstorm on the Pluses and Minuses of the Proposal for a Year-long Blockade

Minuses

- More energy needed/burnout of activists.
- Over-use of activists leading to fewer other actions taking place.
- Takes energy away from Devonport/Aldermaston.
- Might split peace movement/finish off TP.
- Could increase repressive responses at Faslane and/or a back-lash against the wider activist community.
- Faslane Peace Camp could be closed down.
- Possible use of interdicts/prison for main organisers.
- Heavy police presence/tactics – police containment or lack of access to base/groups leading to fall-off of rota.
- No response to blockade, base operates by opening up new gates/ferries.
- 'Successful' project but no change with Trident leading to a feeling of uselessness.
- Impacts on locals through blocking of roads.
- Bad weather/midges.
- Relies on large numbers of arrestables, could fail to attract numbers, recruit for rota.
- Failure of plan may result in depression/lack of hope.
- Long lead-in time and context may change.
- Media might smear and lead campaign against it.
- Increase in terrorism paranoia or even actual terrorist attacks on Faslane.
- Unknown consequences (doubling of MOD police).
- Failure of maintaining nonviolence in such diverse number of participating groups.
- 48 hours may exclude disabled people from participating.
- Financial backing.

- Too big a focus on nukes – an issue too remote and too specific for this kind of mass action.
- Trident might be moved to Devonport.
- Asking too much of Scottish people.
- If clarity of demand is not clear could make side issues take over/dilution of message.
- Weakness of Scottish Parliament.
- Politically naïve.

Pluses

- Trident dismantled.
- People empowered.
- New people join in.
- Revitalises TP, peace movement and wider direct action networks.
- If we do nothing we get even more depressed.
- Example/model of diverse groups cooperating in NVDA together.
- Model for autonomously organised group action.
- Links with many other groups/movements.
- All sorts of mad plans sparked off around the world.
- Lobbying spin-offs/approaches to court.
- Scale and ambition of plan leads to energy boost and communicates our seriousness.
- Safety in numbers/don't start until 100 day rota filled.
- Builds on the work of the peace movement to date.
- Breaks down reluctance to take part in NVDA/civil resistance as part of a wider effort. of many groups doing their bit day by day.
- Responds to demand for creative response.
- Good timing/response to a vacuum-Trident replacement – possible war against nukes in other countries.
- Initial positive response from non-hard-core-activist people.
- Even the attempt at outreach builds public awareness of state violence and rejection of it/educational whatever happens in long run.
- Could be successful even before the first blockade.
- Gives voice to those excluded from the political decision-making process.

- Transforms and strengthens the political scene.
- Circumvents current mainstream political system.
- Good unforeseen consequences.
- Forces us to do things we have talked about for ages, even if hard (outreach/facilitating autonomous action).
- Raises Scottish self-esteem.
- Curiosity about how the legal system will cope.
- International effects.
- Best plan for NVDA against Trident thought of yet.

Letter of 15 June 2006 from Faslane 365 steering group to Strathclyde Police

15 June 2006

Dear Inspector Boyter,

As you are probably aware, as part of renewed campaigns to persuade the UK government to comply with international law and cease the deployment of the Trident nuclear submarine system, groups of citizens taking part in 'Faslane 365' are intending to conduct nonviolent blockades of the Faslane nuclear base from 1 October 2006. Although the plans are not yet certain or definite, we thought we should give you some advance notice regarding liaison with the police.

Although Faslane 365 is a new network, you will know some of the people involved and the nonviolent ethos will be very familiar to you too. What is different is that although there is a steering group for coordination and information sharing, the actual blockades will not be centrally organised and the different blockading groups will be autonomously responsible for how they arrange their particular action. There is a shared commitment to nonviolence by all the participating groups along the lines of the guidelines used for the Big Blockades.

Within these nonviolence guidelines which encourage groups to minimise disruption to peaceful road-users not seeking access to the submarine base, it will be up to each group to decide what level of contact they want with the police before and during their actions at Faslane.

We assume that Strathclyde Police will approach these blockades in a similar way to those previously and will have everyone's health and safety as a priority.

While our steering group will not be in a position to provide overall liaison for the groups, we are in touch with them all and are willing to pass on any information you would like them to have or any concerns you would like them to consider. We will encourage participating groups to get in touch with you in advance and to choose people who will be responsible for police liaison during their stint at Faslane, but we wanted you to know that ultimately it will be up to them whether and how they do this. However, we would like to tell them which police officer(s) will be responsible for liaison from your side. Will it be you, or if not, could you let us know whom it will be and give us contact details to pass on to the groups.

In peace, Jane Tallents, for Faslane 365 steering group

Letter of 28 September 2006 from Strathclyde Police to Faslane 365 steering group

Strathclyde Police, 'L' Division headquarters
Stirling Road, Dumbarton, G82 3PT
28 Sept 2006

Dear Jane,

FASLANE 365 PROTEST ACTIVITY HM NAVAL BASE (CLYDE)

I write in my capacity as Divisional Commander of Argyll, Bute and West Dunbartonshire Division of Strathclyde Police with responsibility for the policing in the vicinity of the Naval Base at Faslane. We have previously met.

As you are aware, I have been directly involved in the policing of these protests for the last four years and I am known to you and some of the other protest organisers from Trident Ploughshares, having had face to face meetings with you in the run-up to previous protest days.

As a general rule I have, throughout this time, taken seriously the democratic right which people have to protest and tried to balance that right with the paramount requirement upon me to ensure public safety and the right of other members of the public to progress unhindered about their business. I believe that the relations between Strathclyde Police and your protest group in the last four years or more would suggest that these rights on both sides have been fairly and impartially dealt with.

Given that the previous protests have been focused on specific single 'days of action' the policing arrangements I have put in place allowed a certain latitude to protesters which resulted, on occasions, in disruption to the local community, particularly in relation to traffic flow on the main route serving Garelochhead and the Kilcreggan Peninsula. For a single day of action, low level disruption has largely been tolerated given that the following day, things would be back to normal.

Clearly the intention of Faslane 365 is to disrupt the base over a prolonged period and therefore the scenario faced by me in planning a police response is wholly different.

There is no doubt whatever that blockading the gates at Faslane to prevent the entry of vehicles will cause significant disruption to other traffic in the vicinity of the Base, preventing the local community going about its lawful business unhindered. I have already received representations from the local community via their elected representatives who are very concerned about access by emergency service vehicles to Garelochhead and the peninsula and disruption to school children and teachers who would be delayed in attending schools both on the peninsula and in Helensburgh.

On no account can prolonged disruption of the community be considered acceptable or the safe workings of the Naval Base be compromised as a result of your protest activity.

To that end my purpose in writing to you as one of the organisers of Faslane 365 is to seek your cooperation in alerting the groups attending that certain restrictions will be necessary.

It is intended to have in place a designated protest area, behind barriers in the vicinity of the main access gates to the Naval Base. These barriers will be positioned sufficiently close to the gates to allow any protesters to congregate on the pavement and from behind which their protests can be made safety. Should any person leave the area behind the barriers and enter the roadway, either the access road bellmouth or the main public road, they will be asked to leave the road. Failure to do so, upon being warned, will render the person liable to arrest. Clearly persons sitting on the road either individually or locked to others, come into this category.

I have been concerned by the deliberate action taken by protesters during the period of the recent Peaton Glen camp, apparently after considerable debate, to block the main A814 road. I would urge your protest groups to reconsider any such action they are contemplating.

From the information on the Faslane 365 website, I note that it is intended that the protests will be nonviolent. You will wish to be aware that the police response to the protest will be proportionate to the situation faced by the officers on the ground. I have previously reinforced to all officers attending Trident Ploughshares protests that they have been nonviolent and will do so again as we prepare for the Faslane 365 protests. Should that situation change, however, I have a duty to protect my officers in attendance.

It is my earnest hope that your objectives of highlighting your cause can be achieved by an entirely lawful protest, and by setting aside a designated protest area for your use I am endeavoring to offer you that alternative. Any unlawful action which results in traffic disruption, however, will require to be responded to as indicated above.

I am aware you have recently been in conversation with Inspector Kenny Boyter from Helensburgh Police Office and should you wish in future days to discuss any aspect of the Faslane 365 protest activity, he would be contactable via that office.

Yours sincerely, E.M. Roger, Chief Superintendent, Divisional Commander

Letter of 30 September 2006 from Faslane 365 steering group to Strathclyde Police

Chief Superintendent Mitch Roger
Divisional Commander, 'L' Division, Strathclyde Police
Stirling Road, Dumbarton, G82 3PT

30 September 2006

Dear Mitch,

Thanks for your letter of 28 September to Jane Tallents asking us to help alert groups participating in Faslane 365 to the restrictions you plan in connection with the blockades.

While the organising of the blockades, including any liaison with Strathclyde Police, is entirely a matter for the autonomous groups who are participating in Faslane 365, we will pass this information on to the groups and we hope that they will find this indication of your intentions helpful.

While in our role as facilitators of the involvement of these groups we are always willing to pass on any further information or suggestions you may have, we cannot speak for the participating groups. However, as you know, the guidelines to which everyone participating in Faslane 365 has agreed are the same as for previous Big Blockades, including that we will move as soon as requested to enable emergency vehicles to pass.

May we also point out that we have no intention to impede ordinary lawful road-users travelling to and from the peninsula. Having been involved in the past with mass blockades at Faslane, we are aware that the level of disruption suffered by lawful traffic is particularly affected by the response and tactics of the police to our intentions to peacefully blockade the gates of the base where nuclear weapons are being deployed, in contravention of international law. We therefore hope that in choosing the police response and tactics you will also commit to minimising disruption for through traffic.

We also trust that you will take into account the level of distress the continued existence of the Trident element of the Faslane base provokes within civic society in Scotland and beyond. This is shown by the diversity of the groups that will participate in Faslane 365, as a look at the website will show. Included are church groups, parliamentarians, groups from urban and rural areas, artists, journalists, writers, academics and many others.

In peace

David Mackenzie, Jane Tallents, Rebecca Johnson, Angie Zelter, Anna-Linnea Rundberg, Adam Conway.
Steering group Faslane 365

Citizen's Complaint

Citizen's Complaint addressed to Strathclyde Police, 'L' Division, at Helensburgh Police Station.

We, resident at various addresses in and around Helensburgh (as specified below), hereby make a complaint regarding the commission of war crimes and crimes against humanity.

Four Trident nuclear-powered and nuclear-armed submarines are based at Faslane in Scotland. Each submarine can carry 16 Trident II D5 missiles, each with eight warheads. One submarine is constantly deployed at sea with its missiles. Since the July 1998 Strategic Defence Review the single deployed submarine carries 16 missiles with three warheads of 100 kilotons each. Each warhead is eight times more powerful than the Hiroshima bomb.

By this nuclear policy, the UK government and NATO violate the rules of international humanitarian law. The effects of the detonation of even a single Trident II D5 missile would be catastrophic. No one launching it could meet the legal tests of proportionality, discrimination or necessity. These facts are well known and the use, or threat of use, of these weapons would qualify as crimes against humanity or war crimes. President Bedjaoui of the International Court of Justice considered that 'Nuclear weapons can be expected – in the present state of scientific development at least – to cause indiscriminate victims among combatants and non-combatants alike, as well as unnecessary suffering among both categories... Until scientists are able to develop a 'clean' nuclear weapon which would distinguish between combatants and non-combatants, nuclear weapons will clearly have indiscriminate effects and constitute an absolute challenge to humanitarian law.'

In addition, it is forbidden to use weapons, which inflict such unnecessary suffering. The death and suffering caused by the use of a Trident missile could never be justified by any conceivable military advantage. Furthermore, its use, however accurately targeted, would have severe effects on neutral states, the environment and future generations, due to long-lasting radioactivity.

The International Court of Justice, in 1996, also clarified for the world community that any threat to employ a means of force that would be unlawful if used, is itself unlawful. However, the UK's nuclear weapons are deployed and are often ready for use at a few days notice and the government of the UK has repeatedly stated that they are willing to use them under certain circumstances. These facts point to an illegal threat.

The following people are thus implicated in the violations described above:

1   Responsible ministers at the political level, and more specifically the Minister for Defence, the Foreign Minister and the Prime Minister.
2   The Chiefs of Staff at the Ministry of Defence.
3   Senior Naval Officers and Trident Submarine Commanders.

We therefore wish you to carry out investigations in connection with the location and the preparation of the potential use of nuclear weapons as well as the preparation and training of nuclear tasks. Please note that, within the context of war crimes, and crimes against humanity, it is not a defence for suspects to state that orders came from a higher authority, that the actions were 'official' or a governmental or legal responsibility, or that they are condoned by national legal systems.

We would like you to focus your investigations at the following locations with the aim of securing evidence of illegal activity relating to nuclear weapons:

1   The Naval Base at Faslane where Trident submarines are based.
2   The Armaments Depot at Coulport where nuclear warheads are stored and fitted onto Trident missiles.
3   The facilities at Aldermaston and Burghfield where nuclear warheads are researched, manufactured and maintained.
4   The regular nuclear convoys which transport warheads from the south of England to Faslane.
5   The Ministry of Defence, Whitehall, London.
6   The Prime Minister's Office at 10 Downing St, London.

We understand that investigating crimes of such a serious and horrific nature, that have been sanctioned by the state for many decades now, will be a difficult task for the police force. However, we believe that the civilian police forces are the correct institutions to be approached to undertake this investigation as it is charged with law enforcement. Due to the location of the Trident bases a significant part of that duty falls on Strathclyde Police. It was agreed at the Lord Advocate's Reference 2001 that, 'A rule of customary international law is a rule of Scots law'. It cannot be right that protesters wishing to stop gross crimes of threatening mass destruction by blockading the base are being charged with Breach of the Peace when Trident is the crime, is a massive Breach of the Peace and is not even being investigated by the police. It is as if the police will sanction a crime if it is huge enough or if it is 'official' government policy and will only concern themselves with minor breaches of the law. This undermines the law and our legal system, which must be seen as impartial and above politics.

We are also concerned that ordinary submariners and soldiers are being led into the commission of war crimes by their involvement in preparations for mass murder. The major difference between a murderer and a soldier is that the killing, and threats to kill, made by soldiers are sanctioned by law and the primary law is customary and conventional international humanitarian law – i.e. the Declaration of St Petersburg, the Hague Conventions, the Geneva Conventions, the Nuremberg Principles. Knowledge of these laws is meant to be taught to every member of the armed forces around the world. These laws are all breached by the deployment of Trident and thus undermine the legal status of the UK's 'defence' forces.

The threat to use weapons of mass destruction on a daily basis (which is what the deployment of Trident actually is if you discard all euphemisms) is a massive breach of customary international law. The work on the successor replacement to Trident is a massive breach of Article VI of the Non-Proliferation Treaty and of the promises given by the UK government in 2000 at the NPT Review Conference to 'unequivocally disarm' its nuclear weapons. These charges are serious and need to be investigated.

We wish you to act as *our* (the People's) Police Force, not merely the *government's* Police Force (this is the difference between a police force in a democracy and one in a dictatorship!) and to fairly and impartially investigate the crime of Trident.

Signed by: Angie Zelter, c/o Faslane Peace Camp, Shandon, nr. Rhu, Helensburgh, G84 8NT, Scotland... there followed several other signatures from local residents.

APPENDIX 7

Trident Renewal, Scotland and the Law

Submissions in Support of the Removal of the Trident Nuclear Weapon System from Scotland

We submit that the Trident nuclear weapon system based at Faslane in Scotland violates the law of all the jurisdictions of the UK, including Scotland, insofar as they all recognise relevant aspects of international law. The deployment of Trident can be seen as preparation for a war crime, namely, for the unrestricted use of a weapon which is inhumanely indiscriminate and causes massive pollution.

This violation of the law is compounded by the UK government's stated intention to replace the current Trident-carrying Vanguard-class submarines with new ballistic missile submarines, as outlined by the White Paper on 'The Future of the United Kingdom's Nuclear Deterrent' published on 4 December 2006 and presented to the UK parliament (Cm 6994).

International Humanitarian Law

This is the sum total of what the White Paper has to say on the UK's nuclear weapons obligations under International Humanitarian Law (IHL): It reflects the tone and content of government statements over several years:

> 2–11. In 1996 the International Court of Justice delivered an Advisory Opinion which confirmed that the use, or threat of use, of nuclear weapons is subject to the laws of armed conflict, and rejected the argument that such use would necessarily be unlawful. The threshold for the legitimate use of nuclear weapons is clearly a high one. We would only consider using nuclear weapons in self-defence (including the defence of our NATO allies), and even then only in extreme circumstances. The legality of any such use would depend upon the circumstances and the application of the general rules of international law, including those regulating the use of force and the conduct of hostilities.

But the UK government's claim that the International Court of Justice (ICJ) 'rejected the argument that such use would necessarily be unlawful in all circumstances' is incorrect and disingenuous.

After stating that a threat or use of force by means of nuclear weapons that is contrary to Article 2, paragraph 4 of the United Nations Charter and that fails to meet all the requirements of Article 51 of the Charter and of International Humanitarian Law is unlawful (Advisory Opinion, para 105, point (2)C and D), the Court declared that 'the threat or use of nuclear weapons would generally be contrary to the rules of international law applicable in armed conflict, and in particular the principles and rules of international humanitarian law'. (Ibid., point (2)E) It then continued:

> However, in view of the current state of international law, and of the elements of fact at its disposal, the Court cannot conclude definitively whether the threat or use of nuclear weapons would be lawful or unlawful in an extreme circumstance of self-defence, in which the very survival of a State would be at stake. (Ibid.)

The President of the Court emphasised that this 'cannot in any way be interpreted as a half-open door to the recognition of the legality of the threat or use of nuclear weapons'. (Judge Bedjaoui, Separate Statement, para 11).

The UK government says that it would use nuclear weapons only 'in extreme circumstances'. It consistently fails to add the ICJ's essential additional criterion: 'in which the very survival of a State would be at stake'. There has been no explanation of how widely or narrowly the government interprets the meaning of 'State survival'. Some government statements suggest that the threshold for use falls well below that of an extreme circumstance involving state survival. For example, the government has often referred to nuclear weapons defending our 'vital interests'. These could refer to conventional UK forces overseas under threat from biological or chemical warfare. It has never been made clear what is meant by 'vital interests'.

We submit that Trident could *never* be used lawfully, even in self-defence. This is because a use of force that is necessary and proportionate under the law of self-defence must, in order to be lawful, also meet the requirements of the law applicable in armed conflict; in particular, the principles and rules of international humanitarian law.

The government accepts that 'The use of nuclear weapons is governed by the same principles of law that govern the use of other weapons, namely the principles of international humanitarian law.' These fundamental principles apply to all countries, even if their survival is at stake, and no state can claim exemption from them. They are 'intransgressible' (Advisory Opinion, para 79). The government merely asserts that it would always comply with these principles. However, it has never given a satisfactory account of the legal reasoning supporting this claim. The explanation given for this is that the policy of nuclear deterrence requires ambiguity. A potential enemy must never know the circumstances in which the UK might use nuclear weapons. Furthermore, the Attorney General's advice to the government is privileged.

The cardinal principles of IHL include the principle of discrimination. According to this principle, states must never make civilians the object of attack and must consequently never use weapons that are incapable of distinguishing between civilian objects and military targets.

Furthermore even a legitimate military target must not be attacked if civilian death or injury, or damage to civilian objects, would be excessive in relation to the concrete and direct military advantage anticipated from the attack. A recent Opinion provided for Greenpeace by Phillippe Sands QC and Helen Law notes that 'The ICJ itself was concerned with the effect of a particular weapon, not just its targeting capability:

> ... humanitarian law, at a very early stage, prohibited certain types of weapons because of their indiscriminate effect on combatants and civilians...' (ICJ Opinion paragraph 21)'. The Greenpeace Opinion goes on to say that '...in order to meet the obligations [of the principle of discrimination] a weapon must be capable of being targeted and its effects must be capable of being predicted and controlled sufficiently so as to be able to discriminate between combatants and civilians.

Nuclear weapons are unique because of their radiation effects. The best evidence of government thinking on this issue is in the 1995 UK written and oral pleadings before the ICJ. The UK argued that if nuclear weapons were used, the intention would be to destroy military targets through their heat and blast. Radiation, said the UK, is only a side effect. There would therefore be no actual intention to 'poison' the enemy through radiation (UK oral pleading 1995 para 3.60).

However, nuclear weapons are 'explosive devices whose energy results from the fusion or fission of the atom.' (ICJ 1996 Advisory Opinion, para 35). Radiation is of the essence. The UK might believe that consequences which are inevitable and foreseeable, but unintended, are not relevant to the legal argument. If this is so, it has to be argued, not merely asserted.

The UK pleadings emphasised the accuracy of small nuclear weapons detonated in isolated areas. These may not violate the IHL principle of discrimination. Whether they did so, it is argued, would depend on the circumstances prevalent at the time.

Targeting may well be accurate. However, the foreseeable *effects* of a weapon must also be taken into account when assessing compliance with the principle of discrimination. No one could reliably forecast the complex atmospheric conditions and the direction of the wind at any given moment. The effects would be so unpredictable that accurate targeting would be irrelevant. No nuclear weapons could be used with any assurance that their effects would fall within the bounds of legality.

An Opinion provided by Rabinder Singh QC and Professor Christine Chinkin for Peacerights in December 2005 argued that:

> The Court's inability to give a definitive answer to the question put to it in the Threat or Use of Nuclear Weapons was based both on its assessment of the current state of international law and on the 'elements of fact at its disposal.' Its determination was made in the abstract without reference to a specific incident of maintenance or replacement of a specific weapons system in the hands of any particular state. Even then, referring to the 'principles and rules of law applicable in armed conflict' it found that: 'In view of the unique characteristics of nuclear weapons ... the use of such weapons in fact seems scarcely reconcilable with respect for such requirements. (1996 ICJ Reports para. 95)

If we consider a specific nuclear weapons system – Trident – the arguments concerning the legal status of nuclear weapons become even more forceful. The Peacerights Opinion goes on to describe Trident in detail (para 29):

> The UK Trident system currently consists of four Vanguard-class nuclear-powered submarines each carrying up to 16 US Trident II D5 missiles. There are around three nuclear warheads mounted on every missile making about 48 warheads carried on each submarine. At least one is on patrol at all times. Trident nuclear warheads are 100 to 120 kilotons each. Even one kiloton, a 'nuclear mini-bomb' would flatten all buildings within half a kilometre with up to 50 per cent fatalities up to one kilometre'. (Lord Murray (Former Lord Advocate of Scotland), 'Nuclear Weapons and the Law', 1998,

available at http://wcp.gn.apc.org/newmurray.html). 'The fireball of a detonated Trident warhead is said to have a diameter of half a mile across while the heat and blast extend miles further.' 'A low-yield Trident warhead would reduce a whole town to rubble.' (Ibid.) Each warhead can be aimed at a different target and each has at least eight times the explosive power of the bomb which was dropped on Hiroshima on 6 August 1945.'

This system is designed and intended to unleash vast heat, blast and radiation; the radiation will cause immediately lethal and long-term carcinogenic, muta-genic and teratogenic effects on human beings and other life forms that cannot be controlled in space or time. The 100 kiloton Trident warhead is designed to detonate as air bursts to cause the maximum damage.

Rabinder Singh QC and Professor Chinkin argue that:

In light of the blast, heat and radio-active effects of a detonation of a Trident warhead, in our view, it is impossible to envisage how the intransgressible requirement of the principle of distinction between combatants and non-combatants ... could be met. The use of a Trident warhead would be inherently indiscriminate. Even if aimed at a military target it cannot distinguish between that and civilians within its range' (para 30).

Even if smaller 1–5 kiloton weapons were used with Trident missiles they would probably be exploded on or near the ground in order to destroy precise targets. Such a strike would throw up enormous quantities of radioactive dust which would be sucked into the stratosphere and come down anywhere – even thousands of miles away. This would irradiate unpredictable numbers of people then and well into the future. The indiscriminate effects of nuclear weapons cannot be limited in space or in time.

The UK government has argued against the view that any use of Trident would be 'inherently indiscriminate'. In doing so, however, it ignores the unpredictability of the effects of nuclear weapons in general and of Trident in particular. Both the UK and the US have consistently asserted that those arguing for illegality claim that all nuclear weapons have certain 'inherent' characteristics which inevitably make their threat or use incompatible with international humanitarian law. 'Many of the submissions made to the Court have [assumed that] any use of a nuclear weapon will inevitably violate the principles of the law of war ...' (UK oral pleading to the ICJ page 40).

However, the ICJ stated that because of the 'unique characteristics of nuclear weapons ... the use of such weapons in fact seems scarcely reconcilable with respect for [the principles and rules of law applicable in armed conflict].' (Advisory Opinion, para 95). We submit that although nothing can be predicted with certainty, we do not have to prove that any threat or use would be inherently illegal under any circumstance. We only need to argue the *improbability* of lawful use in any *plausible* scenario.

Protocol I of 1977 Additional to the 1949 Geneva Conventions is the expression of the pre-existing customary law which binds all states. With reference to precautions in attack, Article 57(1) declares: 'In the conduct of military operations, constant care shall be taken to spare the civilian population, civilians and civilian objects.' Article 57(2)(a) (iii) states that those who plan or decide upon an attack shall 'refrain from deciding to launch any attack which may be expected to cause incidental loss of civilian life, injury to civilians, damage to civilian objects, or a combination thereof, which would be excessive in relation to the concrete and direct military advantage anticipated.' Similar language is used in the *Manual of the Law of Armed Conflict* issued by the Ministry of Defence.

Anyone launching a nuclear strike therefore has a duty of care as laid down in Protocol I. However, the unpredictability of the effects of nuclear weapons makes it impossible to carry out this duty. The UK government has repeatedly been asked how Trident, or its successor, could be used with any certainty that it would comply with the principles of international humanitarian law, in particular the principle of discrimination, but to date there has been no considered response.

The Scottish Dimension

During the Trident Debate in the Scottish parliament on 14 June 2007, Patrick Harvie MSP quoted Professor William Walker:

> there is a unique situation in Scotland. There are nuclear weapons in a land where the mood of the parliament and of the country is opposed to them. The parliament has a right to express society's views. Even if it doesn't take steps to obstruct nuclear weapons ... it can ask questions within the UK. It can raise a voice of dissent from an important new institution within a nuclear weapon state...

The parliament went on to vote by a margin of 71 votes to 16, with 39 abstentions on a motion that 'congratulates the majority of Scottish MPs for voting on 14 March 2007 to reject the replacement of Trident... and calls on the UK government not to go ahead at this time with the proposal in the White Paper.'

This reflects Scottish views at large. An ICM opinion poll carried out in January 2007 found that almost two thirds of Scots opposed the plan to replace Trident regardless of cost. In November 2006, 61 per cent of Scots agreed with the statement 'The Scottish parliament should have the ability to remove nuclear missiles from the Clyde'. In the parliamentary debate Mike Rumbles MSP echoed a widespread principled opposition to Trident and its replacement:

> There is a legitimate argument about whether any UK government would ever use our nuclear deterrent. I think that it is important not only to set out my party's position but to make clear my own views on what is an important moral question for everyone. I cannot envisage any scenario in which use of the Trident missile system would be justified. I am at one with the many leaders of civic Scotland and our churches who have given a moral lead on the issue...

Some MSPs questioned the wisdom of the Scottish parliament debating Trident. The constitutional settlement contained in the Scotland Act 1998 clearly established the boundaries between devolved and reserved issues. Defence policy is a matter for the Westminster parliament. However if, as this submission argues, Trident could never be used lawfully, a different light is cast on the matter.

Scotland, as part of the United Kingdom, and under Scottish law, is subject to the rules of International Humanitarian Law. The Opinion of the High Court: Points of law arising in relation to charges upon which, on trial on indictment in the Sheriff Court at Greenock, 30 March 2001, confirmed that 'A rule of customary international law is a rule of Scots law.'

Moreover, the International Criminal Court (Scotland) Act 2001 makes 'provision for offences under the law of Scotland corresponding to offences within the jurisdiction of the International Criminal Court'. Such offences include Genocide, Crimes against Humanity and War Crimes.

For the purpose of the 2001 Act, 'war crime' means a war crime as defined in Article 8(2) of the Rome Statute. Article 8(2)(b) includes under War Crimes:

> (iv) Intentionally launching an attack in the knowledge that such attack will cause incidental loss of life or injury to civilians or damage

to civilian objects or widespread, long-term and severe damage to
the natural environment which would be clearly excessive in relation
to the concrete and direct overall military advantage anticipated.

As regards the mental element of war crimes, Article 30 of the Rome Statute
provides that a person has intent in relation to conduct when he means to
engage in the conduct; and in relation to a consequence when he means to
cause that consequence or is aware that it will occur in the ordinary course
of events. Similarly, 'knowledge' means awareness that a circumstance exists
or a consequence will occur in the ordinary course of events. These provisions
are replicated in Section 8 of the 2001 Act.

According to Section 29 (Crown application), the Act 'binds the Crown
and applies to persons in the public service of the Crown, and property held
for the purposes of the public service of the Crown, as it applies to other persons and property.'

We know from Article 2, paragraph 4 of the UN Charter as interpreted
by the ICJ that if a particular use of force is unlawful, the threat to use such
force must also be unlawful. It might be argued that the possession of
nuclear weapons does not constitute a threat to use them. However, the UK
does not merely possess nuclear weapons. It deploys Trident-armed submarines on permanent patrol and has repeatedly stated that in certain circumstances it would use those weapons.

Accordingly, we submit that the deployment of Trident in Scottish
waters amounts to a preparation for a War Crime which is justiciable under
Scottish Law. We urge you, as Lord Advocate, to consider the legal points
raised in this submission and give us your opinion on these arguments.

Dated: 8 October 2007

Signed by:

Alina Armstrong, Convener of the Iona Community's Justice and Peace
    Working Group
Meg Beresford, Wiston Lodge
George Farebrother, Secretary of World Court Project, UK
Janet Fenton, Coordinator of Edinburgh Peace and Justice Centre
Kathy Galloway, Leader of the Iona Community
Andrew Gibson, Solicitor
Professor Nick Grief, Professor of Law at Bournemouth University

Ian Hamilton, QC
Rev. John Harvey
Fr Gerard W. Hughes, SJ
Professor Lynn Jamieson, University of Edinburgh
Dr Rebecca Johnson, Director of Acronym Institute
Dr Justin Kenrick, University of Glasgow
Alan Mackinnon, SCND
Robbie Manson, LLB
Rev. David McLachlan
Dr Lesley Morrison, Medact
Ellen Moxley, Founder of the Scottish Centre for Non Violence
Lord Ronald King Murray, ex-Lord Advocate
Patricia Robson, Morningside Justice and Peace Group
Richard J.D. Scott, MA, LLB
Helen Steven, Founder of the Scottish Centre for Non Violence
David Turner, Campaign against the Arms Trade
Robin Waterson, General Meeting for Scotland (Quakers)
Alan Wilkie, World Court Project – Scotland
Dr Ben Young, Jubilee Scotland
Angie Zelter, Founder of Trident Ploughshares and Faslane 365

Letter of 24 April 2007 from Faslane 365 steering group to Strathclyde Police

Faslane 365 steering group
Tel: 0845 45 88 365/07768 312676
Email: info@Faslane365.org
Your Ref:
Our Ref: Strath/MR/01

Chief Superintendent Mitch Rodger
Dumbarton Police Office

24 April 2007

Dear Mitch Rodger,

We are writing to discuss various concerns and suggestions we have about the policing response to Faslane 365. We hope to meet with you and Inspector Gavin Bone to discuss these issues, but intend this letter to clarify our position, particularly with regard to the nature and role of the meetings we have had with you and Inspectors Gavin Bone and Kenny Boyter.

Before we do that however, it is important to reiterate that the work currently going on in HMNB Clyde to support and deploy Trident nuclear-armed submarines is illegal under well established principles and undertakings of both international and domestic Scots law. We remain deeply concerned that Strathclyde Police are either unable or unwilling to confront such egregiously illegal activities. We hope that a way will soon be found to enable you to tackle these crimes, and we look forward to a day when we can support you in doing so. However, in the immediate future we must all deal with the world as we find it and hope we can continue to do so in an atmosphere of mutual respect and nonviolence, even if we disagree about our different roles and responsibilities.

Ongoing Discussions Between Faslane 365 Steering Group and Strathclyde Police

We have become concerned after hearing that autonomous groups planning demonstrations or blockades at Faslane have been told that Strathclyde Police will not consider their reasonable requests on the stated grounds that the steering group has not 'cooperated' with you over certain matters. We would like to continue these discussions, as we regard them as helpful to both sides, but would not be able to do so if the police then use this against blockading groups seeking to liaise with you.

Since an initial meeting with you in October last year, we have had a number of meetings with Inspector Boyter and then with Inspector Bone. From the beginning we explained that while we are happy to talk with you, the meetings are a communication channel only: they are not negotiation or liaison in any way. Faslane 365 is structured so that each of the blockading groups is autonomous, the only unifying conditions are the Nonviolence Guidelines and the shared demand that Trident be taken off deployment and dismantled and the UK cease to possess or deploy nuclear weapons. As the steering group, we have undertaken to facilitate Faslane 365, but we do not have any further responsibility or authority than that. We have never had, nor sought to have, a mandate to negotiate or liaise collectively on behalf of any of the blockading groups. Individual members of the steering group are sometimes also involved in specific blockading groups and may on occasion liaise on their behalf; if this occurs, it is solely in their capacity as part of that blockading group, not as part of the steering group.

We feel that the meetings between members of the steering group and Strathclyde Police can be valuable for both parties, providing their limits are recognised and not abused. What we *can* do is:

Raise any issues or concerns we have arising from incidents we have witnessed or experienced ourselves. We are present at more of the blockades than most people, as most of us are based locally. Thus we may have useful overview and context, and can often raise concerns at an early stage and so prevent them becoming major problems.

Act as a communication channel to feed back any concerns or information from the police that you want passed on to the blockading groups. We have done this on a number of occasions.

What we cannot do, for the reasons outlined above, is enter into nego-tiations or agreements on behalf of blockading groups. We have expressed this position consistently from the start of our meetings and thought that you understood this to be the basis on which we met.

The reason we are raising this issue at such length is that we are concerned that the perception of these meetings is beginning to slide into areas where we have no mandate. In particular, we are worried about certain aspects of the liaison between yourselves and Friends of the Earth Scotland (FOE) over an event as part of the Environmentalists block on 26 April. Our understanding is that they contacted Inspector Bone with a request for a rally, including a large White Elephant, at the North Gate, and the matter was passed on to Operational Planning at Dumbarton. Following discussions, a revised proposal was put by FOE to a constable in Operational Planning who then presented it to you. The response received was that you had rejected the proposal because of the 'refusal' of the steering group to agree that all blockading groups would publicise their blockades on the rota.

We take no position, and express no opinions, on the negotiations between Strathclyde Police and FOE. We are not, and do not wish to be, any part of those negotiations. Our concern is solely with the apparent misinterpretation of our role in discussions with Strathclyde Police. As explained above, we have no mandate to enter into any agreement regarding whether Groups 'announce' their blockades or not. To assume such responsibility would be completely contrary to the structure of Faslane 365. We can pass your concerns on to blockading groups but no more. We hope you will be able to reassure us that you accept the basis on which we are meeting with you and your officers, as we have consistently said from the beginning (and as reiterated above).

Impact of Blockades on Non-Base Traffic

We would also like to discuss a number of issues around the impact of the blockades on through-traffic to and from Garelochhead and the Rosneath Peninsular. I'm sure you are well aware of the strength of feeling locally on this. We have had many discussions with local residents about this before, after and during the 'local demo' on 2 April and on other occasions. Some of the steering group also attended a meeting in Rosneath on 16 April.

We are distressed at the impact of the delays on the nearby communities, and would like to do everything we can to minimise the impact on non-base traffic. But over-riding our worries about the impact on the local community is our compelling need to do everything in our power to prevent the deployment and use of nuclear weapons. These immoral instruments of war have the capability to incinerate millions of human beings and contaminate the Earth with radioactivity, causing starvation, cancers and birth defects in future generations. It is because we cannot allow these illegal weapons to continue to be deployed in our name, that we feel morally bound to continue to do what we can to disrupt the unlawful activities of the nuclear base.

We feel that the policing tactics to date have exacerbated rather than minimised the impact on local traffic. In particular, the deployment of large numbers of police officers at the gates with instructions to prevent people getting into the gateways and approach roads and to prevent people 'locking on' even to the extent of arresting people who are standing on the pavement with tubes are counter-productive, resulting in greater disruption to non-base traffic. This leads to a widespread perception that Strathclyde Police have chosen to prioritise keeping the base open over minimising the disruption to through traffic. This is in stark contrast to the approach taken at the Big Blockades in previous years.

In light of this, we have a number of questions and suggestions:

1   The previous practice was, once a blockade was established, police would direct queuing base traffic to park up somewhere else until the blockade had been cleared. This allowed through traffic on the road to the Peninsular to flow relatively normally while not causing any significant extra disruption to the base, over and above that which we have caused anyway by blockading. This worked well for five years at Big Blockades. *Why has this practice now been abandoned? Could it not be reinstated?*

2   The practice at Big Blockades was to prioritise keeping the road open even if that meant not preventing people getting into the 'bell mouth' at the North Gate or onto the South Gate approach road with lock-ons. Once people were in the gateways and blocking them your officers would take the view that such an obstruction amounted to a Breach of the Peace and would therefore arrest and remove the blockaders. We may not agree with this determination, as the blockaders are upholding international law rather than breaching anyone's peace, but this approach had the virtue of effectively limiting the impact of the blockades on the local community. The current approach of trying to keep people away from the gates at all costs, even to the extent of sometimes arresting people who are simply standing on the pavement, seems to have the opposite effect of maximising the

disruption to the local community while arguably having little effect in reducing the impact on the base. *Could this approach not be reviewed and something closer to the Big Blockade tactics described above be instituted?*

3   If you feel unable to alter the tactics as suggested above, then could the following tactics be considered: *If a group has got a blockade established on the roundabout or on the road, with lock-ons, and the* MOD *Police cutting team advise your officers that it will take more than, say, 20 minutes to remove people and re-open the road then could the blockaders not be offered the opportunity to move, with their blockade, into the bell mouth or gateway so that the main road could remain open?* We think it is very likely that, as long as the base traffic was not allowed past the blockade in the process of moving, most groups would be only too happy to do this. The base traffic would be disrupted, but no more than would be the case if the blockaders remained in situ while being cut free. The traffic to and from the Peninsular would be disrupted to a much lesser extent. Facilitating this approach would not amount to 'allowing' a blockade to happen; but it would show initiative in managing one that had already happened, in order to minimise the impact on local people.

We would also be open to exploring other ways to alleviate the effect on the local community. As you are aware, one of our nonviolence guidelines is that groups will always move for ambulances, etc. However, we would be open to explore if there was some way to allow essential local traffic through as well, providing this did not further restrict our ability to disrupt criminal nuclear preparations on the base. We are thinking here of school buses, local teachers and doctors, carers, etc. If such categories could be identified, then it is likely that blockaders would be willing to let them through, while maintaining disruption of the base itself. Clearly this is something we would need to seek further feedback on from the groups but if you feel it is worth exploring we would be happy to discuss it with you and then seek such feedback.

We recognise that there are many factors in this, including ourselves. We believe that the police are an important factor and that the policing tactics have a significant effect on the extent to which the local community is disrupted. We are constantly re-evaluating the situation to see if there is anything we can do to minimise disruption to lawful traffic while continuing to disrupt the unlawful traffic into Faslane. For example, you may already be aware that we have asked all the blockading groups coming in May not to blockade before 9am so as to make sure those sitting Standard and Higher Grade exams are not disrupted or delayed in getting to school. After hearing the concerns of local residents we are now going further and recommending to all groups coming from now until the end of the exam period not to blockade between 12 and 2pm so as to avoid delaying pupils going in to school for afternoon exams and insure that blockades do not prevent pupils getting to exams or exam preparation classes. If you have any other ideas which could help minimise the knock-on effect of the Faslane blockades onto the local community we would be happy to hear them.

In peace, Faslane 365 steering group

Questions and Answers in the *Helensburgh Advertiser* of 29 March 2007

FROM GRAHAM BARR, COVE

The Trident missile system and its predecessor Polaris are a deterrent but they also create massive employment in the area. Can protesters really justify the loss to the local economy and impact on employment if the system were scrapped? How would they suggest how to combat job losses both in the facility and in support roles as well as the wider impact on the local economy?

FASLANE 365 RESPONSE

The cancellation of Trident would more likely have a positive than a negative impact on the local economy. The Faslane submarine base stands in the way of the economic regeneration of the Gare Loch, impeding marine sports, recreational and new industrial developments that could create far more local jobs than the base employs. If the naval base is kept while Trident is cancelled, research demonstrates that more jobs would be produced by dismantling Trident than continuing its deployment. For more information on this, see the recent study by the Scottish TUC.

The jobs argument should not be used to avoid or obscure the fundamental moral and security case for getting rid of Trident. The real question is, could we ever justify maintaining weapons of mass murder on the grounds that they create jobs? Each Trident warhead is 8–10 times greater than the bombs that killed hundreds of thousands at Hiroshima.

Trident cannot deter the real security threats that we face – terrorism, climate change and poverty – and deploying a further generation of nuclear weapons breaches Britain's international obligations and worldwide efforts to prevent proliferation.

FROM NAME WITHHELD, SHANDON

Do protesters based at the peace camp pay council tax? Do they have planning permission for the buildings there? If not, why not?

FASLANE 365 RESPONSE

Thousands of people from many walks of life have come for Faslane 365 blockades from all over the country and as far away as Australia and Japan. Most pay taxes where they live. The stereotypical view of who the protesters are, what they do, what they think, would be shattered by stopping to talk to any Faslane 365 group. A discussion with any of the protesters would reveal knowledgeable, committed members of many communities who have a deep desire for peace, security and a nuclear free world.

As for planning permission, local people might do better to question the planning process that allows the MOD to erect huge, ugly buildings and structures and close off access to parts of Scotland and its beautiful lochs.

The Peace Camp is temporary. We long for the day when the peace camp can be transformed to a Peace Garden to commemorate the struggle for the abolition of all weapons of mass destruction.

Faslane Peace Camp has been there for 25 years in June and they will hopefully be given a chance to speak for themselves in the *Advertiser*.

FROM ROBERT McINTYRE, ROSNEATH

We are sympathetic to the right to protest but peninsula residents have been badly affected by the protests in terms of their movements being restricted by traffic congestion. People have been held up for medical and other important appointments and children being bussed to and from schools have been affected. Why don't protesters go and protest at Coulport which is where the armaments are actually stored? What is their reaction to the suffering of local residents because of the actions of protesters?

FASLANE 365 RESPONSE

We are sympathetic to the needs of locals and sincerely regret any distress caused by our actions to people not working at Faslane. The emergency services know that all blockaders will move for them in accordance with Faslane 365 nonviolence principles.

Both sides care about the welfare of other people – it's what makes us all human. It's that concern for the health and happiness of all, especially our children's future, that motivates us. We understand how locals just want things to return to 'normal', but nuclear weapons are not normal. Most of the world – more than 180 countries – have chosen not to have them in return for a promise, made in 1968, by Britain and a small number of others with nuclear weapons that they would get rid of them.

Faslane 365 aims to disrupt the 'business as usual' deployment of nuclear weapons and persuade the government to fully implement Britain's treaty undertakings by renouncing these weapons of mass destruction. It is the tailbacks of traffic trying to enter the base that cause the disruption. Local civilians would have clear passage if this military traffic were directed elsewhere, at least until the blockades are cleared.

FROM NAME WITHHELD, RHU

The aim of Faslane 365 was to have a protest per day at the gates of the base. This definitely hasn't happened so would the campaigners say their mission has failed?

FASLANE 365 RESPONSE

The aim of Faslane 365 is not so much to have a protest per day as to facilitate autonomous groups of people to take a stand against the violations of international law which are taking place every day at the base. Blockaders are attempting to stop preparations for war crimes from taking place. Using Trident would kill millions of innocent people. Threatening to use Trident – which is what the deployment of Trident on a daily basis is all about – is also illegal. More than 650 protesters have been arrested for breach of the peace, while they are actually upholding international non-proliferation and humanitarian law and acting as responsible citizens.

Social change takes time and commitment and we will only succeed when ordinary people realise that not everything that is 'official' is lawful or acceptable, and when large numbers use their power to bring about justice and peace.

Meanwhile, even one person standing alone at the gates of Faslane is a reminder to all of us of the hope for a better world.

FROM ROZ, HELENSBURGH

None of the decisions about Trident's future have been taken at Faslane. Why wasn't Faslane 365 held outside Westminster or Holyrood where their presence might have made politicians think twice?

FASLANE 365 RESPONSE

Politicians are thinking twice. The revolt of nearly a hundred MPs at Westminster against government plans to upgrade Trident is evidence of that. Recent YouGov polling showed 65 per cent of Scots thinking that if a majority of Scottish MPs voted against Trident replacement it should not be sited in Scotland and 72 per cent of Scots think Trident replacement is a bad use of public money. Along with the continuing protests at Faslane, this will give the politicians at Holyrood, after the May elections, the strength to insist that Trident is not a 'reserved' matter because illegalities (preparations for war crimes) cannot be reserved. Thus Scottish parliament Bills are expected to be introduced against the basing of nuclear weapons in Scotland.

Quite a few MSPs have joined the blockades at Faslane. And many of the Faslane protesters do protest elsewhere – on the day parliament voted on Trident Replacement protesters demonstrated outside both Holyrood and Westminster. But Faslane is where protesters engage in direct resistance against these terrible illegal weapons that undermine the UK's moral integrity and which encourage worldwide proliferation.

Contacts

ACRONYM INSTITUTE FOR DISARMAMENT DIPLOMACY

Working since 1995 to promote effective approaches to international security, disarmament and arms control. Engaging with governments and civil society, Acronym provides reporting, analysis and strategic thinking on a range of issues relevant to peace and security, with special emphasis on treaties and multilateral initiatives.

www.acronym.org.uk

ALDERMASTON WOMEN'S PEACE CAMP

Established in 1985, the camp remains a symbol of resistance to nuclear madness – and British-manufactured weapons of mass destruction in particular. They are currently campaigning against new developments at Aldermaston, which will allow the UK government to build a new generation of nuclear weapons – a replacement for the current submarine-based Trident system.

www.aldermaston.net

BLOCK THE BUILDERS

The first and only group using concerted nonviolent direct action to physically stop the building work at Aldermaston. We regularly blockade the site in publicly announced actions, and BTB affinity groups have carried out unannounced actions at Aldermaston and at the offices and factories of the companies who profit from the new developments.

www.blockthebuilders.org.uk

EDINBURGH PEACE AND JUSTICE RESOURCE CENTRE

Committed to nonviolence, alternatives to war, human rights and ecological responsibility. Since 1980 the Resource Centre has been working with individuals and groups in Edinburgh on peace and justice issues. They are happy to work with all groups, faith based as well as secular, who are constructively concerned for Peace and Justice. The centre was set up ecumenically.

In maintaining and developing their community base, their aim is to model the principles of a peaceful and just society.

www.pjrc-edinburgh.org.uk

NUKEWATCH

A UK-wide network which monitors the nuclear convoys, informs the public, local authorities and media of their movements and campaigns against them.

www.nukewatch.org.uk

TRIDENT PLOUGHSHARES

A campaign to disarm the UK Trident nuclear weapons system in a nonviolent, open, peaceful and fully accountable manner.

www.tridentploughshares.org